WHAT GREAT TRAINERS DO

WHAT GREAT TRAINERS DO

The Ultimate Guide to Delivering
Engaging and Effective Learning

ROBERT BOLTON and DOROTHY GROVER BOLTON

AMERICAN MANAGEMENT ASSOCIATION
New York • Atlanta • Brussels • Chicago • Mexico City
San Francisco • Shanghai • Tokyo • Toronto • Washington, D.C.

Bulk discounts available. For details visit:
www.amacombooks.org/go/specialsales
Or contact special sales:
Phone: 800-250-5308
Email: specialsls@amanet.org
View all the AMACOM titles at: www.amacombooks.org
American Management Association: www.amanet.org

This publication is designed to provide accurate and authoritative information in regard to the subject matter covered. It is sold with the understanding that the publisher is not engaged in rendering legal, accounting, or other professional service. If legal advice or other expert assistance is required, the services of a competent professional person should be sought.

Library of Congress Cataloging-in-Publication Data

Bolton, Robert, 1929-
    What great trainers do : the ultimate guide to delivering engaging and effective learning / Robert Bolton and Dorothy Grover Bolton.
        pages cm
    Includes bibliographical references and index.
    ISBN 978-0-8144-2006-5 (hardcover) — ISBN 0-8144-2006-0 (hardcover) — ISBN 978-0-8144-2007-2 (ebook) 1. Employees—Training of. 2. Employee training personnel.
I. Bolton, Dorothy Grover. II. Title.
    HF5549.5.T7B5785 2016
    658.3'124—dc23   2015016799

About AMA
American Management Association (www.amanet.org) is a world leader in talent development, advancing the skills of individuals to drive business success. Our mission is to support the goals of individuals and organizations through a complete range of products and services, including classroom and virtual seminars, webcasts, webinars, podcasts, conferences, corporate and government solutions, business books, and research. AMA's approach to improving performance combines experiential learning—learning through doing—with opportunities for ongoing professional growth at every step of one's career journey.

Printing number

10 9 8 7 6 5 4 3 2 1

To our grandchildren, with love always:

Annie Hawkins

Emily Hawkins

Will Gabor

Madison Gabor

Sarah Rose Gabor

Malone Gabor

Mimi Gabor

Jack Gabor

Zoe Peyton Jones

Jeremy Peyton Jones

Lilly Bolton

Ruby Bolton

Matthew Grant-Bolton

Anna Grant-Bolton

Angelique Mukandamage

Rosemary Munkres

Ben Munkres

Contents

Preface

A teacher affects eternity; he can never tell where his influence stops.

———Henry Adams[1]

The fundamentals of any discipline are skills that have been learned from exemplars, honed by mindful practice, and improved by disciplined innovation. In a master trainer, these skills are so deeply ingrained in the trainer's behavior that they seem to be innate—yet they can be analyzed and learned by anyone committed to mastering the craft of training.

This book is based on the Craft of Training workshops that we and our colleagues delivered primarily at Fortune 500 corporations but also in smaller companies and numerous not-for-profit organizations. Over the last three decades, the workshop has undergone numerous revisions and endless tweaking.

In these pages you'll learn how to lead dynamic workshops. In music, the term *dynamics* refers to the degrees of loudness that give expression and meaning to the notes that otherwise might sound mechanical. Dynamics provide the variety that helps the music live and breathe. So, too, the term *dynamic* in the field of training refers to an instructional method that energizes participants through a varied approach that invites lively participation and enhances the learning and retention of the workshop content.

Dynamic training is invigorated by group interaction. In contrast to one-to-one instruction, however, teaching groups of people creates a much more complex set of challenges. Within a group, each person's learning is affected—for better or worse—not only by his or her own thought processes and emotions but also by the complex set of group interactions that influence the learning experience. Dynamic trainers not only master their subject matter but also understand and work effectively with the most important elements of group process.

This leads to the question of what is the best way to grapple with this training material. It cannot be read as one would read either fiction or other nonfiction. The content of the chapters is to be read, studied, tried out, and read again to gain a deeper understanding, and then practiced again and again. This is the way we trained more than sixty men and women over the years who were selected to become trainers in our organization.

The following anecdote will give you an idea of how effective these methods are. A client was seriously considering purchasing one of our courses for a large training group. Wisely, the client decided to send one of his course developers to participate in a workshop and evaluate the quality and appropriateness of the course for the company's needs. The report on the workshop came back to the company as positive on all counts, with one exception: "The course is too complex for any but the most experienced and skilled trainer to lead. This trainer's superb training skills are essential to the effectiveness of the course. Since the rollout is to be large and extend over a year's period and would require more than eight trainers to handle the project, I can't recommend it."

In response, we suggested that the course be given again and led by a younger, much less experienced trainer, and that the same evaluator attend again. That was agreed upon. The second evaluation came back, "I was wrong. These folks have figured out how to train trainers so that the quality of the training remains exceptionally high even in the hands of fairly new and unseasoned trainers."

This book provides how-to descriptions of the training methods those trainers used.

Turn the page and let's begin.

WHAT GREAT TRAINERS DO

FRAMEWORK FOR TRAINING

1

The Challenge of Training

It is a splendid vocation you have chosen—to smooth the way for the march of unappreciated truths, and new and courageous lines of thought.

——Petra in Ibsen's *An Enemy of the People*

As educator John Holt said, "Man is by nature a learning animal. Birds fly, fish swim, man thinks and learns."[1] Some psychologists claim that learning is one of our most universal characteristics.[2] Furthermore, organizations need their members to learn—to develop new skills, to adapt to changing situations, to adjust to shifting needs and opportunities. Robert Kegan and Lisa Laskow Lahey argue that:

> There is no more perfect marriage of interests—between the needs of an organization and the needs of its individual members—than the ongoing growth of people at work.[3]

From this perspective, trainers have an enviable role: our job is to improve the effectiveness of the organization by helping individuals succeed.

Yet training often fails—and on a massive scale. Estimates vary, but one educated guess has American corporations spending about $60 billion on training annually, with not more than 10 percent of what's taught actually resulting in transfer to the job. So the life of a corporate trainer is rarely as ideal as the opening paragraph may seem to suggest. Trainers who choose this career path to help others succeed often find they lack the skills or organizational support required to achieve their own success.

The Untrained Trainer Is Vulnerable to Failure

Anna started with XYZ Corporation six years ago as a customer service representative. Because of her strong task and interpersonal abilities, she soon became a supervisor. Anna spent more time coaching her employees than most supervisors—and with very positive results. It was a natural next step for her to conduct the brief orientation session for all new departmental employees.

When the corporate training department was seeking someone to do supervisory and management training, Anna applied and got the job. She was excited about the challenge.

Challenge it was. Anna found that she was expected to teach nine different courses, most of them one or two days long. She averaged two and a half days in the classroom each week—120 days a year.

Anna's training day began early and ended late. She started with some last-minute preparation, arrived early to be sure the room setup was right, and then greeted people individually as they entered the training room. She taught for six and a half hours, spent her lunch hour chatting with class members, and lingered to talk with a few participants after class. With more than a full day behind her, she then attended to her in-box to deal with the most urgent emails, and then dashed home to a quick dinner and more preparation. When applying for the job she had no idea her days would be so mentally and physically grueling.

The toughest part, however, was that the work was sometimes emotionally draining as well. The groups Anna taught ranged in size from about a dozen participants to thirty or more. It quickly became evident that some participants would rather be almost anywhere else than in the workshop. She knew that some had been sent to training to get "fixed." Often participant resentment was obvious, and it was aimed not only at the person who sent the participant to training, but at anyone associated with the training—especially the trainer, who was the closest target for their ire.

The participants' energy for learning in Anna's classes was low. She tried to overcome group lethargy by making her presentations more spirited. Sometimes the additional effort made a difference; sometimes it didn't. Some training sessions went better than others, but Anna found herself returning repeatedly to the same questions: Why are so many people in my classes just putting in time? Is the problem with them? With me? With the content of the courses?

One week she had to teach a group of young, bright, successful middle managers in a two-day people-management course. A needs assessment indicated that the training was a good fit, but some of the people being sent to the workshop said, "I don't need this," or "I just can't see myself using this stuff." By noon of day one, it was clear to Anna that the participants weren't going to get much out of the training and that she had a long day and a half ahead of her. Anna could feel her stress rising. She noticed the tension in her voice as she responded to some of the more challenging participants. She kept thinking, They don't like me. No one is learning anything. This is a nightmare.

After the class ended, self-doubt and discouragement continued to plague Anna for days. She decided she didn't want to continue this way; either she would find a way to be more effective at the demanding job of training, or she would transfer to another type of work where she could once again experience the type of success she'd had in each of her previous positions.

Corporate Trainers Seldom Receive Adequate Training

An old proverb says, the cobbler's children go without shoes; similarly, many corporate trainers receive little or no training in their craft. It's been estimated that each year more than a million people are given first-time responsibility for training others. For the most part these new trainers are given little, if any, preparation in even basic teaching methods. Recently, the president of a training firm said, "Approximately 80 percent of those people I contact in business [who are] responsible for creating or conducting training programs have never been taught how to teach." All too often, people who have never taught before are expected to make an almost instantaneous transition to the demanding role of trainer.

Too many trainers have to struggle with material they haven't had a chance to fully master while confronting difficult group dynamics they haven't been given the skills to address. When one is struggling with a difficult training session and not doing it particularly well, the whole debacle is happening on center stage, with twenty or more people watching a trainer agonize and try to improvise some way out of a bad situation. Of course, training isn't always this rough, but a few bad incidents in quick succession or a series of mediocre workshops can be very punishing experiences for the trainer.

Word travels fast. Research in customer relations shows that an unhappy customer tells an average of nine people about his or her dissatisfaction. That statistic seems to hold for the training field as well. But while stores deal with individual customers, most of whom don't know each other, trainers work with groups of people who often do know one another. When a workshop goes poorly, half or more of the participants may be disgruntled. In a twenty-participant workshop, that's about nine or ten people each telling several others about their unsatisfactory experience. As many as forty or more people may hear how poorly things went— and many will have heard negative reviews from two or more sources. It only takes a few poor workshops to establish a bad reputation for the trainer. And a bad reputation can be hard to change, especially if future participants come to a training session expecting the worst, thus making it much harder for the trainer to succeed. A vicious cycle like this hurts the individual trainer and the training department alike.

By contrast, effective training can have a transforming effect on the trainees and by extension on the organization as a whole. It assists both individuals and organizations to fine-tune their responses to shifting circumstances. And it energizes individuals and groups by challenging them to extend existing abilities and develop new ones.

Successful Workshops Require a Wide Range of Training Skills

Training is a set of skills that rise at times to an art form. In a master trainer, these skills are so deeply ingrained in the trainer's behavior that they seem to be innate—yet they can be identified and taught. And they can be learned by anyone dedicated to mastering the craft of training.

Anna was lucky. After a meeting at the corporation's headquarters, she ran into Tom, who had been in one of her easier training sessions. Tom greeted Anna happily and told her that he'd just taken a presentation skills course that she would love. She should check it out, he said, as he handed her a copy of the training announcement. Anna went back to her supervisor, laid out her frustrations, and got the OK to take the two-day presentation skills training.

The course itself was helpful—Anna could see many ways to make her own presentations more powerful. Beyond that, the trainer, Katie, was inspiring. Energetic, dynamic, and humorous, she was a walking advertisement for the skills she was teaching. More important, though, the kinds of carping remarks that made Anna so tense and unhappy didn't faze Katie at all. Katie responded to those comments with a verbal response or brief demonstration that somehow made the skills seem more relevant rather than less so. By midafternoon, the critical remarks had faded away and people were celebrating one another's successes. At the end of the day, Anna told Katie how impressed she'd been and found herself blurting out her own discouragement.

"How do you do it?" Anna asked. "It's a battle for me just to stand at the front of the room—and you make it look like fun."

"It *is* challenging work," Katie agreed. "But when you know you can meet the challenges, training is enjoyable."

"I guess I'm not sure I can meet the challenges," said Anna, glumly.

Katie was not only skilled but generous; she offered to meet with Anna to help her think through what she might want to change about her training.

That meeting was a turning point. Katie helped Anna find ways of restructuring her subject matter to make her courses more accessible to participants; she helped Anna see how the presentation skills she was learning could make the training sessions more compelling and lively. Perhaps most important, Katie helped Anna see how her coaching strengths could be used in a training context.

Anna returned to her work buoyed by her sense of current progress and achievable goals that are supported by practical action plans. Success didn't come instantaneously, but Anna was a hard worker, and within months she began to feel adept at using several of the skills required by this craft of training.

Dynamic training doesn't happen by accident. The best trainers have mastered a wide range of interpersonal and cognitive skills and put these skills to work in the service of both the individual learners and the group they are part of. This book is designed to help you become a dynamic trainer.

Preview of the Book

Part I introduces the framework for our approach to training. Following this discussion of the challenges of training, Chapter 2 discusses the two fundamental aspects of training—content and process. Chapter 3 presents a universal structure for skill-building workshops that can help trainers integrate content and process in any skill development area.

Each of the chapters in Part II describes one aspect of the anatomy of a workshop in greater detail. You will learn how to get a workshop off to a good start; involve participants by leading brief and varied activities; you'll learn more about how to organize and present key skills and concepts, use disclaimers to sidestep objections, listen productively to participants, and vary the way you respond to questions and comments. You'll also find detailed accounts of how to demonstrate skills effectively, set up and lead practice sessions, and provide in-the-moment feedback to make practices more effective. Part II concludes with an introduction to workshop evaluation and guidelines for bringing the workshop to a meaningful conclusion.

The four chapters in Part III focus on helping a trainer think on his feet and roll with the punches that training can throw. They highlight the work of the trainer as facilitator: understanding resistance, creating a positive learning climate, managing group process and individual participation, and using emergent redesign to rescue a troubled workshop while you are teaching it. These chapters teach how to manage group process in a manner that maintains workshop productivity and copes with dysfunctional individual or group behavior.

The three chapters in Part IV are designed to help trainers manage their defensiveness and to continue maturing as a trainer. Based on research by numerous investigators we describe "facilitative qualities" that have been found to aid teachers and others in the helping professions be more successful in fostering growth and development in those they serve.

The book concludes with three appendices. Appendix I, Course Preparation Worksheets, contains a series of one- to two-page outlines to guide your preparation for leading activities, making presentations, doing demonstrations, and leading practices.

Appendix II, Adapt the Workshop to Fit the Participants, provides guidelines for adjusting course materials in order to make them a better fit for a particular group of participants. Customizing the material to their needs can improve acceptance and retention of learning dramatically.

Appendix III, Install the Training Properly or Live to Regret It, discusses how important to the success of the workshop are the steps taken well before the training starts.

Now that you've seen the overview of *What Great Trainers Do*, the next chapter will explore the two very basic and intertwined elements that determine the degree of success of any workshop.

2

Content and Process: The Two Intertwined Elements of Dynamic Training

Confluent: Flowing together; blended into one.
———*The American Heritage Dictionary of the English Language*

Every training event is composed of two intertwined elements: workshop content and group process. Content and process are always present in a workshop and the quality of each greatly affects participants' learning.

Content is what is taught. It is the subject matter of the workshop—the knowledge, concepts, methods, and skills that are to be learned. Participants are attending the workshop to learn new content or to develop more mastery in an area in which they already have some competence. Since the content is what people are there to learn, a dynamic trainer needs to be a subject-matter specialist in each course he or she teaches. That's a major challenge for many trainers because the organizations they work for may not provide the time or resources needed to help them master the content they'll be teaching.

Group process, the other component of training, focuses on how the training group is functioning. It is composed of two related aspects of group experience: (1) the emotions the individuals in the group are experiencing, and (2) the ever-fluctuating interaction between participants as they encounter one another, the workshop content, and the trainer.

Process is always present in training and inevitably contributes to or detracts from learning. When managed well, group process supports participants' learning of the workshop content. And, as you might expect, mediocre or dysfunctional process undermines learning. The good news is that process can be observed, analyzed, and managed to serve the learning goals of the workshop. Good process kindles the want-to-learn part of people that makes the learning experience more enjoyable and far more productive.

When looking at a workshop from a process point of view you put the participants and their frame of reference first. You ask yourself:

- What dynamics are occurring in the room?
  - Among participants?
  - In an individual?
  - In your interactions with others?
- What discomfort do you see?
- How safe do people feel?
  - With you?
  - With one another?
  - With the material?
- What are you doing that's helping them learn?
- What is getting in the way?

The content–process distinction, like the brain–mind dichotomy, is conceptual rather than actual. Thinking about content and process as separate but related entities enables us to discuss them independently as we do in this chapter. And it helps us to more skillfully observe, understand, and manage the interactions in the workshops we lead.

Powerful training occurs when content and process flow together and blend seamlessly to foster peak learning. We use the term *confluent training* to designate workshops in which sound content and quality group process flow together, and are blended into one integrated process.[1]

Figure 2-1. Quality learning in dynamic training stems from the integration of sound content and effective group process.

Confluent Training vs. Content-Centered Teaching

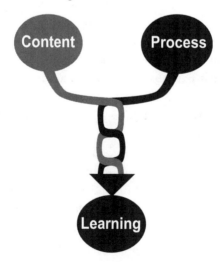

Robin Montz, a ninth-grade social-studies teacher, had always used a traditional, strictly content-centered approach to teaching. In time, however, he was trained in confluent education. Robin then applied the educational methods that integrated high-quality group process with the teaching of the same content that he had taught the previous year. He then compared the grades with the previous year's grades that were obtained when he used traditional methods. He also checked the average intelligence level of the two classes and, as expected, they were virtually identical. Here's a comparison of the results of each approach to teaching essentially the same content with basically the same caliber of student.[2]

GRADE	TRADITIONAL CONTENT-CENTERED TEACHING	CONFLUENT TEACHING AND LEARNING
A	39	**210**
B	83	**72**
C	225	**71**
D	8	**8**
F	10	**2**
Total	365	**363**

Wow!

Of course, the results aren't always this dramatic, but for most training situations a confluent approach delivers far better results than the traditional content-centered approach.

As in numerous public schools, many training organizations have taken a traditional content-oriented approach to teaching and learning, with predictable dismal results. The most commonly cited estimate is that a mere 10% of learning from training is applied on the job. Although there are multiple causes of this depressing finding, a major factor is that so much training is still conducted in the traditional content-centered/process-deficient manner.

Successful Trainers Focus on Both Content and Process

Both content and process require continual attention. Most trainers stay focused on delivering the workshop content but many are much less attentive to group process. However, without ongoing management of group process, a workshop is likely to soon flounder, and when it does, learning inevitably plummets. This chapter is concerned primarily with group process (which is sometimes referred to as "process," "group dynamics," or "dynamics"). Later chapters will enrich your understanding of how to improve your management of group process and your teaching of the workshop content.

When trainers are not tuned in to the interpersonal dynamics of the group, the process aspect of training is invisible to them. *Yet, as we've emphasized, process is always present and always contributes to or detracts from the outcome of the training.* So the trainer who is out of touch with group process is flying blind.

A group's process inevitably changes over the course of a training session. When a training group meets for the first time, it will feel very different from that same group later in the day or on a subsequent day. In later chapters, we'll examine how to create a positive learning environment, observe the process of the group in fairly subtle manifestations, and intervene as necessary to keep the group process positive. For now, though, we'll describe three types of responses to group process when it's threatening to get out of control.

Dealing with Deteriorating Group Process

A large corporation decided to extend its sales training to all customer service representatives in its largest division. The rationale was that since customer service reps are constantly in contact with customers, they have many opportunities for selling additional products to existing customers. The rollout of this training involved several corporate trainers delivering the same course, often in adjacent training rooms. Here's what happened in three of the rooms.

Room 1

Lynn is an experienced trainer who has delivered this same course to sales people eight times in the past year and a half. She knows the material cold; she tells her husband she could do the training in her sleep. But this group is not made up of sales people; it's made up of customer service representatives who are largely unresponsive. They don't respond to her humor, so she cuts back on humor. That's okay: sometimes you get a serious group. She asks questions. They don't answer her questions. She tries asking the same thing another way with no luck. Eventually she answers the question herself and moves on.

Just before the break she tries a little motivational speech. "Sales skills are going to be useful to you in all parts of your life, not just as customer service reps but at home too." She puts her heart into it, but the participants look disengaged. They straggle in late from the first break. And after the break, more than one set of eyes drift off.

Room 2

Alex noted some hostile vibes within the first fifteen minutes of the training, and he's spent the next hour listening to the group members express their anger and frustration. Because he's listening attentively to them, they're not angry with him, but they sure are angry with the company. They feel betrayed. If they wanted to be salespeople, they tell him, they would have gone into sales, where the big money is. But they don't want to be salespeople, with all the stresses of cold calling, presenting the same products over and over again, struggling to close the sale. They want to be customer service reps, with the customer coming to them with problems that they know how to resolve or can pass on to a supervisor.

Alex has heard in detail from most of the group. He knows that Vince once held a sales position and hated it, and that Sue is worried about whether she can succeed at selling. He knows about the stress levels most of the participants are experiencing just from handling irate customers—and what little energy they have for selling products. What he doesn't know is how to get back to presenting the material he's supposed to teach.

Room 3

Like Alex, Herm could see that there was enough trouble in the room to make forging ahead a bad idea. And he realized that pretending nothing was wrong wasn't going to make anything right. He pulled a chair into the center of the front part of the room, sat down, and invited the group to tell him what was going on that made it hard for them to be there. Like Alex, he got an earful. Unlike Alex, though, when the participant's tensions had been lowered by his open-minded listening, Herm returned the focus to the group's training needs. He looked around at the group and asked, "What ideas do you have for addressing the problem?"

After receiving their ideas, he summarized their input. "It sounds like some of you can see an advantage to learning sales skills and the rest prefer to focus on customer service skills. We're fortunate that the same basic skill of listening, which I was about to teach, is essential in both sales and customer service work. I'll go ahead with teaching the listening skills, but instead of using sales examples and role plays exclusively, I'll also teach customer service applications and use some customer service role plays. You can choose whether you want to practice customer service skills or sales skills. The difference will be that I have role plays for sales prepared, but we can create the appropriate customer service role plays together. If this makes sense to you, I'll move right into teaching listening skills. How does that sound?"

The group was amenable to the idea.

Distinctions Among the Three Trainers

Lynn, Alex, and Herm were all experienced trainers who knew their material so well that they could pay attention to what was happening in the room. Most trainers, if confronted with these group process difficulties, would, like Lynn, be tempted to tough it out, make small adaptations in their presentation style, and try to motivate the group by selling them on the usefulness of the skills. As with Lynn, these trainers might not realize they were making a choice to focus on content at the expense of process—although they might well recognize that what they were doing wasn't working. When a trainer focuses primarily on content and pays scant attention to group process, participant learning soon suffers.

Few trainers take Alex's route, which was to focus on process to the exclusion of content. But it's worth noting that this strategy also neglects one of the two dimensions of training, which thereby thwarts the group's capacity to learn. Even though Alex resolved the process issues well, he was at a loss about how to get the group refocused on the content that they were there to learn and the group would soon become impatient with his inability to help them learn how to fulfill their new sales role.

Herm managed, even in this relatively difficult situation, to combine effective group process with teaching the course content. His suggestion to the group is an example of what we refer to as "emergent redesign"—restructuring a workshop while you're in the process of leading it. (You'll learn how to do emergent redesign in Chapter 25.)

When Process Worsens, Restoring It Is the First Order of Business

When a workshop is running smoothly, trainers need to keep alert to the ever-shifting quality of group process while devoting their major attention to teaching the content that the participants came to learn. The early chapters of Part II describe how to keep workshop process in good running order. However, if group process worsens, learning plummets. And when group process heads south, as it did in the three examples just discussed, restoring positive process becomes the trainer's first order of business.

3

A Universal Structure for Skill-Building Workshops

The sole justification for teaching . . . is that the student comes out of it able to do something he could not do before. I say **do** *and not* **know***, because knowledge that doesn't lead to doing something new or doing something better is not knowledge at all.*

———Jacques Barzun[1]

This chapter describes a universally applicable workshop structure for skill-building workshops that can help trainers integrate content and process in any skill-development area. This workshop structure is composed of units, modules, and components.

Units: The overall title of the material to be taught.

Modules: A section of a unit.

Components: The seven parts of a module.

Sorry about the jargon. We avoid it wherever possible but the important parts of workshops need to have labels to facilitate discussing these aspects of our work. Understanding the purpose and function of these major elements of a workshop can increase your training effectiveness significantly.

This is the only chapter in the book that may feel like a tough slog, but let us assure you that knowing the basic structure of a skill building workshop will benefit you over and over again as you deliver, redesign, or design training.

Workshop Structure

Units

A unit is the overall title of the material to be taught and is the largest structural element of a skill-building workshop. Each workshop has an introductory unit, a closing unit, and one or more (usually several) units in between. For example, a workshop on People Skills for Team Leaders has six units:

- Introduction to the Workshop
- Listening Skills
- Influence Skills
- Conflict Management Skills
- Cooperative Problem Solving Skills
- Conclusion of the Workshop

Creating an outline by listing the units of the workshop provides a trainer with a "big picture" view of the course he'll be teaching. Subdividing a training session into units also helps trainers remember the importance of introductions (creating readiness for the learning ahead) and conclusions (summarizing what's been learned, then encouraging participants to evaluate what they've learned and to figure out how, where, and when to apply it). Also, designing a workshop as a series of units makes it easier for participants to learn the workshop content.

Modules

Each unit is made up of several modules that package the content into smaller, more easily learnable amounts of information and skill development. For example, the listening unit in the course mentioned above has six modules:

- Introduction to Listening for Team Leaders
- The Body Language of Listening
- Paraphrase What You Hear
- Respond to Feelings
- Combine Listening and Speaking
- Conclusion

Components

The modules of a workshop typically consist of a sequence of components, which are the basic building blocks of a workshop. In a well-designed workshop you'll generally find seven components, which, for each skill being taught, are sequenced in the following order:

Component 1: INVOLVE This Component employs a brief talk or activity to help participants grasp the relevance of the content being taught. Retention increases when participants grasp the content's relevance. Dynamic training develops the "want to" that readies people for learning the "how to." In sales jargon this is called WIIFM (pronounced *wiffim*)—What's In It For Me?

Component 2: TELL HOW These concise trainer presentations tell the participants exactly how to do the ability being taught, using examples that are pertinent to their life and work.

Component 3: SHOW HOW The trainer demonstrates how to do the skill that was taught in the Tell How component.

Component 4: PRACTICE In this component the trainer sets up and leads practice sessions.

Component 5: COACH In this component the trainer provides precisely targeted and extremely brief individualized feedback and instruction during a practice session.

Component 6: APPLY This is a concise presentation or guided discussion (in the whole group or in subgroups). Sometimes this component is a combination of presentation and group discussion. The APPLY component is designed to encourage participants to consider:

- How they can implement the skill
- Possible barriers to implementation
- How these barriers to implementation might be overcome

This component often concludes with participants developing implementation plans that help them transfer learnings to their back-home situations.

Component 7: EVALUATE In this component the participants' development of the skill being taught is self-assessed, peer-assessed, and/or trainer-assessed. It's also a good time for the trainer to obtain participant evaluations of this module of the workshop and of his leadership of this part of the workshop.

Each component will be explained in greater detail later in the book—usually in a chapter-length treatment. In Appendix I, you'll find Course Preparation Worksheets that you can use to guide your development of a one- or two-page outline of that component for any workshop you'll lead.

In recent decades research has confirmed what many leading-edge educators have long believed—that physical movement, even brief moments of it, improves mental processing. Conventional training generally keeps participants sedentary for long periods of time, which tends to make them lethargic and less involved learners. However, when participants proceed through the seven components, they automatically experience brief periods of movement, which helps keep them invigorated for learning.

These seven components constitute a "learning by doing" process in which every component:

- *paves the way* to a practice session,

- or *is* a practice session,

- or *shows how to improve* the concepts, skills, or behaviors being practiced,

- or *discusses how to apply* the skills,

- or *evaluates* the usefulness of what was taught.

Multiple Rotations Through the Sequence of Components

Neurophysiologist Carla Hannaford writes, "When we first learn something, it is slow going, like beating a path through untraveled terrain."[2] So to master a new skill it's often necessary to cycle through several rotations of the components. One rotation is rarely enough to gain sufficient mastery of a skill to warrant using it in the workplace—or with friends and family, for that matter. For a skill like reflective listening, we find that it takes three rotations through relevant parts of the process for most participants to become proficient enough for the skill to become a useful part of their communication repertoire.

In the first rotation through the components the Evaluate step is omitted.

The First Rotation
Involve ➡ Tell How ➡ Show How ➡ Practice ➡ Coach ➡ Apply

The second rotation through the components usually omits the Involve, the Evaluate, and often the Apply components.

The Second Rotation
Tell How ➡ Show How ➡ Practice ➡ Coach

The third cycle through the components also omits the Involve component but usually includes the Apply and Evaluate components that are typically deleted in the previous rotation.

The Third Rotation
Tell How ➡ Show How ➡ Practice ➡ Coach ➡ Apply ➡ Evaluate

It's worth repeating that, to learn many skills, *three rotations through the relevant components* are usually required. However, in our admittedly unscientific review of skill training programs, we've found few workshop designs that contain sufficient practice and coaching components for participants to acquire adequate proficiency to warrant their trying to put the skills to work in their back home environment.

Capitalize on the "Morning-After Experience"

In the morning after a day of training in which there are three rotations through the components, do whatever it takes to make time to squeeze in a fourth practice immediately after the introduction to the workshop day. And provide time enough for a quick debriefing. To greatly reduce the time required for this practice, it is not preceded by the other components that typically come before a practice, nor is it followed by the components that generally follow a practice. That's why it's termed a practice-only session.

In just about every workshop in which we're able to schedule this no-frills, first-experience-of-the-day practice, nearly all the participants have a much more successful practice than any they had in the workshop previously and a much greater success than we initially expected.

Several months after we first experienced the effectiveness of the first-experience-of-the-day practice, one of us read the nineteenth-century French mathematician and theoretical physicist Henri Poincaré's strategic use of his subconscious mind. Regarding his struggle to resolve a math problem, Poincaré wrote, "I turned my attention to the study of some arithmetical questions, apparently without much success. Disgusted with my failure, I went to spend a few days at the seaside." Then, one day as Poincaré strolled along a bluff overlooking the ocean, the solution suddenly came to him "with brevity, suddenness, and immediate certainty." In a chapter titled "Mathematical Creation" in his Foundations of Science (1904), Poincaré noted that when he was stymied by a difficult problem, he benefited from getting away from it for a while, as then the solution would often come to him. If, for instance, he went away to the oceanside for a few days, when he returned to the problem the answer that had eluded him came sharply into focus. Although Poincaré was referring to complicated and profound mathematical invention, the same subconscious process can foster increased learning in multiday workshops. We call it, the "morning-after experience."

Here's how the morning-after experience works:

1. Participants make a *significant effort* to learn a new ability.
2. The participants leave the workshop and, other than possibly doing a little preparation for tomorrow's training session, they focus on other aspects of their life.

3. While their conscious mind is focusing on other things, and later as they sleep through the night, their subconscious mind is at work integrating the new learning into their repertoire.

So we recommend making it a rule, whenever possible, to arrange for a practice the first thing after the opening of the second, third, fourth, and fifth days of a workshop so trainees can enjoy the fruits of the "morning-after experience."

An Engaging and Productive Blend of Consistency, Repetition, and Variety

People usually learn best in workshops that have the following attributes:

- They are structurally consistent.
- They entail sufficient repetition (in this case, several rotations through the pertinent components):
  - To enable participants to develop the skill to the point where they can use it competently.
  - For participants to feel confident enough about their level of skill acquisition to use these newly developed abilities in their real-life situations.
- They include ample variety to maintain interest and involvement.

Structural Consistency

All units are structured in essentially the same way. Similarly, every module is organized like every other module. Furthermore, each Component 1 is organized like every other Component 1, each Component 2 is organized like every other Component 2, etc. This structural consistency makes it much easier for a trainer to learn a new course or deliver a familiar one. Equally important, this repetition of structure enhances participant learning. And it makes it easier for training designers to create or revise a course.

Content Repetition

Repetition often is an essential element in learning but, as you've probably experienced, it's often boring. And boredom tends to kill learning. In our Craft of Training workshops, when we recommend designing structural consistency into the organization of a workshop, someone typically asks, "But won't all this structural repetition bore participants?" And someone else will likely add, "And won't it bore the trainers too? They'll surely find this approach too lock-step as well!"

Fortunately we can respond, "Not in our experience. Here's why." And then we say something like the following about content repetition:

> Dynamic training relies on content repetition in order to facilitate deeper levels of learning and greater recall. But, in dynamic training, the repetition occurs several components later. For example, the Tell How component is always separated from the next Tell How component by three or four other components, as you'll see by looking at the diagrams earlier in this chapter. And the repetition virtually always is part of a message that includes useful new information.

Variety

Although structural repetition doesn't induce boredom, well-designed variety perks up a workshop. Develop a diverse assortment of examples for your presentations. When it's time to demonstrate a skill, you may be able to alternate between video demos and live ones. And you can have participants work in dyads on occasion, in triads some of the time, occasionally in small groups, and once in a while in whole-group settings.

Consistently Excellent Results

Clients want to get consistently excellent results from training. Obviously, there's no foolproof structure for training effectiveness. But this type of workshop organization comes closer than anything we know of for providing dependably high-quality outcomes. And, since this workshop structure is a very efficient path to skill acquisition, participants appreciate it too.

While some trainers are initially skeptical about this much structural repetition, once they have experience with this framework they usually make it their go-to workshop structure. In fact, we've found that trainers appreciate this consistency of structure, which makes their training much easier to learn and deliver. And they're delighted to find that this training design generates high levels of participant involvement, creates hands-on learning which transfers well to participants' back-home situations.

PART II

DEVELOPING A DYNAMIC WORKSHOP

4

How to Open a Workshop

You never get a second chance to make a first impression.

———Will Rogers

In an ideal world, participants would enter a workshop feeling calm, secure, re-laxed, open, and ready to take in new ideas and skills. In the real world, many do. However, it's wise to assume that a number of participants will feel a bit anxious about attending the course, concerned that they might be called on to speak in front of the class, worried that they may not measure up to others in the class, or appre-hensive about meeting new people. Some will inevitably be distracted by the thought of work piling up while they're away. Others may wonder why they were sent to this particular training. Is it a reward? A punishment? The first step to being shown the door? So, instead of entering the workshop with an open-minded approach to learning, many trainees feel guarded until their experience provides them with pos-itive answers to one or more of three crucial but usually unspoken questions that are frequently on the minds of people entering a training event:

- Will I be safe—not be put on the spot or otherwise made vulnerable?
- Will it be worthwhile—something I can really use?
- Will it be reasonably engaging—or will I be bored stiff?

When learners feel unsure of the answers to these questions, they tend to be closed to learning. Their defensiveness is often expressed by being remote and un-involved, forming exclusive subgroups, questioning the applicability of what's being taught, and so forth. When these anxieties are not defused, the resulting defensive behavior can transform what was meant to be a positive learning experience into a trainer's nightmare.

So without directly addressing the three unspoken questions that are often on participants' minds as they enter a new learning experience, the trainer's friendly manner can create a safe, welcoming climate. And her brief, but carefully crafted preview of the course content and its benefits can stimulate the expectation that this might turn out to be a worthwhile use of their time. Then, too, the brisk pace of the opening combined with your somewhat revved-up energy deployed to get the workshop off the ground will undercut the possible expectation that this is likely to be a tedious experience.

The way the opening of a workshop responds to participants' unexpressed concerns helps set the tone for what follows. So, in this chapter we highlight the critical importance of the opening minutes of a workshop. Then we show how to respond indirectly to the unspoken questions mentioned above while covering the usual introductory workshop topics:

- Who the trainer is
- Who the other participants are
- What material will be covered
- How the training will be managed

Provide Prework

Sending prework gives participants a head start on learning the workshop material. And prework generally helps them get a more specific sense of what the workshop will be about. Prework can include reading materials that explain why this training is needed, what will be covered, and what end results are expected. Prework can also involve a brief quiz on the subject matter to gauge where participants stand prior to the training, or participants can be asked to list questions they would like answered during the training.

Be Aware of the Lasting Effect of First Impressions

When you lead a workshop made up of people whom you've never met, be alert to the power of first impressions. If you start off on the wrong foot with a group, it can be difficult to recoup. Researchers at Princeton University found that people make snap judgments about a person's competence, likability, and trustworthiness in less than a second![1] Furthermore, these first impressions tend to be long-lasting. News analyst David Brooks's survey of research on initial impressions of other people found that

> these sorts of first glimpses are astonishingly accurate in predicting how people will feel about each other months later. People rarely revise their first impression; they just become more confident that they are right.[2]

Thus, when you stand in front of a group for the first time, before you ever say a word, participants will have made an initial assessment of how competent, likable, and trustworthy you are. It ain't fair! But since human nature usually works that way, we do well to take this phenomenon into account when opening a workshop.

Here are ten things you can do to create a positive first impression while getting the workshop off to a good start:

1. Dress Appropriately

We'll provide more specifics on this in Chapter 10, but it's appropriate to briefly mention the point here. Make sure your wardrobe fits the occasion. Considerable social psychology research indicates that people are more trusting of people who look like and dress like them. Every organization has its own dress code and it's a sound practice for trainers to follow it. Kim Campbell, former Prime Minister of Canada, put it this way: "Does fashion MATTER? Only if you're out of it."[3] And the savvy social activist, Dorothy Day, when preparing her followers for antiwar demonstrations, told the men to wear neckties and jackets. Like all wise change agents, don't let your garb undermine your message.

2. Begin Your Work Before the Workshop Starts

Arrive at the workshop site at least a half an hour before the starting time so you can be sure the room is set up properly and you are ready to welcome and chat with the first people to arrive. Greet the early arrivals, introduce yourself, and learn something about them. As participants continue to arrive, introduce yourself to as many people as you can. Invite them to have a cup of coffee or tea if that's available. Introduce a few newcomers to one another and then begin acquainting yourself with some other new arrivals and get them acquainted with one another. These small efforts help set the stage for greater participation during the workshop.

3. Create a Seating Arrangement Conducive to Participation

A dynamic workshop should seldom have more than twenty to at most twenty-five participants. Arrange the chairs in a semicircle with a chair reserved for the trainer at one end of the semicircle and with the door to the rear of the group (preferably) or to the side so anyone who must enter or leave during the session can do so with minimal disruption. Make sure all participants will be able see and hear you and one another. And check charts, audiovisual screens, etc., to be sure that they are visible and readable by everyone.

It's important to have a flexible seating arrangement for highly participative workshops. We strongly recommend against having people sit behind or around tables unless tables are absolutely necessary. When people are seated at tables, movement is restricted and communication is inhibited. When using a table-less seating arrangement, you may initially get a few complaints about the lack of tables but people tend to adjust quickly. If tables are required for some activities, consider putting them against the wall and arrange the chairs as described in the previous paragraph. If tables are needed at some point in the workshop, the participants can move their chairs to the nearby tables that are positioned near the back wall.

When participants arrive at the workshop, the table-less room arrangement subtly announces that the workshop will be an interactive experience.

4. Provide Healthy Snacks

Many organizations provide coffee, tea, and something sweet when people arrive at the workshop and for the morning break. Increasing numbers of people, however, are health conscious about their food choices. Exercise whatever influence you have to provide some healthy snack and beverage options. One size does not fit all!

5. Display a "Welcome" Flip Chart

Create and display an attractive "Welcome" flip chart with the course title and the word *Trainer* followed by the name you like to be called and your last name.

6. Give a Two-Minute Warning

As you approach the starting time, give a two–minute warning that the workshop is about to begin. That gives participants time to wrap up their conversations and find their seats.

7. Get Off to a Good Start

Start well and the participants will be revved up for the journey ahead. Start poorly and you'll find yourself needlessly fighting an uphill battle. So give some thought to how you will transition seamlessly from chatting casually with participants before the workshop to giving the workshop an energetic beginning. Start at the announced starting time as this will signal the norm of punctuality, a norm that can be important to the success of the workshop.

Training veteran Bob Pike says, "Creative trainers recognize that they need to do at least three things with an opening if they are going to raise the BAR in their training:

Break preoccupation through involvement.

Allow networking to reduce tension and to increase retention.

Relate the opening to the content so that participants see the relevance of the opening. It makes a point. It is not a waste of time."[4]

After a brief welcome which should take no more than a minute or two, a quick ice-breaker helps people relax and feel more at home in the group. Polling, one of the more effective ice-breakers, simply involves asking for a show of hands to provide participants (and the trainer) with information about the other people in the room. This involves the participants from the get-go, provides you with useful information about the group, and fosters networking as participants learn a bit about one another. Here's one way to go about it:

Before we get started let's take a minute to learn a bit about each other. Raise your hand if:
- You just got back from a vacation.
- You're going on a vacation soon.
- You wish you were on vacation right now.
- You're originally from:
  - The northeast
  - The southeast
  - The northwest
  - The southwest
  - The middle of the country

As you speak, *demonstrate* what you want people to do. Timing is important here. For example, *raise your hand* as you say,

Raise your hand if: . . .

Perhaps you can use sports questions according to the season you're in. For example:

- How many of you are Yankees fans?
- How many are Red Sox fans?
- How many think the Giants are going to win the Super Bowl?

Interspersing some banter in reaction to some of the group's answers gets the class off to a relaxed, light, and humorous start. As described in Chapter 5, it's often helpful to include a brief get-acquainted activity in the opening minutes of a workshop.

8. Focus on Factors That Contribute to an Effective Beginning

After the polling, people will begin to feel a bit more at ease, so it's time to cover the factors that contribute to a solid beginning of a workshop:

- The trainer's self-introduction
- The content overview
- The teaching methods that will be used
- The workshop ground rules
- The participants' self-introductions
- The announcement of workshop logistics

In a twenty- to twenty-five-person workshop you should be able to complete this type of introduction in twenty-five to twenty-eight minutes.

Trainer Self-Introduction

If the option of having someone introduce you is offered, decline it. An introduction by someone else won't achieve the connection you want to make with the group. Only you can do that. So make it a rule to introduce yourself.

Your self-introduction should address the two primary questions participants generally have about a workshop leader:

1. Who is the trainer as a professional? Summarize your qualifications for leading this workshop.
2. Who is the trainer as a person? Briefly describe a personal interest of yours or something the participants wouldn't know about you unless you told them.

An effective self-introduction responds to the qualifications issue and the human issue. Both topics can be covered in less than two minutes. This may sound like a short amount of time to introduce yourself, but it can be done and will enable you to move quickly to the next part of the introduction. It's important to avoid getting behind schedule in the opening minutes of a workshop.

Customize your self-introduction for each workshop you do. Customization begins with knowledge about the group you'll be leading. Is it made up of seasoned managers who have been in countless training sessions? Or are they new recruits fresh out of college? Perhaps there's a mix of age and experience. Specifically, what work do they perform? What company-wide problems are they facing? With this knowledge you can adjust what you say to meet what you think their expectations will be. To a group of old hands you can emphasize your solid professional experience as well as your current work. To a group of newer employees you can place less emphasis on your experience and more on what you are doing now.

For the personal side of your introduction, think about the degree of informality and the depth of self-disclosure that will be appropriate for this group. Being too informal with a group that's looking for more of a professional self-introduction can be a negative, just as a stiff formality can bring yawns from others. Since considerable self-disclosure can be off putting to some participants, it's best to err on the side of too little at the opening of a workshop. If you think more self-disclosure is desirable, you can always add some as the training proceeds. Like salt in a recipe—easy to put in, hard to take out.

Although you'll customize your introduction to each group you work with, the basics will nearly always be the same. So refine the basics of your self-introduction so that it makes a strong contribution to the opening of your workshops.

Keep in mind that participants will soon be introducing themselves to the group. Your self-introduction is, in part, a demonstration of what's appropriate when participants introduce themselves. The length, the kind, and the depth of self-disclosure, as well as the degree of formality will register on them. And when their turn comes, participants will at least partially take their cue from your self-introduction.

A brief self-introduction might go something like this:

> My name is Alexander Moore but people usually call me Sandy. I think we all agree that the effectiveness of any course depends partly on the trainer. So I'll tell you a bit about myself.
>
> I've been a member of the organizational development staff here at Shannon Industries for six years. This workshop is a favorite of mine because participants find it so practical.
>
> Before joining Shannon, I worked as a customer service manager at a large public relations firm.
>
> My wife and I have two children; John is a high school sophomore and Kim is in eighth grade. I put lots of miles on my car going to the sporting events they participate in.
>
> Something that you wouldn't know about me if I didn't tell you is that I am an avid fly fisherman and can hardly wait for the season to begin.

Content Overview

Participants are reassured and they learn better when they're given a brief, well-thought-out plan of the workshop. For a one day or shorter training, consider using an uncluttered bulleted or numbered outline on one sheet of newsprint. If the training is longer than a day, provide a one-sheet overview of the total workshop and a one-sheet outline of the current day. Post the skeletal outlines of the workshop and of the current day's agenda side by side for participants to refer to from time to time.

Some trainers like to tell the following fable in their workshop opening.

> A country fair is held each year in a town far away. One of the big events is a woodcutting contest. And every year for the past twenty years the same man won it. That man is getting up there in age—he must be about seventy, give or take a couple of years. Last year he was challenged by a strapping young weight lifter.
>
> In the morning-long contest, that young man never broke his pace, never paused for a breath, never stopped to give himself a break. He was a marvel of muscle and endurance.
>
> The old man, by contrast, disappeared behind the corner of a barn for five minutes out of every hour. When the contest was over, however, the old man had won again. The young man couldn't believe it—but there were the two huge stacks of logs to prove it.
>
> "Just one question," he said to the old man. "Why did you stop for five minutes every hour?"
>
> The old man replied, "I was sharpening my axe."

The trainer then concludes with a statement like, "I think of this workshop as time to sharpen your axe, a place for honing your _____ skills so when you get back to your workplace you'll be more effective than ever."

Teaching Methods

At the beginning of a workshop, participants will want to know what they'll be doing and how they'll be involved. As you explain the teaching methods you'll be using in the workshop, participants will be better able to sense what's in store for them and they'll begin to relax a bit more. At the conclusion of your rundown of the workshop teaching methods you may want to invite their comments by saying something like, "Any questions about the workshop methods?"

Workshop Ground Rules

Workshop ground rules (sometimes called workshop norms) are standards of behavior that contribute to a positive learning environment. Most trainers have settled on their own set of norms that help optimize their workshop's effectiveness. Below are a handful of guidelines that are widely used. The capitalized words in the visual below are posted throughout the workshop; the words in lower case letters approximate what the trainer adds about the ground rule.

GROUND RULES

- EVERYONE IS IN CHARGE OF THEIR OWN LEARNING. If the course is not meeting your needs, let's talk about it.

- IT'S OKAY TO MAKE A MISTAKE. That's a normal part of learning.

- BE SUPPORTIVE OF OTHER PEOPLE'S EFFORTS TO TRY THINGS OUT AND LEARN.

- CONFIDENTIALITY: When you are outside of the workshop, it's okay to talk about your own experience in the workshop but not about someone else's experience.

- BE ON TIME. That will help us stay on a tight schedule, which was designed to get you out on time.

Add a norm about electronic communication that's congruent with that of the organization you are training in.

Keep the number of ground rules to a minimum—if there are too many, some folks will undoubtedly forget some of them. And a number of the participants may consider you a control freak.

Since ground rules describe how group members agree to operate in the workshop, be sure to get the group's buy-in to the ground rules before moving on to the next topic. You might simply ask, "How does this sound to you?" or "Does this make sense to you?"

When these ground rules are agreed to at the beginning of a workshop, they prevent needless unproductive behavior. Participants begin self-correcting themselves on the basis of norms that they agreed to at the beginning of the workshop.

Refer to the ground-rules visual from time to time. Occasionally, reiterate a particular ground rule when it's especially applicable. For example, when announcing the first break, remind participants about the "be on time" ground rule.

Participants' Self-Introductions

At the beginning of a workshop most of the participants want to know, "Who are these other people?" Be sure to take timing into consideration when planning how participants introduce themselves. We've seen training manuals that schedule two hours for the opening of a one-day workshop with most of that time spent in participant introductions. That's more than a quarter of the workshop!

Keeping the self-introductions brief enables the group to move quickly to the substance of the workshop. You can compensate for the brevity of the introductions by fostering an interactive workshop environment that enables participants to learn more about one another at the same time that they are engaged in learning the workshop content. This brief but ultimately thorough approach to getting participants acquainted with one another is a great workshop timesaver.

It's useful to have a bulleted visual outlining what you'd like participants to include in their self-introductions. Here's one option:

Self-Introductions

- Your full name

- What you like to be called

- Where you live (unless it's an in-house training)

- Your company (unless it's an in-house training)

- Your work responsibilities

- What you hope to get out of this training

- Something others wouldn't know about you unless you told them

---

While this outline provides a mix of professional and personal information, the only point that allows for much self-disclosure is the last one. Participants have the freedom to say things like, "My golf handicap is twenty and I've been working hard to lower it." Or "My interest is in my three boys, ages twelve, fourteen, and seventeen, and their activities. I spend a lot of my free time going to their events."

Play the Name Game

The Name Game follows the self-introductions. It's an effective and widely used community building activity for groups of up to 25 people. Here's how it goes. You ask for a volunteer to begin by saying the name he likes to be called. The participant to that person's right repeats the first person's name and adds the name that he or she likes to be called. The next person repeats the names of the first and second person and adds their own. This process continues until the last person repeats everyone's name in the group and adds his own. This introductory activity can be challenging and fun at the same time. When you use the Name Game you can count on two things—that everyone in the group will be working hard to learn everyone's name and that they'll be having a lot of fun trying. You can ease any performance anxiety by interjecting comments like:

> You can see that the volunteer who goes first has a much easier job than the person who goes last and has twenty-some names to remember. But you folks who speak early, stay focused on learning names because you'll want to know the names of the people you'll be working with in various activities throughout the workshop. Don't worry if you are at the end, and have to recall twenty names. We're not going to hang you out to dry. We'll help you out when you need assistance with a name.

How to Quickly Learn Everyone's Name

People appreciate it when the trainer learns and uses their name. And it pleases and impresses them when you can repeat everyone's name at the completion of the Name Game. Even if you are really bad at remembering the names of new acquaintances (like the male coauthor of this book), the following method will help you learn every participants' name and put their names and faces together by the time the introduction to the workshop is concluded:

- If possible, before the workshop begins read the participants' list and become somewhat familiar with the names of the folks who will be attending the workshop.
- As people gather for the workshop and during the self-introductions, concentrate very hard and learn as many names as you can.
- Then, during the Name Game, every time a new name is mentioned, mentally repeat each name that's been mentioned along with the new name.
- Once in a while you might want to ask the whole group to repeat all the names given so far. That will aid recall and reduce the pressure a bit.

This way of opening a workshop builds community fairly rapidly so you can quickly move to the substance of the workshop. As mentioned earlier, additional community building experiences can be distributed throughout the workshop.

The Announcement of Workshop Logistics

The introduction to the workshop generally concludes with a brief summary of workshop logistics. Here's where you succinctly announce nitty-gritty details like starting time, closing time, when and how long the breaks will be, the location of beverages and snacks (when available), the time and length of the lunch break, the location of rest rooms, and any safety information. Keep the announcements brief and brisk.

This is often a good time for a ten-minute break. People are ready to stretch their legs. They're now able to put a few names and faces together, so they'll be a bit more comfortable getting acquainted with others during the break. If you have a standardized way of letting folks know when breaks end, describe it to the group now. Then, when the break is over, use that method to call participants back into session.

9. Be Yourself Plus

Without trying to become someone you're not, it's wise to embody the following characteristics throughout your leadership of a workshop and especially when you are getting a workshop off the ground:

Be conversational. By being conversational in your delivery you avoid taking on a pedantic teacher role, which is the kiss of death for trainers.

Be purposeful. Your highly focused introduction to the workshop conveys that something important is afoot. And your demeanor of relaxed purposefulness communicates, "We're moving now. Get on board for the good stuff ahead."

Be energetic. Opening a workshop effectively requires concentrated energy from the trainer. You are trying to get the group coalesced and moving. Put some oomph in your voice and vigor in your body language to energize the group for peak learning.

Be open-minded. Listen receptively and respectfully to different points of view. Teach with conviction but avoid being evangelical about the workshop content. We like the way one of our colleagues avoids stirring up resistance while nudging participants to experiment with what he's teaching:

> I'm not asking you to buy what I'm advocating but I hope you'll rent it long enough to see if it works for you.

At this point you begin transforming a gathering of individuals who may not know one another into a purposeful learning community. Embodying the above characteristics will help you transform a group of strangers into a fellowship of learners.

This approach to the opening of a workshop is designed to:

- Have everyone's name spoken and heard.
- Have every participant speak in the group as a way of breaking the ice for future participation.
- Enable each person to learn a bit about everyone else in the workshop.
- Proceed quickly to the meat of the training.

10. Begin Again and Again

Community needs to be reestablished each day of the workshop. A group that was cohesive in the late afternoon or in the evening generally needs some time to regain a sense of community the following morning.

Informal comments by the trainer at the opening of the second day (and subsequent days) can start to rebuild the climate that was created earlier. Asking if anyone can recall the names of all of the participants—or the names of half of the participants—or the names of any participants can add a light note while helping people get reacquainted. Some trainers like to suggest that participants take a different seat on each of the remaining days of the course so everyone will build stronger relationships with a larger number of group members.

Asking if anyone used something they learned yesterday will begin leading the group back to the substance of the workshop. Additionally, the following items need to be addressed:

- A summary of participant evaluations that were completed at the end of the previous day
- A brief review of yesterday's content and a preview of today's material
- Participant's questions, issues, and comments on previously taught material
- An invitation for comments on the "overnight effect" (which was discussed in the previous chapter)
- A transition into what comes next.

A Summary of Participant Evaluations

Post the numerical feedback from yesterday and, if your day-end evaluation form asks for this information, read a few characteristic comments regarding what was most valuable and what was least valuable. When you read this to the group, keep an objective tone of voice and don't editorialize. This is a moment for the participants to step out of their own experience and see how things are going for others. If the feedback leans heavily toward the negative, you can ask for any ideas for making today more effective than yesterday. If the feedback is largely positive, you can ask if there are any comments or questions that anyone would like to add. If an assignment was given, ask how that went.

Review and Preview

This is the time to recap where we've been and summarize where we're going. Yesterday's schedule can be posted and briefly reviewed. Then give the schedule for today and show as many links to yesterday's content as you can to demonstrate how the course hangs together.

Debrief the "Overnight Effect"

In multiday workshops it is not unusual for a participant who had a hard time accepting yesterday's material to show up the next morning with a more receptive mindset. And participants who were having difficulty learning the skill being taught often do much better in a practice on the following day. Sometimes the conversation a participant has with his spouse leads him to see things differently. Many times, however, assimilation takes place overnight as the information one struggled with during the workshop session begins to sink in.

In conclusion, covering all the bases for opening a workshop sets the stage for a smooth transition into the real meat of the course.

5

Using Activities to Engage Participants

A teacher who is attempting to teach without inspiring the student to learn is hammering on cold iron.

——Horace Mann, "The Father of American Public Education"

Joan offered a one-day workshop on how to plan and put on a great wedding and expected to give that same workshop to new groups in the future. Participants were engaged couples who were facing the challenge of planning their own wedding. She spent the first two hours of the workshop explaining in grim detail the major and minor details that could derail the smooth functioning of the wedding plans. She designed the workshop this way to show the types of problems that participants could encounter and to explain how her services could help them avoid most of the problems and resolve any that might arise. However, the opening of the workshop was such a downer that a number of the couples left the workshop before the lunch break, and those who remained felt overwhelmed by the innumerable problems she described. The workshop was clearly in trouble and never did recover.

Another workshop was scheduled for the following month and Joan was determined to avoid the pitfalls she just encountered. So she asked Ted, a trainer friend, to help her figure out a better way to help the participants of her next class discover the avoidable pitfalls that often bedevil weddings. Ted suggested that instead of making a presentation, Joan could use an activity to involve the group in coming up with the same type of information that she presented to the first group. Following Ted's suggestions, Joan asked the couples to form into groups of six and talk about some problems in weddings that they'd attended. Problems could be a major disaster, such as the florist having the wrong date for the wedding so no flowers were present. Or it could be as minor as some flowers being wilted. It was okay to discuss anything the participants noticed that they were sure was not what the bride and groom wanted. A volunteer was to take notes of the problems and be ready to report to the group.

At first the conversation was muted. But soon the momentum changed; the noise level rose and bursts of laughter punctuated the conversation. And rather than being a wet blanket, the discussion of negatives became an energizer for the participants who now were eager to learn how to steer clear of potential problems.

As the above incident demonstrates, the skilled use of appropriate activities can

- involve participants in the subject matter,
- relate them to each another, and
- enliven the group.

Activities also add a bit of spice to a long training day, and, by getting people out of their chairs and moving around, they often recharge people's energy.

This chapter discusses the common characteristics of proficiently led activities and describes an eight-step method for leading them well. Particular attention is given to step 5, Giving Directions, since experience shows that's the step most likely to be done poorly. Next you'll find suggestions for varying the ways to form subgroups. And you'll learn how to conduct mini-activities, which, in a very brief amount of time, inject a shot of energy and a welcome change of pace into a workshop. Appendix I has an activity worksheet to guide you through the creation of a one-page outline for virtually any activity that you'll ever use in a workshop (other than the very brief mini-activities that we'll describe later in this chapter.)

Common Features of Learning-Full Activities

Effectively led activities share these characteristics:

- They have a definite educational purpose.
- They follow a specific set of steps.
- They generate information for discussion.
- They are debriefed to enhance learning.

Lawrence Shulman asserts that "learning begins with student engagement."[1] Well-selected and -conducted activities provide a great way of stimulating that engagement. Well-designed and purposeful activities help participants become involved more quickly, increase their interest and energy, and accelerate their getting acquainted with each other.

It's great to develop or come across an activity that's lively, enjoyable, brief, and is related to the content you are teaching. However, the occasional use of mini-activities that don't contribute to the *content* of the workshop but that enhance its *process* by reviving participant's energy is a viable educational purpose.

But don't overdo using activities. You've undoubtedly heard the phrase, "Too much of a good thing." That certainly applies to the use of activities in a workshop. By all means avoid diluting your workshops with activities that contribute little or nothing but "fun and games."

A Step-by-Step Method for Leading Activities

There are three phases to leading an activity:

I. Introduce the activity.
II. Conduct the activity.
III. Debrief and conclude the activity.

The phases are composed of a total of eight steps. These three phases and this set of eight steps can be used in the same order for just about any activity you'll ever lead:

I: Introduce the Activity
1. Get the group's attention.
2. Transition in.
3. State the purpose.
4. Provide a preview
II: Conduct the Activity
5. Give directions.
6. Observe and guide.
III: Debrief and Conclude the Activity
7. Debrief the experience.
8. Conclude the activity.

I: Introduce the Activity

Step 1: Get the Group's Attention

The first thing to do when leading an activity is to get the group's attention; go no further until you have it. Don't start speaking until all eyes are on you and all mouths are closed. You may be thinking, That's a no-brainer; why mention it? We note it because speaking before having the whole group's attention happens more often than you might think. Novice trainers are especially prone to begin giving directions when participants are still moving or chatting.

Many trainers have developed their own special way of getting the group's attention that helps them avoid sounding like the workshop police. Some ring a small handheld dinner bell, some clap their hands, others use a sound from their cell phone, one of our colleagues plays a few notes on his miniature trumpet, some use a gentle-sounding chime, and still others flick the light switch off and on. Consider developing your own signature attention getter. However you do it, get people settled and don't rush into giving directions until you have everyone's attention.

Step 2: Transition In

Throughout this book you'll read the words *transition in* and *transition out*. Using transitions to make a smooth shift from what came before to what you're moving into will improve the workshop's flow and will prevent participants from getting lost in what otherwise might appear to them to be disconnected material. As the following example demonstrates, good transitions are succinct:

> This morning we discussed the difference between a *managerial role* and a *leadership role*. Then you viewed a DVD showing how people function in each role. Now you'll have a chance to discuss how to apply this information to your work.

Clear and succinct transitions link the multiple parts of a training together and are an important contributor to workshop effectiveness.

Step 3: State the Purpose

Briefly explain your rationale for using the activity. People are more likely to become involved in an activity when they're clear on why they're being asked to do it. The statement of purpose can be as simple as the following:

> This activity will help you discover additional opportunities for taking more of a leadership role in the organization.

Step 4: Provide a Preview

Give a succinct summary of what they'll be doing. For example:

> For the first ten minutes you'll be working alone on an activity in your workbook. Then, for the next twenty minutes, you'll be in groups of four discussing the ideas you developed in your alone time.

II: Conduct the Activity

Step 5: Give Directions

Incomplete or unclear directions create confusion and can destroy an activity's effectiveness. When giving directions make sure they're presented in sequential order. Because giving explicit directions is so crucial to conducting activities (and practices), you'll find further guidelines on giving directions later in the chapter.

Step 6: Observe and Guide

When the directions have been given and participants are engaged in the activity, the trainer's function temporarily recedes into the background. However, the trainer is still in charge of the group. This is not a time to review your notes about what's coming next. You are still "on duty" as the leader of the workshop. This temporary shift in function is from having a more directive role to being an observer and guide. Let participants know that you'll be walking around to see how they're doing and that you won't interrupt to guide their work unless they absolutely need help.

As you move about the room, monitor the activity to ensure that each subgroup is progressing as expected. Look for successes as well as any difficulties that participants are encountering. As you observe the various subgroups, think about debriefing questions that will help people draw pertinent learnings from their experience.

If you think a subgroup is stuck, you may decide to intervene briefly to get it back on track. If a group is floundering because the participants don't understand the directions, you can provide clarification to get them started. However, you may find that some participants would rather discuss content than do the activity. It's rarely appropriate for a trainer to teach content during an activity. If you give into that type of request, you'll be chipping away at the time for the participants to discover the learnings that can best be gained from doing the activity.

III: Debrief and Conclude the Activity

Step 7: Debrief the Experience

Debriefing is a word that's used for surfacing lessons from what was just experienced—in this case, participants' involvement in an activity. If participants are dispersed throughout the room, you can either have them debrief where they are or ask them to return to their regular seats. Then, when you have their attention, invite them to reflect on their experience.

The most widely used debriefing question is:

What did you learn from his activity?

It's not a bad question, although if asked repeatedly throughout a workshop it can become predictable and not sufficiently thought provoking. Fortunately, you can do much better. The learning potential from effective debriefing is so significant that Chapter 6, Debrief to Harvest the Lessons, is completely devoted to this skill and includes many examples of debriefing questions.

Step 8: Conclude the Activity

Some trainers plunge directly from the end of an activity into the next module. Instead, make sure you

- summarize the learnings, and
- transition out to the next piece.

A summary followed by a transition out might look like this.

Summary: This activity provided an opportunity for you to focus on the differences between a manager's role and a leader's role and to assess which of these roles you tend to
gravitate toward.

Transition: Now it's time for a break. When you return we'll discuss emotional intelligence
at work and its importance for your development as leaders. See you in ten minutes: 11:35
workshop time.[2] Check your watches. Right now workshop time is 11:25.

More Tips on Giving Directions

Because giving unambiguous directions is essential to leading an activity effectively,
here are some how-tos for giving directions. The directions for an activity should be
given one at a time and in actionable chunks that are separated from the next chunk
by a brief pause. For example:

You'll need your workbook and something to write with.
    (Pause while people get their materials.)
Now, move into groups of four positioned as far away from other groups as possible.
    (Pause while they move.)
Open your workbook to the activity on page 8 labeled *Key Functions of Managers and
Leaders.*
    (Pause while they turn to page 8)
Read the directions. You have seven minutes to do this part of the activity.

Assist the participants with their time management. Tell them

   1.   when five minutes remain,
   2.   when the activity is half over, and
   3.   when there's one minute to complete the activity.

If an activity has several steps, post the number of minutes as well as the time when
each major step should be completed. Present instructions both verbally and visually
(unless they are very brief and easy to remember).

   When giving directions it's usually desirable to use a previously prepared chart,
overhead, handout, or electronic visual summarizing the directions. Unless you've
provided a handout, make sure that there's a visual of the directions posted where
participants can refer to it while doing the activity.

Sequence the Directions

When giving directions for activities, be sure you give them in sequential order. The
following steps for providing information about doing an activity are listed in the
order in which they are usually given:

1. What participant's will be doing
2. What materials, if any, will be needed: workbook, pencil, handouts, etc.
3. Where they'll be doing the activity (unless it's obvious)
4. How many people they'll be working with
5. Who they'll be working with
6. Criteria (if any) for selection of people to work with. Some examples:
   a. No reporting relationships
   b. Someone you haven't worked with yet
   c. A number of other options are mentioned in the next section of this chapter
7. Instruct participants to move into their subgroups now. When they've regrouped, continue giving directions for the activity.
8. How long the activity will take and how they'll know when the time is up
9. What your role will be
10. Conclude your directions by asking if there are any questions.

When it's written out like the above, this may seem like a cumbersome process with too many steps to remember. But it's a natural flow so you'll be able to learn it quickly. And you can use these steps for leading every activity that you'll ever want to use (other than mini-activities, which will be discussed shortly). Once you've used this process a few times it can be your standard operating procedure for leading activities and you'll soon be able to recall it effortlessly.

Vary the Way You Form Subgroups

Many activities (and practices) involve forming subgroups. Try to create different combinations of learners each time you break into smaller groups. Doing so will contribute to the cohesiveness of the workshop. Subgroups may be as small as twosomes or threesomes or as large as five to seven people depending on the nature of the activity. Experience has shown that when there are more than seven people in a group, some are apt to get lost in the group and may not participate.

Put some variety into your method for quickly moving participants into small groups. Here are a couple of options for pairs and triads:

- "Get together with two persons sitting near you."
- "Find someone you haven't worked with yet."

For larger groups of uniform size you can count-off around the room. For example, if you want groups of four ask someone to start by saying "1" and then go around the room "2," "3," "4"; "1," "2," "3," "4," etc. With this and the other ways of forming subgroups the last group may not have the full quota of participants. Figure out in advance whether that would pose a problem and if so determine how you'll deal with it.

In creating subgroups larger than dyads and triads, keep in mind that the smaller the group, the greater the participation. Also smaller groups typically consume less workshop time than larger groups. When possible, limit the size of larger subgroups to five to seven people.

When it's okay for the subgroups to be of varying sizes, you might consider an alternative way of forming the groups like one of these:

- Geographical: Where you live (or where you were born): Northeast, Midwest, Mountain states, etc.
- Energy level: morning person, afternoon person, evening person, late-night person
- Favorite meal: breakfast, lunch, dinner, evening snack
- Color preference.
- Birth order: oldest children in one corner, middle children in another corner, youngest children in the third corner, only children in fourth corner
- Birth month
- Arrival style: typically arrive at appointments early, on time, a bit late
- Degree of organization: very organized, moderately well organized, disorganized
- Work role

If subgroups are likely to be larger than four or five people, consider having a particular location in the room for each subgroup for noise control purposes. If, for example, you have a group of twenty-five participants and the subgroups are formed according to people's favorite season of the year, you could designate a given corner of the room for each season.

Consider Using the Preparation Worksheet for Leading Activities

When author Bob Bolton's daughter, Betsy, was fresh out of college she joined Ridge Training, our company, before moving on to graduate school. During her time with the company, she made countless improvements in the trainer materials that we provided for our trainer network. One enhancement, the Activity Worksheet, was immediately adopted as a practical and user-friendly workshop preparation aid. The somewhat revised version found in Appendix I will help you implement the contents of this chapter.

Occasionally Reenergize the Group with a Mini-Activity

There are numerous mini-activities that don't require a full set of directions and take only a few minutes. Their purpose is to grab the participants' attention and illustrate something important that you're about to teach. They often make a modest contribution to community building and they typically have an energizing effect on participants. Mini-activities (sometimes called recharge activities) can be used to introduce and heighten interest in learning the material that comes next, as you'll see in the example below of the use of a mini-activity to introduce a module on conflict management.

In contrast to leading longer activities, a trainer only has to do two things when leading a mini-activity:

1. Give clear directions.
2. Debrief the activity.

For example, with no transition-in at the beginning of a module on conflict management, the trainer asks if someone can explain what "free association" is. When the trainer is sure everyone understands the concept of free association, she does two things listed above.

1. Give Clear Directions

"I want you to free associate to the word 'conflict.' Call out the words that come to mind and I'll write them on the chart."

People say words like "fight," "anger," "upset," "discord," "trouble," "war," "resolution," "bad news," "disturbance," "disagreement," "discuss," "hurt," and "disaster."

Although someone might contribute a positive word like "discuss" or "resolution," negative words always predominate. The trainer then says, "While most of you mentioned negative words in association with *conflict*, the premise of the approach we'll be learning is that conflict has the potential to be positive. Other than the positive words *discuss* and *resolve*, which are on the chart already, what words can you think of that reflect the desirable outcomes of many conflicts?"

People say words like "peace," "reconciliation," "agreement," "harmony," "blend," "accord," "calm," "negotiate," "discuss," "conciliation," and "understanding."

2. Debrief the Activity

The trainer pauses briefly for the contrast between the negative and positive associations to sink in and then debriefs the mini-activity.

The next chapter on debriefing will help you maximize learnings not only from every activity you conduct but from throughout the workshop.

6

Debriefing to Gather the Learnings

Experience is not what happens to you, it is what you do with what happens to you.

——Aldous Huxley[1]

The word *debrief* came into popular usage during the early space programs. When the astronauts returned from outer space, the first thing they did was participate in an after-action review session so that findings from the mission could be captured while the experience was still fresh in their minds. Learning about those journeys to where no one had ventured before was riveting, and the information gathered in the review was so useful that the practice was widely adapted by consultants, educators, managers, and executives.

In these pages the word *debrief* is used for *after-the-fact review discussions* about a training event or some part of it. More specifically, debriefing (sometimes termed "processing") is a discussion that's designed to *generate discussion about what happened in, learning that occurred during, and/or reactions to*

- an activity,
- a demonstration,
- a skill practice,
- a presentation, or
- another workshop event,

as well as *to achieve closure at significant transitions,* such as the end of

- a module,
- a day, or
- a workshop.

In other words, to generate maximum learning in your workshops, you'll be leading lots of debriefing sessions. So it makes sense to learn how to conduct debriefs effectively.

The Benefits of Debriefing

When done well, debriefing is an amazingly versatile and powerful training tool that not only helps produce and solidify learning but also enhances group process.

Debriefing generates and consolidates learning by:

- Reinforcing key concepts
- Helping people learn from their own experience
- Enlarging participants' learning by making the collective experience of the group available to each participant
- Airing misunderstandings and buried objections so they can be addressed
- Improving the transfer of learning

Debriefing enhances group process by:

- Increasing participation
- Generating two-way communication between the trainer and participants
- Providing knowledge about participants' grasp of the subject matter and satisfaction with the workshop
- Helping build a sense of community

Debriefing Reinforces Key Concepts

An effective debrief raises important learning points, thereby reinforcing the information that's most important to remember.

Debriefing Helps People Learn From Their Experience

Debriefing is a way of learning from experience, which makes it an especially powerful training tool. As Blaise Pascal, the French philosopher and mathematician, put it, "We are generally the better persuaded by the reasons we discover ourselves than those given to us by others."[2]

Debriefing Makes the Collective Experience of the Group Available to Each Person

Hearing how other participants experienced an activity broadens one's own learning. For example, in a whole-group debriefing, some subgroups that have had successful experiences will not only testify to the usefulness of what's being taught but may also relate some helpful how-to information. Other subgroups may struggle or fail to use the new abilities effectively, and a good debriefing will inform the whole group about pitfalls to avoid.

Debriefing provides information from one's peers. And on at least some issues, a peer's input may be considered more significant than that of the trainer. For instance, when the issue is applicability, a colleague is often deemed more credible than the trainer. A participant who might doubt that the trainer is a good judge of whether what's being taught will work in the "real world" will probably pay a good deal more attention to the same point made by a fellow trainee.

Debriefing Airs Misunderstandings

Misunderstandings often arise when people are learning new material. Also, some participants may doubt the practicality of using the methods and skills being taught but decide not to mention their skepticism. But when misunderstandings and objections aren't raised, they remain unaddressed and, therefore, persist as ongoing obstacles to learning. Debriefing airs many of these misunderstandings and objections so that they can be resolved and no longer hinder learning.

Improving the Transfer of Learnings

During debriefing sessions some participants are likely to describe how they're thinking about applying their new learnings at work. Others might want to ask about the application of what they learned in a specific situation. This tends to prompt others to think about how they might use what they've learned back on the job.

Debriefing Increases Participation

When debriefing, participants briefly describe their own experience of or reaction to what just transpired. Since each participant is the best authority in the room concerning his or her own reaction, speaking during a debriefing is one of the easiest and safest ways of participating in a workshop—a benign way to dip one's toe in the water. And once a participant has spoken in the group, it's much less daunting to speak up again or ask questions thereafter.

Generating Broader Participation

Many people are shy about speaking in a group—especially a group of strangers, which is often the case in training situations. In a debriefing situation, it's much easier for a shy person to speak since he is describing his own experience or point of view. And, remember, he is the world's greatest authority on that. Furthermore, everyone's input is expected to be succinct—so one's comments can be very brief. Once a person speaks a sentence or two in the group, it's much easier to speak again. The first time they talk in the group they "break the ice." and it's easier to participate after that. Then too, the more people who are participating the easier it seems for shyer folks to join in. So good debriefing sessions help create an interactive environment.

Providing Knowledge About Participants' Grasp of the Subject Matter and Satisfaction with the Workshop

Debriefing sessions provide the alert trainer with an awareness of how well participants understand the material that was covered and how invested and sagacious they are in thinking about how to apply it. So participants' debriefing sessions can be a useful evaluation time for the trainer.

Debriefing Helps Build a Sense of Community

Debriefing provides a way for people in a group to pay shared attention to shared events. When participants reflect on and discuss what they are experiencing, the cohesiveness of the group tends to be enhanced and the sense of community strengthened.

How to Debrief

Here's a six-step process for leading debriefing sessions:

1. Reestablish the large group focus. If people have been in dyads, triads, or subgroups of other sizes, ask them to return to the large group. (Some trainers remain standing during a debriefing; others prefer sitting, hoping to communicate nonverbally that they are shifting their role from presenter to listener. Both ways work.)

2. Direct a question to the whole group. Usually no more than three questions are needed in a given debriefing. Some trainers ask basically the same question two or three times. That just muddies the water. Get your question right. Then ask it. Then be silent and wait for the participants' responses. (You'll find a number of debriefing questions later in this chapter as well as in some subsequent chapters.)

    Note: Steps 3 through 5 are bracketed to indicate that you will cycle through these steps several times before proceeding to step 6.

3. Pause and wait. You are asking for opinions, reactions, learning, and feelings. Participants often need a bit of time to decide whether to respond to the question and, if so, how they will phrase their response. The pause may seem like an eternity to the trainer—but not to the participants. Discipline yourself to silently wait out the pause. After someone speaks, pause again and continue pausing after each person's input until you sense that everyone who wanted to contribute has spoken.

4. Listen attentively to the speaker. Then acknowledge the statement with a reflection such as, "You noticed _____. Or, "So your learning is _____. When reflecting, you are not presenting, so soften your voice from a presentation mode to a quieter listening mode.

   Another option is to simply say "Thank you" or nod your head.

   Occasionally you may decide to note similarities and differences.

   Avoid teaching. If someone asks you a question during a debriefing you can write it on the Question Parking Lot Chart (discussed in Chapter 13) and say you'll respond to it later. Or, if a more timely answer would be appropriate, you may wish to respond as soon as the debriefing is concluded.

   Avoid evaluating the question or comment: eliminate even positive evaluations such as "Good point."

5. Invite other participants' responses. Direct your attention to another part of the room and ask, "Anyone else?" After someone answers you may want to look to yet another part of the room and again ask, "Anyone else?" or "Anything else?"

6. Transition to the next part of the workshop. Make a clean shift to what comes next. Resist the impulse to continue teaching about the part of the workshop you are wrapping up.

Since debriefing is a period that's designated for participants to speak, it's a natural time for them to ask questions and raise issues about the course content. Some trainers answer the questions on the spot. But that approach cuts into the participants' opportunity to mine the experience they just had. Furthermore, when a trainer answers participants' questions during a debriefing, it tends to turn future debriefings into question-and-answer periods, with the result that in subsequent debriefings participants will have less opportunity to learn from the experience they just had. It's important to remember that debriefing is a form of learning from experience that generally is a much more potent form of learning than occurs in the typical question–answer periods.

How to Sequence the Speaking in Dyads and Triads

In some workshops, such as those in which communications skills are taught, debriefings of dyad and triad experiences are often done within those small subgroups.

Sometimes these debriefings are most effective when participants speak in a predetermined order. The following sequence often works well:

1. The person on the receiving end of the skill training speaks first; he's the best authority on what if felt like to be the recipient of the training.
2. The skill user speaks next; her perspective on the challenges and satisfaction (or dissatisfaction) with using the skill is reported.
3. When there is an observer (as in a triad practice) the observer speaks last.

Debriefing Questions for Various Parts of a Workshop

It's easy for trainers to fall into the habit of asking the same two or three debriefing questions over and over again. But when you recall the number of debriefings in a typical workshop, it becomes obvious that relying on the same few questions repeatedly will soon bore everyone, including the trainer.

Having an assortment of questions you can choose from will make your debriefing more interesting and learningful. The questions below can help you put more variety and specificity into your debriefing sessions. When prepping for a workshop, you'll probably find that some of these questions will work well for you with little or no revision. But to do effective debriefing, you'll need to revise many of the questions to address the content of your training. And it's crucial to come up with many of your own questions that will relate specifically to the subject matter you are presenting and the particular group of participants that you are teaching.

Occasionally, in place of a question, you may decide to use a sentence stem, such as, "Please listen to this sentence stem and finish it in your own way. 'Something I'll do differently after this workshop is _____.'"

Although the questions below have been placed in an appropriate category, a number of the questions are equally applicable for debriefing some other parts of a workshop.

Questions for Debriefing an Activity

- Let's go around the group and hear what you learned from this activity. Who'll start?
- What insights did you gain from this experience?
- What did you notice about _____?

Questions for Debriefing a Demonstration

- What stood out for you in this demonstration?
- What looks difficult about this? What looks fairly easy?
- What was the most useful thing you observed?

Questions for Debriefing a Practice

- How did it go for you?
- What did you do well in this practice?
- What was most difficult for you in this practice?
- What worked? What didn't?
- Were there any surprises?
- If you did this again, what would you do differently?
- How might you use this knowledge/attitude/skill/process?

Questions for Debriefing a Second or Third Practice of the Same Skill

As you've seen in Chapter 3, we've found that to learn a fairly complex skill, three or more practices are often required in order to unlearn the old, habitual way of doing things and become somewhat proficient in the new way. Here are a few questions for debriefing a second or third practice of the same skill:

- What came easier for you than in the previous practice?
- Was anything more difficult than in the previous practice?
- Tomorrow we'll practice this skill again. What do you want to remember to be sure to do in that practice?

In addition to these three questions, many of the other questions in this chapter can be used for debriefing a second or third practice.

Questions for Debriefing a Presentation

Although trainers seldom debrief a presentation, it's sometimes a valuable use of time.

- How practical do these concepts/methods/skills, etc. appear to you?
- What's your reaction to this way of _____?
- What strikes you as the strengths of this approach? The weaknesses?
- How does what you just heard match, expand, or challenge what you previously thought/did?

Sentence Stems for Debriefing at the Conclusion of a Module, a Half-Day Session, a Day, or a Workshop

- My biggest takeaway from this module is _____.
- Today I learned _____.
- Something that I'm going to do as a result of today's session is _____.
- I expected _____ and I got _____.

- Among the most valuable things I learned in the last two days was
  _____.

A Preface Can Enhance Some Debriefing Questions

When the context of a debriefing question is implicit, a preface is superfluous. But sometimes when you ask a debriefing question the context may not be obvious from the activity, demonstration, practice, or other workshop event that you are debriefing. When the context is not apparent you'll get better responses to a question when you preface it. A good preface adds clarity and specificity to a debriefing question. For example:

> *Preface:* "You learned a six-step process for leading debriefing sessions." [That's a lot to remember so display the six steps.]
>
> *Debriefing Question:* "Any ideas about what you could do to help you recall all six steps of what to do in a debrief?"

One last thought about debriefing: the more you encourage participants to articulate their thoughts and reactions about what they are learning, the greater the likelihood that they will use what you're teaching when the workshop is over.

7

Organizing Your Presentations

Everyone may speak truly, but to speak logically, prudently, and adequately is a talent few possess.

——Montaigne[1]

Dynamic trainers excel at two sets of presentation skills: organizing their presentations and delivering them. In this chapter, we'll focus on how to organize dynamic presentations. Chapter 10 provides guidelines for delivering dynamic presentations.

Five Options for Delivering Training Presentations

There are five commonly used approaches to delivering training content in workshops:

1. Use video presentations.
2. Read the presentations from the training manual.
3. Memorize the presentations.
4. Use off-the-cuff delivery.
5. Deliver the presentations extemporaneously based on easy-to-remember outlines.

This chapter briefly describes the first four options and why, although each of them is used frequently in training, we find them ill-suited for dynamic training. The bulk of the chapter describes a more dynamic approach—presentations that are designed to be easily remembered for extemporaneous delivery.

Option 1: Use Video Presentations

Many courses are sold with video presentations. Most of the videos are written by content experts and narrated by professional speakers. You may wonder, Why not use these top-notch video presentations instead of going through the hard work of outlining the talks, learning them, and delivering them in your workshops?

An obvious drawback to videotaped presentations is that they can't be tailored to the specific needs of the group you're teaching. And unless you are financially willing and able to reshoot the video many times to fit specific divisions or departments, you'll find yourself in the position of showing videos that don't fit the participants' situations. Even if you could afford to create new video presentations for every client, the medium is incapable of responding to the fluctuating moods and needs of a group. Furthermore, having content delivered by video makes it less imperative for the trainer to learn the material well. And participants are likely to wonder, "If she knows this content, why can't she tell us herself?"

Then, too, watching a video presentation tends to induce greater passivity in participants. Their energy declines visibly in response to most video presentations and the last thing you want to do is turn participants into couch potatoes.

Option 2: Read the Presentations from the Training Manual

When a training program lacks video presentations, some trainers *read* the talks to the group—a guaranteed sleep inducer!

To make matters worse, much training material is written for the *eye* rather than for the ear. But writing something that's to be used in public speaking is far different from writing that is designed for a person to read silently to herself. If a training program was not written for the ear you'll have to alter the material significantly for use in oral presentations. The twentieth-century American poet T.S. Eliot said, "If we spoke as we write, we should find no one to listen."[2]

Option 3: Memorize the Presentations

This isn't a feasible option for trainers, although we've known a few who have attempted it. Memorizing entire talks for a day-long or multiday workshop requires far more time than most of us have. Besides, if anything unpredictable happens during the workshop, as it often does, this approach to delivery will likely leave the presenter unprepared to handle the unexpected. And if the workshop is running behind schedule, the trainer will be ill equipped to ad lib his way through a greatly condensed remainder of the talk.

Option 4: Use Off-the-Cuff Delivery

This approach works well for some people in some situations but is too haphazard for leading a workshop. It is especially unsuitable for Tell-How presentations in which the instruction needs to be highly specific, carefully sequenced, and very succinct.

Option 5: Deliver the Presentations Extemporaneously

Dynamic trainers make it a practice to deliver virtually all presentations extemporaneously. By this we mean giving presentations that are

- carefully prepared, and
- spoken without significant reliance on notes.

Because extemporaneous talks are delivered without notes, people sometimes equate *extemporaneous speaking* with giving an *impromptu presentation*. But as we use the terms there is a world of difference between these two approaches to presenting:

- Impromptu speaking refers to presenting
  - without preparation or
  - rehearsal.
- Extemporaneous presentation, by contrast, is
  - based on intensive preparation and
  - thorough rehearsal.[3]

The rest of this chapter discusses creating easily remembered outlines for extemporaneous presentations.

Stating the Content Clearly

Your delivery responsibilities begin by making sure the content you are communicating is understandable to the people you are addressing. Although this seems like a no-brainer, when you know a subject in depth but most or all of the participants are subject neophytes, it can be challenging to put the course content in terms they can understand. But it can be done and it's one of the challenges of training to do it well.

Ludwig Wittgenstein, the Austrian-born British philosopher, stated,

Everything that can be thought of at all can be thought of clearly.
Everything that can be said can be said clearly.[4]

So work at phrasing your content so that it is easily understandable to everyone in the room.

Standard Presentation Structure

Learning is enhanced when content is organized in a manner that helps trainees understand and recall it easily. Ever since Aristotle, most treatises on public speaking recommend dividing presentations into three sections:

- The *introduction,* which sets the stage for the meat of the presentation
- The *body,* which contains the substance of the talk
- The *conclusion,* which succinctly reviews and wraps up the presentation

This time-tested format works well for most training presentations. The following pages describe an effective way of creating presentation outlines using this three-part structure.

Begin by Outlining the Body of the Presentation

It makes sense to be clear on what the body of your talk is about *before* you plan your introduction or conclusion. Get the main teaching points down on paper. When you're sure you've got the key points of your presentation, add sub-points when relevant. Mentally label each point and sub-point with a *brief* phrase and put those phrases in the appropriate places in your outline.

Next Outline the Introduction of the Presentation

When the body of your presentation has been outlined, you are ready to develop a brief introduction. The introduction should capture people's attention and "tell them what you're going to tell them." Introductions usually have three parts:

- A *transition into* the presentation
- A *benefits statement* or other relevant attention getter
- A *preview*

A Transition Into the Presentation

Transitions are sentences or phrases that help participants follow your reasoning as you proceed through your talk. Although you usually *develop* the body of the presentation prior to developing the introduction, you obviously *deliver* the introduction first. To begin the introduction, you'll want to prepare a transition to bridge:

- From what the participants have been doing;
- To the presentation you are introducing.
    Having practiced how to _____, let's now turn our attention to applications.
    In our last component we covered _____; now I'll explain _____.

A Benefits Statement or Other Relevant Attention Getter

At the outset of your talk people want to know, "What's in it for me to learn this?" So, give the bottom line at the top of your talk. That whets participants' appetites for what's coming.

Here are some other types of attention getters:

- A question.
- A dramatic statement.
- A quotation.
- A statistic.
- A brief demonstration.
- A visual.
- Two opposing points of view.

Of course, the attention getter should be brief, pertinent to the subject matter of the presentation, and of interest to this particular group.

A Preview

"Tell them what you are going to tell them" and do so as succinctly as possible. Using a visual that you prepared ahead of time, state each point in the order in which it will be given.

There are times when one or even two parts of the introduction may be eliminated. For example, at the conclusion of the previous component you may have indicated what's coming next, so a transition would be redundant. And, if you can't find a good attention getter, don't use one. Good attention getters aren't easy to come by and using a poor one is worse than using none at all.

The Body of the Presentation

The body of a Tell-How presentation succinctly and specifically describes how to do the skill or method that will be portrayed in the demonstration and what participants will do in the upcoming practice. (See next section for tips on developing well-organized presentations.)

The Conclusion of the Presentation

Generally there are four parts to the conclusion of a presentation:

- A wrap-up signal
- A crisp review
- A summary of the benefits (when benefits have been mentioned)
- A transition out of the presentation to what's coming next

A Wrap-Up Signal

Trainers often segue into the conclusion by sending a signal that the presentation is drawing to a close:

"The last thing I want to note . . ."

"Finally . . ."

"In conclusion . . ."

A Crisp Review

"Tell them what you told them" and do it concisely. Often a review is essentially a carbon copy of the preview that you prepared for the introduction. If that's the case, when reviewing the points that were made you can use the visual that you used in the introduction. A good review provides participants with mental Velcro that helps the points stick in their minds.

A Summary of the Benefits

In the introduction you explained the benefits of employing what you've been talking about. Now give a concise reminder of those benefits.

A Transition Out

This generally is a one- or two-sentence statement that links the presentation you are concluding to what's coming next.

More Tips for Developing Well-Organized Presentations

Soundly organized presentations make life much easier for the trainer—they have a logic that makes them easier to recall and deliver. Good organization also makes it easier for participants to learn and use the content being taught. The following suggestions are designed to help you structure the body of your presentation:

1. Learn the subject matter thoroughly.
2. Slant the presentation to the group you're working with.
3. Keep it simple.
4. Make it brief.
5. Help participants avoid commonly made mistakes.
6. Develop the presentation in reverse.
7. Make it interactive.
8. Create a well-crafted skeletal outline.
9. Use "signposts" to guide participants through the presentation.
10. Flesh out the talk with illustrative material.

11. Personalize the presentation.
12. Make the presentation condensable.

1. Learn the Subject Matter Thoroughly

The fifteenth-century English poet John Dryden's advice to writers applies equally to twentieth-first-century trainers: "He, who proposes to be a writer, should first be a student." You owe it to the participants in your workshop to be a subject matter expert in the material you are teaching. Do whatever it takes to achieve state of the art knowledge of that topic. Zig Ziglar, a popular speaker and author says, "I came to realize that the more I knew about my subject, the more creative I could be in my presentations."[5]

Disciplined reading generally is an important part of learning the content of a course. *The Book of Common Prayer* of 1662 outlined how to absorb the written word productively: "READ, MARK, LEARN, AND INWARDLY DIGEST."[6]

2. Slant the Presentation to the Group You're Working With

Slanting is a term that journalists use for the process of gearing an article to the profile of a newspaper's or magazine's readers. Slanting is crucial to making the material interesting and applicable to the intended recipients.

An article about a famous athlete that would be appropriate for *Sports Illustrated* would be slanted very differently to appeal a typical reader of *People Magazine*. Although salespeople may not use the term, the effective ones slant their sales pitch to their clients. As a British real-estate salesperson explained, "We don't sell houses. We match lifestyles." Similarly, dynamic trainers match their presentations to the needs, interests, and applications of the participants they're working with.

Trainers often find themselves delivering essentially the same content to very different occupational groups. Before the workshop begins, learn as much as you can about the specific group you'll be teaching. Will it be composed of executives, middle managers, team leaders, or some combination of them? Are all the participants from one part of the organization, such as accounting or sales, or will people from several departments attend the workshop? What's the culture like in that part of the organization? How are participants apt to feel about having to attend the training program? Has the organization as a whole or this part of it had some significant successes recently? Any upsetting news? When you find yourself presenting to different occupational groups or different organizations don't skimp on your effort to slant the material to each group.

When more extensive adaptation than slanting is advisable, you can retrofit a workshop more extensively. Appendix II provides guidelines for revising a workshop to make it applicable to a different population or the same type of population when it faces altered circumstances.

3. Keep It Simple

When summing up the annual meeting of the World Economic Forum in Davos, Switzerland, news analyst David Brooks, wrote, "If there was one trait the best of them possessed, it was a talent for simplification. They had the ability to take a complex situation and capture the heart of the matter in simple terms. . . . They took reality and made it manageable for busy people."[7]

4. Make It Brief

In communication, as in architecture, less is often more. William Strunk, Jr., in his classic, *The Elements of Style*, stresses that "vigorous writing is concise." And Nobel Prize–winning Yiddish author, Isaac Bashevis Singer, said, "The wastebasket is the writer's best friend." This guideline applies in spades to training presentations. So identify the bare minimum of information that participants need to know in order to be successful in the next practice. Then ruthlessly prune everything else away.

Dynamic trainers typically limit their workshop presentations to seven minutes or less. Anything more is considered overkill.

5. Help Participants Avoid Commonly Made Mistakes

It's been said that an expert is someone who knows some of the worst mistakes that can be made in his field, and how to avoid them. The same can be said of effective trainers. They know the mistakes that are made most frequently when learning a particular subject and they teach participants how to avoid those pitfalls. They not only say, "Do this"; they also counsel, "Make sure you avoid doing that."

Conscientious trainers carefully observe practice sessions to see what participants learn easily as well as where participants have problems using the skill being taught. The next time they deliver the workshop, they focus less on what was easily mastered and devote more attention to the material that participants found most difficult. Their commitment to help trainees avoid making predictable mistakes drives them to continually fine-tune what they teach.

6. Develop the Presentation in Reverse

In Chapter 3 (where we discussed the structure of dynamic workshops) we noted that when *leading* a workshop the following three components are taught in this order:

1. Tell how
2. Show how
3. Practice

When *developing* a workshop, however, it's best to proceed in the opposite order—you begin your preparation focused firmly on what will be done in the practice:

1. Determine what concepts, attitudes, and/or behaviors people will employ in a successful *practice.*
2. Next, plan the best way to *show how* to do those behaviors.
3. Finally, create a *tell-how* presentation that describes what the learners will be seeing and hearing in the *show how* and will be doing in the *practice.*

7. Make It Interactive

To advance learning and avoid the glazed eyes and vacant stares that often result from one-way presentations, make your talks interactive. A vital part of your presentation is deciding how you will involve the participants. What questions will you ask? How else will you stimulate interactivity? Chapter 14 will help you facilitate energizing communication in your workshops.

8. Create a Well-Crafted Skeletal Outline

Frederick W. Robertson, one of the most highly regarded preacher of the nineteenth century, said, "If the thoughts are rightly arranged, the words will take care of themselves. But all depends on the effectiveness of the outline."[8]

After you've practiced a new presentation, redo the outline and make it more succinct. After another practice or outing with the talk, redo the outline again, condensing it still further. Make each successive outline more bare bones than the previous one.

In the next chapter we'll discuss how one of the world's greatest orators, Winston Churchill, typically used an outline when making a presentation, although on many occasions he never needed to refer to his notes. We know a number of exceptionally effective trainers who use essentially the same process.

9. Use "Signposts" to Guide Participants Through the Presentation

In public speaking lingo, "signposts" are words, phrases, or sentences that steer participants through a presentation in ways that enhance their sense of the presentation's flow and their comprehension of what's being communicated. The most frequently used signposts are numerical:

"There are three compelling reasons to act on this immediately:

"The first, and most significant, reason is _____.

"A second factor is _____.

"Third, _____."

The excessive use of numerical signposts, however, soon becomes wearisome. You'll be more effective when you use some of the many other ways of phrasing your signposts:

"For example, . . ."

"Another point to consider is . . ."

"Let me also mention . . ."

"This can't be overemphasized . . ."

"I want to stress . . ."

"Let me underscore . . ."

"Furthermore, . . ."

"On the other hand, . . . "

"Now, let's look at the downside . . ."

"A case in point is . . ."

"In conclusion, . . ."

10. Flesh Out the Talk with Illustrative Material

Keep on the lookout for anecdotes, quotations, and other material related to the main points of your presentations. A good story is especially potent in making a point memorable. Once you've outlined the presentation, add carefully selected examples, quotations, statistics, and so forth. Just be sure not to overdo it.

Trainers who teach often hear practical and sometimes humorous stories told by a learner who has put the skills or methods of the course to work. Keep your ears open for these stories that can enliven future presentations. Let the class feel your respect for the participant whose story you are telling. And, unless you've received permission to use the anecdote, be sure to disguise the story enough so it could never be linked to the person who told it or to the organization in which it happened.

Devise a filing system or other type of collection method that works for you. People typically begin by listing all the topics they think they will be covering in their talks. Arrange them alphabetically or in whatever order works for you. Most professional speakers develop a computer file or filing cabinet file for each topic. Then they download from the Internet, or scan, photocopy, or clip items from newspapers, magazines, and books. They also type up experiences they've had and events they've heard of, and file them away. It's a lot of work, especially when you are setting up your system. But if you read a lot and collect interesting vignettes that you read, have witnessed, or heard about, soon you'll have an invaluable and continually growing body of illustrative material. Our filing system has provided us with presentation examples for more than three decades, and it has certainly been worth the considerable time and effort it took to develop and maintain it.

If you use a handout that quotes any published material of more than fifty words per quote, secure permission for use. News items from newspapers are an exception to this legal requirement. However, written permission is required for cartoons, editorials, and regular features.

11. Personalize the Presentation

In all likelihood, some of the workshop presentations you give will have initially been written by someone else. It's great to have much of the research, organizing, and writing done for you. However, the life experience and mode of expression of the person who developed the presentation will have been different from yours. To be effective, you'll need to personalize the presentation—recast it into your own words and use examples from your own experience and research as well as from practice sessions that you've coached.

12. Make Your Presentations Condensable

In a dynamic workshop there's lots of participation, so managing workshop time can be challenging. There will be many occasions when you'll need to shorten a presentation. So, plan ahead for that eventuality. If you don't plan what you'll do when you find yourself in a time bind, you're likely to:

- Make poor on-the-spot decisions about what to cut.
- Rush through the material. Although you may be able to talk faster, any effort to speed-talk probably will make the situation worse. Your being in a time bind won't cause participants' rate of learning to accelerate. And they probably won't appreciate the stress that your hurry-up effort injects into the workshop.
- Continue teaching past the announced closing time. Not the best way to win friends and influence people.

Just about any well-crafted presentation can be put into a nutshell. So when time is short, rather than rush your talk, cut it. *Figure out ahead of time how to make each presentation condensable.* In that condensed timeframe, state the most significant points that you want to make and very briefly say why each point is important. That way you should be able to cut a seven-minute presentation to a two-minute or shorter speech. It's that simple. With a bit of experience, you'll be able to quickly make every presentation condensable.

When your outline is complete, you can create workshop visuals (Chapter 8) to use when delivering your presentations extemporaneously (Chapter 9).

8

Creating and Using Flip Charts

Even though we live in a world of multimedia, PowerPoint and webinar meetings, the basic flip chart is so useful you cannot get rid of it! . . .

——Graham Jones[1]

I n previous chapters we focused on the verbal aspects of presenting. In this and the following chapter we'll suggest ways to enhance your presentations with two visual aids that are frequently used by trainers:

- Flip charts (also called easel charts) created prior to the workshop.
- Trainer-built charts created by the trainer while conducting the session.

Here's a bit of history for you. John Patterson, the founder of National Cash Register Company (NCR) and the creator of the first sales training school, was one of the first executives to grasp the importance of visual aids in the workplace.[2] His early sales experience led him to believe that the eye is more impacted upon than the ear. After reviewing the research of the day, Patterson found that the optic nerve is twenty-two times stronger than the nerve controlling hearing. On the basis of that information, he bolstered his sales presentations with blackboards and easel charts. His use of these simple visuals was enormously successful. Knowing a good thing when he saw it, Patterson put easel pads and charts in all NCR showrooms, factories, and offices to support selling, manufacturing, and training. His firm's mastery of presenting with flip charts was a significant contributor to NCR's early success.

In the following years, the humble flip chart became one of the training field's most frequently used visual aids. With the advent of slideware, however, trainers downplayed the role of flip charts as an aid to learning. Although flip charts are about as low tech as you can get, they are surprisingly useful in dynamic training. The informality of charts is a good match for the learning climate you are trying to create in a dynamic workshop. One of the biggest payoffs from using charts is that, of all major visuals aids, such as slides, overheads, videos, and movies, flip charts have the least negative effect on group process. In dynamic training, that's a huge plus.

Additionally, flip charts can be used to stimulate group interaction. You can write participants' comments on a chart or have participants work in groups using flip charts in various parts of the room. If you have an important classroom interaction, you can use charts to facilitate the conversation—taking brief notes to summarize key points of the discussion. And you can post the charts for later reference.

Among the benefits of using flip charts, many trainers would put at the top of their list the fact that charts make great cheat sheets. You can lightly pencil in notes to yourself to use as reminders during your presentations.

Guidelines for Creating Pre-Made Flip Charts

Pre-made flip charts have become the dinosaur of the training world. Still, we include a section on pre-made charts for the few trainers out there who may still use them. If that's not you, skip on to the section on trainer-built charts. And, if you're not interested in charts of any kind and are strictly a PowerPoint user, move right on to the next chapter where the focus is totally on that subject. Here are some basic rules of thumb for creating easy-to-read charts:

- Use heavy chart paper—sufficiently opaque that the printing on the chart beneath it cannot be seen. Or use a blank sheet between charts.
- Use paper with faint lines on it to make your writing more orderly.
- Title the charts with four-inch-high letters.
- Make the letters of the chart's content two to three inches high. If you are developing charts on a computer, use sans serif type because on charts (and slides) it's easier to read for short lines of text. (A sans serif typeface has virtually no embellishments, while a serif typeface has small flared-out embellishments which makes it easier to read in longer documents like the chapters of a book, but is less suitable for use on the bulleted points on a chart.)
- For titles and for emphasis, you may want to use all CAPITAL LETTERS. (Emphasis can also be added with underlining or color.)
- For the points, using upper- and lower-case letters improves readability.
- Make bullets about half the size of the letters that follow them.
- Leave lots of white space.
- For the text, use a six-by-six format: no more than six lines and no more than six words on a line. Some trainers discipline themselves to use a five-

by-five format: no more than five lines and no more than five words per line. Condensing content for either of these formats takes time but it is well worth the effort.

- Choose your words very carefully. Mark Twain's advice is especially pertinent to presentation visuals: "The difference between the almost right word and the right word is the difference between the lightning bug and lightning."[3]
- Use two or three, but no more than three, colors per page. Rely on dark colors for lettering—black, dark blue, teal, forest green, purple, or brown. For bullets and highlighting, red, orange, yellow, or pastels are appropriate.
- When using illustrations, keep them simple.

Guidelines for Creating Charts While Teaching

The ability to build your own charts as a part of your presentation demonstrates a strong command of the subject matter and, when not done too frequently, can be interesting for the participants to follow. Here are a few tips to keep in mind:

- When writing on a chart, have the easel on your nondominant side so your back is to the least number of participants.
- When you expect to create a specific chart while teaching, pre-think *what* you will put on the page, *how* it will look when it's written, and *when* you will draw and/or write it.
- Use dark colors like those mentioned earlier—black, dark blue, teal, forest green, purple, or brown. For bullets and highlighting, red, orange, yellow, or pastels are appropriate.
- Make each point succinct. Don't write complete sentences unless they're no longer than five words. Condense each point as much as possible. Use only one line per point.
- Write quickly; you'll lose contact with the class if you get too engrossed in developing the chart.
- Use broad-tipped markers that are water based and won't soak through the paper. Bring your own magic markers if you want to ensure that you have what you need and that the markers are in good shape.
- When writing, minimize talking as much as possible. A group's attention quickly wanes when a trainer talks to her chart pack.
- It can be very distracting when the trainer presents while holding one or more markers in his hand. So, make sure you put the marker down when it's not in use.
- Some trainers are poor spellers and the charts they create while teaching highlight that disability—one that some of us find impossible to correct (says the male author of this book). Some trainers who are afflicted with

inept spelling jokingly refer to it as "creative spelling" and quote President Alexander Hamilton, who said, "It's a damn poor mind that can only come up with one way to spell a word."

Use the Surround System for Posting Charts

In multiday workshops, at the lunch break and at the last break of the day, trainers often attach key charts to the walls of the room in the order in which they were used. This approach literally surrounds the participants with the course content. And it provides an excellent visual summary for reviewing the subject matter of the workshop. Select only the most important charts so participants aren't overwhelmed with too much visual information.

You may want to develop a simple mental or written wall plan that specifies what charts will be included in your summary and where the charts will start. Typically the charts are posted with the bottom of the charts about four feet above the floor. When wall space is limited, the charts can be posted one above another.

Attach a Chart to the Wall

When trying to attach a chart to the wall, many presenters find themselves awkwardly fumbling around as they try to hold the chart and the masking tape and perhaps a marker or two while affixing the masking tape to the chart and fastening the chart to the wall. It's seldom an elegant moment. To avoid that clumsy-looking hassle, before tearing the page from the chart pack:

1. If you have a marker (or anything else) in your hand, put it down.
2. Attach the pre-torn pieces of masking tape to the top corners of the chart.
3. Then, with only the chart in your hands, tape it to the wall.

Walk the Walls

Just before or after the lunch break and immediately prior to the end-of-the-day debriefing, you may want to invite participants to "walk the walls" to review the content that was covered. Or, with the class seated, you may "walk the walls" reading aloud the content of the selected charts.

As the epigraph at the beginning of the chapter states, "The basic flip chart is so useful you cannot get rid of it!" Perhaps after having been reminded of its many uses, you won't want to.

9

Creating and Using PowerPoint Slides

No one in business today could pretend to be facile in business communications without Power-
Point. It's like being able to read.

——Clarke Caywood

PowerPoint software solved many of the problems associated with what used to be expensive and time-consuming processes of creating and editing slides. Today, at 95 percent of market share, PowerPoint dominates the presentation software market, having been installed on more than one billion computers. The latest research indicates an estimated 350 PowerPoint presentations are given *every second*![1]

Advantages of Using PowerPoint in Dynamic Training

The advantages of using PowerPoint include ease and speed of slide preparation and revision, and portability. Slides can be put together for a new training presentation or the revision of an existing one by fairly quickly adding new material, deleting what's inapplicable, and adjusting the terminology as needed. Another benefit is that the use of PowerPoint can increase the presenter's believability; an Arizona State University study found that using PowerPoint makes ideas seem more credible. Ease of duplication is also a great advantage. With a click you can send your presentation to someone for an e-copy. And, finally, there's no more risk of not knowing where your charts are or if your charts fit the easel stand that has been provided. You know you have your slides on your computer as well as on your thumb drive if you have compatibility issues.

PowerPoint Is Often Used Ineffectively

Although in many cases you may inherit the slides to support the course that you're teaching, it's wise to be able to create your own when you need to or want to. But be alert. There are many pitfalls to avoid when using PowerPoint. As the disparaging phrase "Death by PowerPoint" suggests, this technology has often been improperly used. In the hands of many people, PowerPoint deteriorated from being an aid to being a crutch. PowerPoint designer William Earnest says, "Presentation slides have become the most misused tool in the history of communication."[2]

It's no wonder that PowerPoint and other slide systems seldom are used well. Researchers discovered that the average user received only a half hour of instruction on how to create and deliver PowerPoint presentations. And in many organizations, poorly conceived and ineptly designed slides are so commonplace that mediocrity of slide use often is an unspoken corporate norm.

Furthermore, the ease of development of PowerPoint slides can lead to hurried design, which often results in the following:

- Poorly developed content. Yale professor and design expert Edward Tufte has written extensively about the undisciplined thinking that the use of PowerPoint often encourages.[3] Complex ideas and intricate skills are frequently reduced to simplistic and ill-conceived bullet points.
- Insufficient editing often contributes to a lack of clarity. As noted in Chapter 7, a really good talk generally has been outlined, re-outlined, written, edited, tweaked, and perhaps honed some more. But few people put their slides through a rigorous revision cycle. And once a slide presentation has been created, however ineptly, people often seem to be reluctant to revise or delete slides.
- An overabundance of slides. Many PowerPoint presentations consist of slide after slide in rapid succession. When subjected to slide overkill, participants often feel that they are being bludgeoned with too many visuals and inundated with too much information.
- When creating slides, many presenters use noncontributory animation and clichéd graphics, just because they're available. These often detract from the clarity and focus of the teaching points and further contribute to the mental and eye fatigue that causes audience members to zone out.

It doesn't have to be this way. The next section provides guidelines for creating and using slides effectively, which, when followed, will help you avoid the problems we just discussed.

Guidelines for Creating Effective PowerPoint Slides

1. Start early. Most good presentations evolve through several iterations. So give yourself sufficient time to revise both the slide content and the design.

2. Plan your slides before you open PowerPoint. PowerPoint is an excellent tool for creating finished slides but it's a poor place to begin developing them. Rather than going directly to your computer, begin with a scratch pad. Presentation designer Julie Terberg says, "I always start with pencil and paper. I'm freer that way." Slide-ware expert Rick Altman seconds the motion. In *Why Most PowerPoint Presentations Suck and How You Can Make Them Better,* he writes, "Where do people go wrong? Often, their fatal errors occur in the first 10 seconds of a project: they put hand to mouse, after which it becomes exceedingly difficult to think creatively."[4] And we would add that doing so makes it unlikely that they will develop a tight, well-organized presentation.

    Consider using this four-step process for developing your slide presentations[5]:
    a. Outline
    b. Write
    c. Sketch
    d. Produce
    Take time between each step to allow your subconscious to ponder the content and design. You'll be delighted with the greatly improved finished product.

3. Limit the number of slides. You can probably improve your presentations by ruthlessly cutting the number of slides that you use.

4. Develop the slide title first, if you're using one. This usually is the most important part of the slide, so work at getting the phrasing right. The title is not only important in its own right; it should influence the rest of the slide content and design. Limit the title to one line with as few words as possible.

5. Follow the six-by-six rule: no more than six lines and no more than six words per line. If you have more than six points, eliminate one or more points or combine two points into one. A few words that summarize the point generally are more impactful than a full sentence. As Rick Altman says, "Something almost magical happens when you reduce the amount of words on a slide. Everything seems snappier. . . . Audience members absorb information more efficiently, and you most likely will project more energy."[6]

6. Rarely use sub-bullets. They clutter the slide and overload the mind.

7. Make sure the slide can be easily read. Researchers at the University of Michigan found that students were more likely to do something such as begin an exercise or prepare a recipe when the instructions were in an easy-to-read font. Here are some keys to making your slides readable:

   a. Select a sans serif typeface such as Arial, Tahoma, Trebuchet MS, or Veranda. Use upper and lower case letters for greater readability. Have your letters measure about ¼-inch high on the completed slide, for example, 24-point Arial type.

   b. For the slide title, use **boldface type** or ALL CAPITAL LETTERS to make the title stand out.

   c. Use dark text on a light background; that combination is most readable and least demanding on the eyes.

   d. Avoid busy backgrounds that drown out the content.

   e. Create visual consistency in all of the above.

   f. Have someone else do a final edit.

   g. Sit in the back of the room and scroll through your slides.

8. Use quality art work. Make sure the illustrations measure up to the quality of the other aspects of your training program. It's better to have no illustrations than to have tacky ones.

   A combination of text and visuals often creates the most powerful and enduring impact. In contrast to providing only text, using text and pictures significantly increases trainees' understanding. Slide designer Bruce Gabrielle reports, "There is 40 years of research showing that adding pictures to a text document can make the message easier to understand, easier to agree with, and easier to remember later. This is called the *picture superiority effect*."[7]

   Illustrations of people should include men, women, and a sensitive mix of ethnicities in appropriate garb, such as business suit, blue-collar uniform, medical white coat, etc. Some clip-art icons avoid that problem by using cartoon figures with no gender, ethnic, or clothing issues.

9. Generally display one point of the text at a time. Many presenters make the one-point-at-a-time approach their default to slide design. As Nancy Duarte explains in her book *slide:ology*, "I prefer to have text build sequentially, as I'm not sure why anyone would want the audience to jump ahead. Remember, if the audience can see your bullets, they know the points you are going to make. They'll get bored or agitated waiting for you to catch up with them."[8]

   By the way, it's okay to use one approach with charts and another with slides. Just be sure you have a reason for your decision, since a curious participant might ask for your rationale.

10. Don't animate the slide. The whole point of using visuals is to increase learning, and several research studies found that the use of slide animation decreases learning. Researchers speculate that viewing animated slides requires extra mental activity, which interferes with comprehension.

   Another problem with animation is that few PowerPoint users employ animation effectively. Every poll about PowerPoint's most annoying characteristics lists inept animation in the top five complaints.

Guidelines for Presenting Effectively with PowerPoint Slides

A few of the following guidelines may seem too obvious to mention; we include them despite their being common sense because a sizable number of presenters do not follow them to the detriment of their presentations.

- Be familiar with the order of your slides.
- Place the equipment where it will have the least negative impact on viewing.
- Position yourself in relation to the screen so you are not blocking the screen and so you are situated where you can use a laser pointer to call attention to the screen.
- Avoid the most common mistake that trainers make with their body language when using slides, which is facing the image on the screen and talking to the screen as they explain the slide with their back to the audience. When you present with slides, feel free to glance briefly at the slide from time to time, but *when you speak, face the participants.*
- Don't have the slides showing all the time. It's generally more effective and more personable to introduce and close a presentation with no slide showing. And when you don't need the slide copy showing, provide a visual break by whiting out or blacking out the screen. When you're in slide show mode, pressing the "W" key turns the screen white; pressing the "B" key turns the screen black. With the screen blank participants will direct their visual attention to you.
- If possible, use a wireless remote. Most models allow you to move forward and backward, as well as to blank the screen. Have a place to put the remote down when not in use, such as the ledge of the easel stand.

An awareness of the many cons of using PowerPoint and knowing how to use all of the pros can help make your presentations memorable and up to date.

10

Fine-Tuning Your Delivery

The human brain starts working the moment you are born and never stops until you stand up to speak in public.

———George Jessel

Plutarch, the first-century Greek essayist and biographer, tells us that, in ancient Greece, Demosthenes had a burning desire to sway audiences with his speeches. Initially, however, he was so inept at delivering his orations that people mocked him when he spoke and laughed him out of the assembly. An actor finally told Demosthenes that it was "of little or no use for a man to practice public speaking if he neglected delivery."

Demosthenes took the advice to heart and went to a subterranean cave where he stayed for weeks at a time slaving in solitude to master delivery skills. To protect himself against the temptation of going out in public and thereby skimping on his practices, he shaved one side of his head so he would be too embarrassed to be seen in society. He rid himself of his stammer by speaking with pebbles in his mouth. His shortness of breath was conquered by declaiming poetry while running uphill. In time, Demosthenes' delivery became so powerful that he is remembered as the greatest orator of classical antiquity.

The great orator never forgot the key to his effectiveness. In his later years when was asked, "What aspect of oratory is most important?" he replied, "Delivery first, delivery second, and delivery third."[1]

The type of presenting that you and we do as trainers is far different from that of a professional orator. But in our work, too, good delivery greatly enhances our results. So ratcheting up your delivery will make a significant contribution to the effectiveness of your training.

This chapter discusses eight keys to effective delivery:

- Establish home base.
- Speak extemporaneously.
- Use the body language of presenting.
- Manage the vocal aspects of delivery.
- Employ additional ways of enhancing your delivery.
- Rehearse your presentations.
- Avoid becoming stale after delivering the same presentation enumerable times.
- Target *one* improvement at a time.

Establish Home Base

Before beginning a presentation, decide where you will stand. That will be your home base—the location from which you will speak during most of your presentation. Being centered in that location for the bulk of the time will help members of the group stay focused on you and will contribute to your success in employing the body language of presenting.

Speak Extemporaneously

Dynamic trainers deliver virtually all of their presentations extemporaneously. This means giving presentations that are both carefully prepared and spoken without referring to notes. Just because you so not use notes does not mean you are speaking off the top of your head. Speaking extemporaneously requires intensive preparation and careful rehearsal.

For a refresher on how to organize talks for extemporaneous presentation, refer back to Chapter 7.

Use the Body Language of Presenting

Your body language includes everything the group *sees* you doing. Here's how to increase the impact of your presentation body language.

The Posture for Presenting

When you are about to begin speaking, walk to your home base confidently and with an erect yet relaxed posture. Plant your feet under your shoulders, point your toes forward, and distribute your weight evenly on both feet. This will help you look and feel grounded. It's also a good stance for gesturing as well as for making eye contact with each individual in the group. A not insignificant plus is that this posture conveys self-assurance.

Don't Pace Back and Forth or Walk Randomly About

Obviously, you're not going to remain at home base for the whole talk. But do avoid the pitfall that many trainers fall into—pacing back and forth or other ways of walking aimlessly about when they're presenting. Indiscriminate pacing may put you more at ease but it's distracting to listeners and it limits your ability to fully employ the body language of good presenting.

There will be times, of course, when in the midst of a presentation you will need to leave home base to walk to a visual aid or some other part of the room. The guideline for walking while making a presentation is as follows:

> When there's a need to move, walk purposefully to your destination and establish that, at least temporarily, as your new home base.

Coordinate Your Body Language with Your Content

Communication researchers tell us that our body language can be even more influential than our verbal language. So it's important to synchronize your body language with what you are saying. While maintaining the posture for presenting, use the rest of your body language, especially your hand movements and facial expressions, for emphasis. Avoid making motions that are not coordinated with your content—things like shifting your weight from foot to foot or clasping your hands in front of you or behind your back.

Gestures: How to Handle Your Hands

People seldom pay any attention to their hands—until they stand up to make a presentation. Suddenly the hands become a problem! People who are puzzled about what to do with their hands when presenting typically hold them in ineffective positions or make arbitrary gestures that detract from the presentation. Some people hide the darn things in their pockets—and worse, start to fumble with loose change and keys that they find there. Haphazard movement of your hands robs you of one of your most valuable resources for emphasis—gestures.

It's been said that gestures are a vocabulary other than speech that speaks to the brain through the eyes. Spirited communication usually entails the use of gestures as well as facial and vocal expression. So use your hands purposefully in the expressive zone, the area directly in front of you between your waistline and chin. This is where gestures are best seen and have the greatest impact. Don't pre-think your gestures other than determining to do most of your gesturing in the expressive zone. Spontaneous gestures support the content of your talk and enliven your presentation. When you aren't gesturing, let your hands rest naturally at your sides. This resting position conveys openness and relaxed confidence.

Eye Contact

Your eyes are among your most important speaking tools. Eye contact draws people into the presentation and helps you relate to individuals while you are presenting.

Relaxed and natural eye contact involves people and supports your message. Sustain it long enough (three to five seconds) to really connect with one participant at a time. This type of eye contact helps you convert a one-to-many situation into a series of one-to-one interactions. It's a good way of relating directly with each member of the training group.

Distribute your eye contact equally to all parts of the room. Research indicates that the typical presenter spends significantly more time looking at the people on one side of the room than at those on the other side. The speaker's nondominant side is usually favored.

Some kinds of eye movement are more distracting and annoying than helpful. Avoid darting glances, constant scanning of all the eyes in the room, or prolonged stares at one person. And don't use the lawn-sprinkler approach to eye contact—sweeping the group with your eyes without making real contact with anyone.

Facial Expression

There are more than two hundred muscles in your face, which makes the face capable of an amazingly wide range of expression. Use this enormous capability to enhance your delivery and support your message. Let your face show the genuine enthusiasm you feel for the importance of what you're teaching. And when presenting on a topic that participants often struggle with, let your facial expression show your sense of the seriousness of the moment. We realize that facial expressiveness is much easier for some people than for others. But everyone has some range of facial expressiveness. Don't underutilize this important aspect of delivery.

Clothing and Grooming

Although clothing and grooming aren't part of your body language, they are part of your visual impact so we'll mention them here. In the novel *Orlando*, Virginia Woolf writes: "Vain trifles as they seem, clothes have as they say, more important offices than to keep us warm. They change our view of the world and the world's view of us."[2] So attention to your wardrobe is a not insignificant part of your preparation for leading a workshop.

Each trainer has his own individual style of dress and grooming, which conveys to the group a bit of who he is. Stay mainly with your own style while also considering a few ways you might enhance your image. Your appearance should support your professional role as leader of the workshop and not be a front-and-center distraction.

Let the formality of the group and the facility in which you'll be working influence the degree of formality of your clothing. Even in the most informal group, however, you will probably do well to stick to what's called "business casual" rather than dress down to the most informal attire in the room. Make sure your outfit will stay together through the workshop day: having to straighten garments or tuck them in are needless distractions from the message being delivered.

Your hands are on display as you gesture during a talk and as you distribute materials or do other functions. Whether you prefer to keep your nails on the short side with a no-fuss look or prefer a more manicured look, the key is to be sure they are clean.

A good-hair day gives your image a boost; a bad-hair day detracts from your image all day long. Make sure your hair won't require much attention while you are in the workshop. Get it right; then leave it alone.

This discussion has barely scratched the surface of this important topic on which book-length treatments are available.

Manage the Vocal Aspects of Delivery

The way you use your voice can affect your presentation dramatically. In terms of vocal quality, what you say should be

- conversational,
- hearable,
- delivered at a comfortable rate, and
- emotionally congruent with the content.

Conversational

Dynamic trainers maintain a conversational manner. When presenting to a group, you'll probably have to talk a bit louder than usual but otherwise speak in essentially the same manner you would use when talking with a few friends.

Hearable

Participants shouldn't have to strain to hear you. Talk loudly enough so everyone in the group can hear you comfortably—but no louder. On a scale of one to ten, with one being a whisper and ten a shout, your basic presenting volume might be about a six, but anything from a three or four to an eight or nine can be appropriate when used briefly to give greater emphasis to a particular part of your message. Varying your volume at times helps maintain participants' interest and can add emphasis and emotional color to your presentation.

Some speakers have trouble with sentence endings. They reduce the volume as they proceed through a sentence. After listeners work hard for a time to hear the full sentences, they often give up and simply tune out if the fading volume continues.

Speech coach Dorothy Sarnoff advises, "If your voice lacks vitality, vigor, enthusiasm, intensity, that's because you're not energizing it, not supporting your voice with the pressure of your breath."

Delivered at a Comfortable Rate

Make sure your rate of speaking is comfortable for people to listen to. Then, vary the rate at times to emphasize a point or to show a bit more emotion. A quicker than normal rate can express excitement, urgency, or enthusiasm. A slower rate than is typical for you can subtly communicate, "Listen up; this part is especially important."

Some presenters annoy participants by speaking too quickly, too slowly, or by always speaking at the same rate. Invite a colleague to attend one of your presentations and give you feedback on your delivery, including how comfortable they are with your rate of speech.

Emotionally Congruent with the Content

The ability to vary your voice enables you to express emotions more effectively. When prepping for a presentation, be conscious of the tone as well as the words. Think about the degree of importance of each part of the content. Then, when you come to a particularly crucial point or essential detail in your presentation, you can signal its importance with your vocal emphasis as well as with your wording when you say things such as the following:

"I want to stress the fact that . . ."

"Here's how you can avoid this difficulty."

"What's most important here is . . ."

Employ Additional Ways of Enhancing Your Delivery

Be Brief

We made this point in Chapter 7: Keep your delivery brief and on point. Unfortunately, we've learned from experience that some people can go into a workshop with the outline of a short presentation and end up delivering a long talk. They often lose their audience along the way.

Listen to the Group While Delivering Your Talk

A good presentation is always a dialogue—a give and take between presenter and participants. Think of it as a conversation—not a performance. While you are presenting be sure to use the antenna you've developed over your lifetime to read the group's reaction to what you are saying. Although your listeners may be totally silent, you can read their response from their facial expressions—a furrowed brow, a squint, or a frown—and other body language.

Invite participants into dialogue at times. Ken Bain's *What the Best College Teachers Do* summarizes a fifteen-year-long research study of how master teachers teach. By and large they listen intently as they teach:

> Most of the teachers we studied frequently used rhetorical questions, even if it was no more than to ask, "Does this make sense?" They watched their students' reactions, read their eyes and other body language, and adjusted what they said to the enlightened, confused, bewildered, or even bored looks they saw in the classroom. . . . They asked for feedback from students, stopped to ask for questions, and paused for ten seconds at a time, looking at students.[3]

Rev Up Your Energy

Sound energy management begins long before the workshop. We all know what it takes—regular exercise, good nutrition, sound sleep habits, and effective stress management. When you've practiced good energy management, you can tap into that energy pool to invigorate your delivery.

When a training program has gone well, it's predictable that on the evaluation forms a number of participants will comment on the enthusiasm or energy of the trainer. Enthusiasm is partly conveyed by the amount of energy the trainer is putting into the leadership of the group. If you aren't enthusiastic about what you are presenting, why should anyone else care?

Handle Pauses Confidently

Many trainers, especially novices in the field, become nervous when they need to pause even briefly during their presentation. To them, a pause of just a few seconds seems like an eternity.

To relieve the stress of these brief periods of silence, people often fill the pauses with "Umm," "Uh," "Ah," "You know," "Er," "Like," "I mean," etc. Because those expressions are often used to fill what to the speaker is an awkward-feeling pause, they're often called "fillers." Many people use the same filler over and over again. When a person relies excessively on filler it becomes a verbal mannerism. And any mannerism is a distraction to communication.

The use of fillers is so detrimental to delivering a presentation that Toastmasters, an organization focused on improving the presentation abilities of its members, appoints "Ah Counters" to tally the number of "ahs" and other fillers cluttering each member's talk. You can be your own Ah Counter by listening to some tapes of your talks and noting the number of fillers you used. This is one area of presenting in which awareness of the problem often spurs improvement.

When pauses aren't ruined by fillers, they can have a very constructive role to play in the delivery of a talk. Mark Twain, one of the most effective presenters of his era, loved pauses and milked them for all they were worth. Regarding the power of the pause he said, "The pause—that impressive silence, that eloquent silence, that geometrically progressive silence which often achieves a desired effect where no combination of words howsoever felicitous, could accomplish it."[4]

Well-used pauses

- provide group members with a short period in which to absorb the preceding part of the speech,
- communicate confidence on the speaker's part, and
- create a brief but useful time for the speaker to think about how she'll phrase the next part of her talk.

So make a concerted effort to avoid cluttering your pauses with fillers. Through your "Ah Counting," determine how many fillers you average in a seven-minute talk. Then set a doable goal for reducing your use of fillers and monitor your success in reaching that goal.

Manage Verbal Slip-Ups

In every workshop, you'll likely fumble a word or two—probably more. Everyone does. When novices make a verbal slip-up, even if it's as irrelevant as mispronouncing an inconsequential word, they tend to stop and say the word again, this time pronouncing it correctly. However, rectifying an unimportant misstatement interrupts the flow of their speech. Often the correction mars the delivery more than the misstatement did. So, when you make a minor slip-up, ignore it. People don't expect you to be perfect. If the slip-up is significant, correct it in a businesslike way and proceed with your talk. Don't make a problem out of a minor glitch.

Don't Rush When You Are Behind Schedule

Another predicament that trainers often encounter is falling behind schedule. In their effort to catch up, many trainers' begin talking faster. That rarely helps and it generally injects more stress into the workshop. Rather than speeding up your delivery when you are running late, cut something out of the talk. If you have had time to implement the suggestions in the previous chapter, you've already made your presentation condensable.

Rehearse Your Presentations

It's been said that the reason there are so few good speakers in public is because there are so few good rehearsers in private. Resolve to be a good rehearser. For virtually everyone, impactful extemporaneous delivery requires much productive practice.

You've developed the outline of your presentation (Chapter 4). In this chapter you've learned—or relearned—a number of ways to improve your delivery. Now it's time to make and review audio video recordings of practices of your presentation until you've mastered its delivery. You'll get more out of your practices if you space your practices out a bit instead of having back-to-back practice sessions. With thorough and mindful preparation, when you walk into the training room you'll have the reassuring feeling of "been there, done that."

Avoid Becoming Stale After Delivering the Same Presentation Enumerable Times

In our Craft of Training workshop, we're often asked, "How can I retain my enthusiasm when I have to give the same presentation time after time?"

That's a problem that people in a number of professions need to solve. In the 1930s, William Gaxton starred in a long and successful run of the musical *Of Thee I Sing*. He occasionally felt the sameness get to him. After an especially perfunctory performance, George S. Kaufman, the director of the show, left the theater during the performance and sent Gaxton a telegram that read, "Watching your performance from the rear of the theater. Wish you were here."

By contrast, Yul Brunner played the King in 4,625 performances of *The King and I* and is said to have relished each performance. In the 1880s, Russell Conwell delivered his "Acres of Diamonds" talk more than six thousand times and founded Temple University with the proceeds. He must have been able to keep his delivery pretty spirited to rake in enough money to found a college!

Here are some tips for keeping your delivery invigorated despite having given the same presentation repeatedly.

- Remind yourself that although you may have given this presentation dozens of times before, *this will be the first time that these people have heard it.*
- It helps to replace some of your illustrations with new ones every once in a while. Research the subject matter thoroughly and collect examples,

quotations, and other illustrative material for each point. Keep adding to this storehouse of illustrative material. Soon you will be using basically the same outline over and over again, but you will be drawing from your stash for fresh examples and quotations. We've always used that method and found that over time it helped us cull the least effective illustrations and quotations, while adding ever more pertinent and interesting ones. Training from the overflow enables you to develop talks that combine the tried and true with refreshing new material. But even more important, the new material will help keep you involved and interested in your presentations even after you've given them innumerable times.

- When you've given essentially the same presentation for the umpteenth time, you're in an enviable position. Since you now have the content down pat, you'll be able to focus fully on the participants and on the nuances of delivery that will enable you to connect more powerfully with them.
- Remember that a professional is a person who does his best even when he doesn't feel like it.

Target *One* Improvement at a Time

This chapter has suggested numerous steps you can take to improve your delivery. Don't try to tackle all of them—or even several of them at once. Many people have tried that but few have succeeded. Instead, select one aspect of your delivery to work on. Target one that can leverage a significant improvement in your performance. If, for example, your posture is poor, it can throw a number of the other aspects of your body language off kilter.

Probably the best way to get feedback on your delivery is to have someone make a video recording of one of your live presentations. Then view it and determine what single change would produce the greatest enhancement in your delivery. Alternately, you could work on an improvement that would be easier to make and that would still result in a significant improvement in your delivery.

Once you've targeted an improvement and achieved it you can rest on your laurels for a bit. Or, if you're feeling gung ho, you may want to immediately select another area of improvement to work on.

11

Using Disclaimers to Sidestep Resistance

Address the disagreement before it addresses you.

——David Peoples[1]

When trainers lead workshops, they're typically focused on the benefits participants will receive from learning the concepts, attitudes, methods, or skills
of the course. Many participants, however, will likely be very satisfied with their
present approach. Otherwise they probably would have tried to change it years ago.
Besides, their current mode of operation has undoubtedly become habitual and,
therefore, ultra-easy to use. But now headquarters, or the training department, or
some other distant entity has decided to pull them out of work to teach them something that many of them aren't remotely interested in learning. Some people who
are scheduled to attend the course may doubt that what you'll be teaching will work
in their corner of the workplace—let alone improve things. These are a few of the
reasons why resistance to change is often a natural and predictable reaction to being
sent to training.

One of the best ways to avoid preventable resistance is through the use of disclaimers. This chapter shows how to create and use disclaimers to circumvent much
unproductive resistance and preventable objections. In the rather rare instances when
a disclaimer does not subvert the expected resistance, you can rely on the methods
taught in Chapters 22, 23, and 24.

Disclaimers are brief statements that raise and respond to predictable objections
before participants raise them. Jay Heinrichs, an authority on the art of persuasion
says, "A good persuader anticipates the audience's objections."[2] Ideally, you want to
raise the participants' concerns before they do. You'll dodge a lot of resistance when
you beat them to the punch.

Resistance to Using Disclaimers

Some trainers are reluctant to use disclaimers in workshops. For example, Gabe, one of our colleagues, was leading a module on disclaimers in a Train the Trainer workshop. The course was customized for hospital trainers who would soon be teaching a series of workshops on how to use a new set of computerized medical procedures. This meant saying goodbye to their old familiar ways of processing things on paper and learning how to use new software, not to mention having to spend weeks entering old information into their computers—information that was already stored conveniently in their files. And all this additional work would be on top of their regular duties.

Not surprisingly, the grapevine had it that many of the people who would be attending the workshop were wary about the change. They were loath to spend a whole week at a training workshop since their regular work would pile up each day they were in class. And most of them worried about making mistakes while struggling their way up the learning curve of working with the new software.

To diffuse some of the resistance, Gabe recommended that the trainers use a disclaimer when they sensed that some participants were disgruntled about having to attend the workshop. One trainer who was participating in the class asked, "Why would I state arguments *against* learning the content that I'm teaching?" Others in the group expressed vigorous agreement with his concerns.

Disclaimers Are Time-Tested Presentation Tools

Gabe wasn't at all fazed by the objections; in fact, he expected them. Similar concerns had been raised each time he trained people in how to employ radically different procedures from those they were accustomed to using.

He explained that although the term *disclaimer* is relatively new in this context, this oratorical device has long been used by savvy presenters. For centuries, leading public speakers have known that when a presenter mentions the existence of points of view contrary to that which he is advancing, it generally has the paradoxical effect of strengthening his argument. For example, in the first century of the Common Era, Quintilian, in his *Institutio Oratoria,* extolled the "extraordinary value" of what we in the twenty-first century term disclaimers, "whereby," as he put it, "we forestall [i.e., prevent or undercut] potential objections."[3]

An additional benefit of using disclaimers is that when the presenter raises the objection, the timing and phrasing of the potential objection can be controlled. But when a participant raises an objection, the timing may be inopportune. And when a disgruntled participant raises an objection, the language may be loaded. So it's best to preempt potential objections with disclaimers. When teaching a concept or method that may be met with resistance, raise the issue first, get all the objections out on the table, and respond to them. Then, when you have addressed the probable concern, make your point.

A Two-Part Format for Disclaimers

The following format can help you create disclaimers:

1. *The Concern:* State a concern, doubt, or objection that people often raise (or that you think they might raise) regarding the point you are about to make. Or, as you'll see later in the chapter, a disclaimer can be used in relation to a point that you just made that some in the audience may view with skepticism.
2. *The Not-to-Worry:* Assert the value of the approach being suggested despite the reservation that was raised.

Although it may be tempting to ignore participants' skepticism about the value or practicality of what you are teaching, it's usually foolhardy. If you try to run roughshod over participants' objections, they generally stiffen their resistance. A better option is to be proactive in dealing with probable objections by using disclaimers to address potential negative reactions *before* participants raise them.

As the chapter title indicates, disclaimers are used to sidestep potential resistance. Here's an example. Years ago, when the microwave oven was a new culinary appliance, most good cooks looked down their nose at it. So when one of the notable cookbook authors of the time, Barbara Kafka, decided to write a book about microwave cuisine, she knew she had to address the strong prejudices against what, at the time, was a new, revolutionary, and widely unappreciated approach to cooking. Therefore, early in the book's introduction she inserted a disclaimer. Although she didn't use the term, she began with the concern. She concisely summarized the most frequently stated objections that people were making against microwave cooking. Since at one time, Kafka had held those beliefs herself she wrote in the first person:

The Concern

For many years, I was wrong about the microwave oven. I saw it abused in bad restaurants, and I thought that was the best it could do. I ate potatoes "baked" in it and rebelled at the lack of quality. I read the manuals that came with the ovens and was repelled by what I saw.[4]

She got the reaction she hoped for from readers. She convinced them that she was well aware of the kinds of problems with microwave cooking that had dissuaded them from using what at the time was a newfangled type of cooking. In four sentences she opened their minds and enabled them to take seriously what she would be telling them about the benefits of this strange new way of cooking.

Kafka then proceeded to the second part of her disclaimer which we term the not-to-worry, which asserts the value of the approach being suggested despite the reservation that was raised:

The Not-to-Worry

> I am a recent convert. . . . I am not about to give up my copper pots, my cast iron wood-burning stove, or my barbecue; but I have a new friend in my kitchen, the microwave oven, and I use it more and more every day. I hope you come to enjoy it as I do.[5]

Readers' resistance to microwave cooking dissolved when they read that disclaimer. If a cook like Barbara Kafka uses the microwave every day, why would middling cooks like her readers not experiment with it? Undoubtedly, many of them gave it a shot, and went on to use their microwave daily.

What Disclaimers Do for Trainers

Disclaimers are a handy training tool for avoiding potential resistance. For example, in an upcoming workshop for supervisors, Mary will be showing a video demonstration of philosopher John Dewey's cooperative problem-solving method—a method that's applicable to virtually any occupation. Unfortunately, the only demonstration video she has access to was developed for accountants. Based on previous experiences, Mary is concerned that some participants may claim that they can't relate to the video because it portrays the skill being used by folks in a different occupation. She decides to sidestep that potential complaint with a disclaimer. In her introduction to the video she addresses the concern:

> You'll be seeing the skills used in a setting that's different from the one you're accustomed to, so you may find the film a bit difficult to relate to.

Then she addresses the not-to-worry:

> But that should only be a minor distraction because the skills you will be learning can be used effectively in any setting. Furthermore, after the video demonstration, all examples will be from your work situation.

Before-the-Fact Disclaimers and After-the-Fact Disclaimers

There are two types of disclaimers:

- Before-the-fact disclaimers
- After-the-fact disclaimers

Before-the-Fact Disclaimers

As in the examples above, before-the-fact disclaimers raise and respond to predictable objections before participants are likely to air them in an activity, presentation, demonstration, practice, or other workshop event. Before-the-fact disclaimers are great time savers since it takes far less time to state a disclaimer than it takes to handle an objection. With the few short sentences of a typical disclaimer you generally can skillfully avoid having to give a considerably longer response to a question or objection that's likely to be raised. Besides, if you wait until after the concern is raised, many of the participants will have already formed inaccurate opinions, and it will take additional time to dislodge their ill-founded doubts. Before-the-fact disclaimers are applications of the proverb, "An ounce of prevention is worth a pound of cure."

Another benefit of using before-the-fact disclaimers is that they help create a more harmonious workshop ambience by reducing the amount of resistance that the group struggles with.

The trainers we work with love before-the-fact disclaimers because they make the trainees' learning more efficient and the trainers' work much easier and more productive.

Here's another example of how a before-the-fact disclaimer can dissolve resistance. After the publication of Dale Carnegie's *How to Win Friends and Influence People,* the author was invited to New York City to speak to a club of sophisticated editors, publishers, and advertising executives. His biographer, William Longgood, was among those who advised him not to go, saying, "They're the toughest bunch in America, they'll eat you alive." Despite the adamant advice not to go, Carnegie accepted the invitation and went to New York City to present to the hostile crowd.

The event was analogous to David confronting Goliath. But instead of using a sling and a stone, Carnegie relied on a disclaimer:

The Concern

> I know there's considerable criticism of my book. People say I'm not profound and there's nothing in it new to psychology and human relations. This is true.

The Not-to-Worry

> Gentlemen, I've never claimed to have a new idea. Of course I deal with the obvious. I present, reiterate, and glorify the obvious—because the obvious is what people need to be told. . . . I am told that you are a hostile audience. But I plead "not guilty." The ideas I stand for are not mine. I borrowed them from Socrates, I swiped them from Chesterfield, I stole them from Jesus, and I put them in a book. If you don't like their rules, whose would you choose? I'll be glad to listen.[6]

That disclaimer won the hostile audience over and the once-unreceptive crowd gave Carnegie a deafening ovation.

After-the-Fact Disclaimers

Occasionally it's useful to employ a disclaimer to counteract objections that participants may have *after* you've made a point in a presentation, done a demonstration, or led a practice. Here's an after-the-fact disclaimer that author Robert Heilbroner used in his book, *The Worldly Philosophers*. The problem Heilbroner faced was establishing the *relevance* of his chapter on the theories of Adam Smith, the father of modern economics, who wrote his famous *An Inquiry Into the Nature and Causes of the Wealth of Nations* in 1776—more than two centuries earlier. After presenting Adam Smith's account of the economics of the sixteenth century, Heilbroner employed an after-the-fact disclaimer:

The Concern

And today? Does the competitive market mechanism still operate?

The Not-to-Worry

This is not a question to which it is possible to give a simple answer. The nature of the market has changed vastly since the eighteenth century. . . . But for all the attributes of modern society, the great forces of interest and competition, however watered down or hedged about, still provide the basic rules of behavior that no participant in a market system can afford to disregard entirely.[7]

Using Disclaimers in Training

Disclaimers are so useful in training that some of our colleagues who regularly teach train-the-trainer workshops use a chart that reads:

DISCLAIMERS are a trainer's best friend.

A Before-the-Fact Disclaimer in a Workshop

Here's the before-the-fact disclaimer (the concern) that Gabe used in the hospital Train the Trainer workshop:

Some of you might be feeling a bit reluctant to be here today. You're already on overload without adding something new to your crowded schedule; you may have already had your fill of our computer-oriented world, and many of you are undoubtedly thinking of the fact that whenever computer changes are installed in a work situation there is a learning curve.

Heads started nodding affirmatively.

Could anyone say more about that?

Participants put their feelings into words. Gabe listened and reflected participants' comments. Then, he added the not-to-worry:

> You'll be glad to know that although there is an upfront investment of time and effort, you'll experience benefits that will make your work more error-free, take a shorter amount of time, and will bring you and your department up to today's standard for our industry.
>
> The downside will be short-lived while the upside for each of you and for the hospital will go on for years to come.
>
> I'm not suggesting that you're home free. However, you will have to face much less resistance than if you plodded ahead without addressing the participants' concerns.
>
> By the way, if you can come up with ways that will make the class more practical, easier to learn, and generally better for you, please share your ideas.

An After-the-Fact Disclaimer in a Workshop

In a Listening Skills workshop, after the first practice of reflective listening, the trainer used this after-the-fact disclaimer:

The Concern

> Did anyone have to struggle not to ask questions, give advice, or make other comments? Was anyone so busy trying to attend, follow, reflect, not ask questions or make comments that they had trouble even hearing what the speaker was saying?

Many participants responded that that they had indeed struggled with those problems during the practice. The trainer then stated the second part of this disclaimer:

The Not-to-Worry

> The early stages of learning a new skill are generally the most difficult because you are trying to break old habits at the same time that you are trying to develop new ones. Your brain is on overload. Tomorrow, though, when you practice reflecting again, I think you'll find that you are doing it much better and that you feel more comfortable with this way of responding to what people are telling you. Give it a little time.

Tips for Developing Disclaimers

For workshops that you lead more than once, keep track of points of resistance and develop disclaimers that could help you circumvent them in your next outing with the workshop.

For workshops that you'll be leading for the first time, you will probably be able to guess at some parts of the workshop that are likely to generate significant resistance. For example:

- When teaching a method that will require more time to implement than using the current practice
- When teaching a skill that some participants believe would be scoffed at in the workplace
- When teaching a method that many of the participants' bosses don't practice and might not value—or might even disparage

As a trainer you undoubtedly will face a career-long encounter with resistance to change. By learning how to use disclaimers, or how to use them more effectively, you'll gain an incredibly useful tool for diminishing needless resistance for the rest of your training days. Disclaimers can also serve you well in the conversations in your "civilian life" outside of your training role.

12

Listening Actively to Stay in Tune
with Participants

Several of the previous chapters discussed the speaking side of communication in training. Now it's time to focus on listening—a crucial yet greatly underappreciated training ability. It's a fundamental training skill—even in the many aspects of a workshop where the trainer's dominant role is speaking. Active listening is crucial for successful application in twenty-three of the chapters and two of the appendices in this book.

With its contribution to effectiveness in each of the above aspects of workshop leadership, you can see that, in dynamic workshops, listening ranks right up there with effective presenting as an indispensable training tool.

Most Trainers Are Better Talkers Than Listeners

Good listening is a rare skill in our society. Few of us were brought up in households where the parents were good listeners and the kids experienced a rich listening environment in which they absorbed the ability by osmosis. In fact, the opposite is the norm.

Although every person of sound mind and a functional auditory system can listen, the average person doesn't absorb half of what he's told. Years ago, research at the University of Minnesota, Florida State University, and Michigan State University, and duplicated over time at several other universities, found that "immediately after the average person listens to someone talk, he remembers only about half of what he heard—*no matter how carefully he thought he had listened.*"[2] Communication scholars at American University in Washington, DC, found that the average television viewer got only one-third of the points covered in a typical newscast.[3] As Dr. Lyman Steil, a founder and past president of the International Listening Association, says,

> It can be stated with virtually no qualification that by any standard set, people in general do not know how to listen.[4]

Thus, it's not surprising that many people in our vocation are better talkers than listeners.

Effective listening is

- a set of learned skills
- for demonstrating that you understand the speaker's thoughts and feelings
- from the speaker's frame of reference.

Three Sub-Skills of Effective Listening

Your training can be greatly enhanced by mastering the three core skills of listening:

- Attending
- Following
- Reflecting

Attending Skills

Attending is the body language of good listening. This skill gets you physically involved in the interaction. Competent listeners pay attention and they show it in their body language. Both the speaker and the listener are positively impacted by these aspects of good attending:

Lean in. Without excluding the rest of the group, face the person who is talking and lean slightly into the interaction.

Open position. When not gesturing, keep your arms relaxed and at your sides; when sitting, rest them in your lap.

Gestures. Use purposeful gestures; avoid random or habitual gestures and nervous mannerisms.

Eye contact. When a participant asks a question or makes a comment, maintain eye contact with her. In group situations, when you reply, break eye contact with the participant and speak to the group.

Facial reactions. When listening, let your concentration on what's being said register on your face. When someone expresses satisfaction over a practice that went really well or skepticism about applying what he or she is learning, let your features show that you are tracking with the speaker.

Overall posture. A posture of relaxed alertness is appropriate for most listening situations.

Good attending shows the participant that you are tuned in to what he's saying. Research shows that good attending improves the listener's concentration[5] and comprehension.[6] It also tends to increase the speaker's fluency,[7] which makes your listening easier and more pleasurable. As Kathleen Singh says,

> Our simple attention, offered to another person, is the most underused of human resources, one of the least costly, one of the most freely available, and—without a doubt—one of the most powerfully beneficial.[8]

Following Skills

There are three following skills:

- Door openers
- Brief encouragers
- Head nods

The first two following skills get you vocally involved in the interaction, and occasional coordinated head nods support your vocal involvement.

Door Openers

Door openers are succinct invitations for a person to begin speaking or to continue speaking. A door opener can simply be an open question:

What are your thoughts about this?

Some door openers are prefaced by a short summary of what the person just said:
Preface:

I'm wondering if you're uncertain about whether this would work in your setting.

Open question:

Would you say more about that?

Sometimes door openers are prefaced by a brief description of the other person's body language:
Preface:

You look relaxed and satisfied, now that the conference you were leading is over.

Open Question:

How did it go?

Brief Encouragers

Brief encouragers are

- one- to three-word statements, such as "I see," or
- empathic sounds, such as "Mm-hmm."

They enable a trainer to participate in the conversation while keeping the interaction focused on the participant and what he's communicating. A number of other words and short phrases can be used to let the speaker know that you are following what he's saying:

"Tell me more."	"Really."	"Gosh."
"For instance."	"Oh."	"Darn!"
"Then?"	"And?"	"Go on."

Head Nods

Nodding your head occasionally is a noninterruptive way to signal that although you are not responding verbally, you are paying attention to what's being said. Sometimes brief encouragers are accompanied by head nods.

Reflecting Skills

What most distinguishes good listening from average listening is a cluster of skills known as *reflective listening*. Reflections are concise restatements of the core of the speaker's message in the listener's own words. You don't need to reflect everything participants say—just the main points. Reflections can sometimes be used in casual interactions but are invaluable for doing the following:

- Showing that you understand what was said in significant conversations
- Fielding participants' questions
- Responding to important subject matter concerns
- Receiving feedback
- Getting the conversation back on track when a misunderstanding has occurred
- Handling disgruntled feelings and hostile comments
- Responding to other emotionally laden issues

We're convinced that *reflective listening is a "must have" set of skills for trainers.* Unfortunately, as UCLA's Dr. Gerald Goodman notes, this aspect of listening is "the missing link in communication because so few people reflect what they hear."[9] So, it's crucial to make sure you've mastered this key skill.

There are four kinds of reflections, all of which are important tools for trainers:

- Paraphrases (reflections of content—the *facts* that were expressed)
- Reflections of feelings (reflections of the *emotions* that were expressed by the participant's wording and/or body language)
- Reflections of meaning (reflections of *feelings and the related content*)
- Summary reflections (succinct restatements that capture *the thoughts and feelings of a whole interaction or a major part of it*)

Paraphrasing

A paraphrase is a succinct restatement of the factual content of the speaker's message in the listener's own words.[10] It's useful in many conversations that are somewhat important to one or both parties and have a moderate level of intensity. Here's an example.

Participant:

It seems to me that there isn't much payoff for restating what the participant says, and to be frank about it I would feel pretty foolish doing that.

Trainer's paraphrase:

You're skeptical about the value of paraphrasing.

Using a "You-Focused" Sentence Starter

Beginners at paraphrasing often unconsciously slip into the speaking role. When that happens, their attempts at paraphrasing generally begin with "I" or "I've" and end up as statements of their own opinion. For example, "I've had a similar experience." Or, "I doubt that would happen." Also, putting the word "I" at or near the beginning of your paraphrase can lead to the use of bloated and hackneyed sentence starters such as, "What I think I hear you saying is . . ." or "If I get what you are driving at . . ."

Using a concise you-focused sentence starter helps keep your reflection focused on the speaker and her point of view:

"*You* think . . ."	"It's important to *you* that . . ."
You're concerned that . . ."	"*You'd* prefer . . ."
"As *you* see it . . ."	"From *your* standpoint . . ."

Notice that each of these starters is very brief. And they all include the word "you" or some variation of it like "you're" or "you'd."

Avoid using the same sentence starter for all of your paraphrases; using the same starter repeatedly makes your listening sound odd and the repetition soon becomes monotonous.

As you gain experience with paraphrasing, you'll find that this skill is even more effective when the you-focused starters are omitted. Using sentence starters is a temporary crutch to help keep your responses directed to the speaker's concerns instead of jumping in with your own comments. As our friend and former colleague, Dr. Rick Brandon, says, "Sentence starters are like training wheels on a child's first bicycle—a big help when learning but a handicap once you get the hang of it."

Make Your Reflection a Statement, Not a Question

Many beginners at paraphrasing are uncertain of the accuracy of their paraphrases so to be on the safe side they word their paraphrase as a question. They lead off with queries like, "Do you mean . . . ?" or "Are you saying . . . ?" That's okay once in a while if you are truly unsure of your paraphrase, but as a habitual way of paraphrasing it can be irritating to the speaker. And sentence starters with unnecessary phrases make conversations drag out needlessly since the speaker is asked to repeat a part of his message that the listener has already digested.

Sometimes listeners phrase their paraphrases as statements but turn their voice up at the end of the sentence. Unfortunately, the upward inflection at the end of the sentence changes what was said from a statement to a question. So turn your voice down somewhat at the end of each paraphrase as you would at the end of a typical sentence.[11]

Although we recommend using statements rather than questions when saying back what you heard, you certainly don't want a paraphrase to sound cocksure. You may have misunderstood the meaning, so you want the speaker to be able to say, "That's not quite what I meant. Let me put it this way . . . " Although an effective paraphrase is not dogmatic, it's not overly tentative either; it's a firm response as befits a good sounding board.

When you're paraphrasing (or using other kinds of reflections), leave a short pause between the participant's statement and your reflection to make sure she has completed that aspect of what she wanted to say.

You'll usually be able to reflect at natural breaks in the conversation. Occasionally, however, a participant will talk at length without pausing. When that happens, you'll need to cut in with something like, "You're giving me a lot of information. Let me make sure I understand it." Then paraphrase what was said and quickly return the focus of the workshop to the whole group. If it seems that the participant is likely to monopolize the conversation, postpone further discussion by suggesting that the conversation be continued on the next break, at lunch, or after class. (For more on monopolizers, see Chapter 15.)

Paraphrase Until You Get a "Yes"

Master trainer Ed Lisbe realized that when a paraphrase is on-target, the speaker typically replies with some form of yes. That is, she may do the following:

- Say "yes"
- Nod affirmatively
- Say "mm-hmm"
- Signal that your paraphrase was on the mark
- That's what's meant when we say "reflect until you get a yes."

Reflecting Feelings

When the speaker's feelings are more intense than normal, reflecting feelings is the listening skill of choice.

When reflecting feelings, avoid beginning your reflections with the words, "You feel" followed by a feeling word like "sad," "mad," or "glad." That's not the way people generally talk about feelings in their everyday conversations. Furthermore, by the end of a workshop, participants will be turned off by the needless and monotonous repetition of the words "you feel." Rather than lead off with, "You *feel* surprised that . . . ," you can simply say, "You're surprised that . . ." Omitting the words "feel" and "feeling" from your reflections helps the reflections fit seamlessly into the conversation.

Reflections of feeling often work better when you avoid using feeling words such as "angry," "afraid," or "happy." Instead, rely mainly on figures of speech, which sound more natural and down to earth.

Here are some examples of figures of speech that you can use in place of "positive" feeling words:

"It was just what the doctor ordered."

"You were on cloud nine."

"That really hit the spot."

"You're tickled pink."

"That was the frosting on the cake."

"You're in seventh heaven."

"You felt like a new person."

Here are examples of figures of speech that you can use in place of "negative" feeling words:

"That put you on your guard."

"His criticism took the wind out of your sails."

"You're caught between a rock and a hard place."

"You're up in the air about whether to give that a try."

"You got hot under the collar."

"Then you hit the ceiling."

When reflecting feelings, make sure your voice and facial expression are compatible with your verbal statement of feelings.

Reflecting Meanings

Reflections of meaning feed back to the speaker a concise summary of what she just expressed including both *the feeling* and *the situation or the thought that prompted the feeling*. People often state the feeling at the beginning of a reflection of meaning:

> What a *relief* [feeling word] that *the evaluations were so good* [situation that prompted the feeling].

You can inject a bit of variety in your reflections by sometimes reversing the order of the sentence by leading off with a description of the situation that triggered the feeling and noting the feeling toward the end of the sentence:

> *Spending all that time in meetings* [situation that prompted the feeling] was a *downer* [feeling word] for you.

Reflections of feeling and reflections of meaning are invaluable training tools. And the more difficult the situation you find yourself in, the more valuable they'll be.

Summary Reflections

Summary reflections succinctly wrap up a whole conversation or a major segment of a conversation. You'll rarely have sufficiently extensive conversations during the actual class time to use summary reflections during the workshop. But there will be times when you'll have longer conversations—with a manager who is talking with you about tailoring a workshop to the needs of his division, an after-class conversation with a dissatisfied or an especially appreciative participant, or when listening to some fairly lengthy input from a colleague in a staff meeting.

Later in the book we'll discuss how to integrate these listening skills into your training in ways that will greatly reduce participant resistance and will enable you to skillfully manage the most challenging training situations that you'll face.

The Listening Spirit

Carl Rogers, one of the most influential psychologists of the twentieth century, emphasized the importance of having an attitude that supports quality listening. That attitude, which we think of as the *listening spirit*, consists of respect, empathy, and genuineness. When you have good listening skills, as described above, and they're supported by the listening spirit, you have a very powerful and widely applicable training tool—one that will also serve you well in other aspects of your life.

13

Responding to Questions, Comments, and Objections

Most human beings, especially well-educated ones, buy into something only after they have had a chance to wrestle with it. Wrestling means asking questions, challenging, and arguing.
——John Kotter[1]

There is an oft told story about a physician, active on the speaking circuit, who typically traveled to engagements in his chauffeur-driven limousine. During the presentations the chauffeur sat at the back of the room. One day while driving to one of these events, the chauffeur said, "You know, I've heard your talk so often I know it by heart." The doctor replied, "That's wonderful; since I'm feeling a bit tired today, why don't you give the talk for me?" So the doctor sat at the back of the room and the chauffeur strode to the podium and gave the speech. He did so well that no one had any inkling that he wasn't the scheduled speaker. When he finished presenting, however, the audience began asking questions. When the first question was asked, the chauffeur hadn't the vaguest idea about how to handle it. After a few anguished moments, he said, "The answer to that question is so obvious that my chauffeur can tell you what it is. "James," he said, gesturing to the physician at the back of the room, "Would you answer this gentleman's question?"

Like the chauffeur, many a trainer finds that dealing with questions and comments can be one of the most difficult parts of giving a presentation.

Handling Participants' Questions

The skill of responding to questions is a key component of the trainer's craft. Not surprisingly, the trainer's credibility often increases or decreases during question periods. As Elaine Biech notes, "In some cases, the effectiveness of your presentation is evaluated more on how well you handle the questions that come your way than on the talk itself."[2]

Fortunately, handling questions and comments is a skill that can be mastered fairly easily. And, when you are open to receiving questions, you give participants a chance to react to your ideas, which enables you to clarify misconceptions and add to what you've said. When questions from participants are handled well, the training becomes more interactive, which tends to increase participants' interest and generates positive energy in the room.

However, many novice trainers find that dealing with participants' questions is a nerve-wracking experience. Even seasoned trainers sometimes find it difficult. You may have witnessed an experienced presenter being peppered with so many questions that his talk began to sound disjointed. He may even get derailed and lose track of where he is in the presentation. Talkative participants may attach lengthy preambles to their questions or attempt to engage the trainer in a dialogue that eats time and bores the other class members. Probably the biggest difficulty for many trainers is when a disgruntled participant asks a loaded or hostile question that's a veiled attack on the trainer or the course material. This chapter, together with Chapter 15, shows how to avoid many of these situations, how to manage them when they do occur, and how to be at your best when responding to any question, comment, or objection.

Establishing Ground Rules for Asking Questions

A good first step for avoiding problems in dealing with questions is to set a few ground rules for asking questions. The guidelines can be altered for a particular presentation, but the established set of ground rules provides a baseline from which to depart.

Two frequently used guidelines are:

- State when you will take questions.
- Establish a time limit for question periods.

State When You Will Take Questions

When questions are asked during a talk, it often breaks the flow of the presentation. Simply announcing the following guideline will usually prevent that from occurring:

Please hold questions and comments until the end of each presentation.

There are times, of course, when it's appropriate to take questions during your presentation. This approach is usually employed in small informal groups. When you're okay with taking questions during your talk, you might announce:

Feel free to ask questions as they occur to you. You won't be interrupting—in fact, you'll be adding to the presentation.

Establish a Time Limit for Question Periods

This ground rule is useful if the group continues to ask questions well beyond the typical amount of time for a question period (a maximum of five to eight minutes is a common norm). If excessive questioning occurs, you might want to set a time limit by saying:

> In order to end the workshop on time we have to start limiting the time spent on questions to ___ minutes per question period.

If questions are still coming at the end of the time period, you can say:

> We've covered some important ground in this question-and-answer period. It looks like there are still more questions. In view of the time, we need to move on. However, I'll be available during the first ten minutes of the lunch break and immediately after the close of the workshop day to discuss any further questions with you.

Prepare to Respond to Likely Questions

Sound preparation is required for dealing knowledgably and succinctly with participant questions and comments. Two aspects of preparation are particularly important:

- Anticipate issues that are apt to be raised.
- Develop concise answers to frequently asked questions.

Anticipate Issues That Are Apt to Be Raised

Review your presentation and think of questions that are likely to be asked. Presentation coach Andrew Gilman points out that the president of the United States can typically predict nine of ten issues that reporters will ask in wide-ranging presidential press conferences where all aspects of domestic policy and foreign affairs are fair game.[3] So it seems like a doable task for a trainer to anticipate most of the issues that are likely to be raised about the much more focused content of a particular workshop presentation. You may not be able to do this with 100 percent accuracy, but, especially if you've taught the course before, you should have a fairly good idea of what questions may be asked. Trainers who teach presentation skills know that someone is likely to ask, "What's wrong with putting my hands in my pockets when I present? It looks relaxed and comfortable." If they're teaching reflective listening they can be fairly sure that issues such as sounding mechanical or coming on like a psychologist will be raised. And in a people styles course, some participants will be dubious that people of every style can be successful.

Develop Concise Answers to Frequently Asked Questions

Since you should be able to anticipate many of the issues that will be raised, you can create succinct, well-worded, prepared answers to regularly asked questions. These predictable questions will probably be asked in many outings with a given workshop, so work at getting the wording as concise and as memorable as possible. Once in a while, work at simplifying, shortening, and otherwise refining your answers to those frequently asked questions.

In addition to preparing answers to predictable questions, you can benefit from spending some time increasing your general knowledge of the subject matter of your course. Get acquainted with information in books and articles beyond what the training manual says about the subject you are teaching. The combination of broad research and the use of crisp, prepared answers provide a good base for handling participant questions.

Invite Questions Productively

The typical way of inviting questions after a presentation is to ask,

Are there any questions?

Unfortunately that question usually produces a long, lethargic silence. So many experienced trainers presenters prefer to ask,

Who has the first question?

Though this wording is only slightly different from the relatively unproductive, "Are there any questions?" the recommended question tends to pull more and better questions from participants.

A key moment in a Q-and-A period is the silent interval between inviting questions from the class and the moment when the first question is asked. This interval is often termed "wait time," although if you follow the approach advocated in this chapter, "thinking time" would be a more appropriate label. Especially for beginning trainers, this brief pause can seem like an eternity and many trainers end pauses prematurely and therefore unproductively. Educator Peter Johnson says, "On the face of it, remaining silent seems quite trivial, but research shows that extending thinking times is positively related to more student talk, more sustained talk, and more 'higher order' thinking."[4]

Here are some tips to help you manage these brief periods of silence in a relaxed and polished manner:

1. After you invite questions, stand erect, be silent, and look calmly at the group. Your poise will free participants up to think about their questions and whether they want to ask them.

2. Even if no questions come after several seconds, remain calmly silent.

3. If after fifteen to twenty seconds no one asks a question, "paraphrase" what's happening in the group and then repeat the question. For example:

    > Sometimes it's hard to put concerns or questions into words. But just in case something comes up, take a little more time. . . . [pause]. . . . I'll wait a bit more in case someone has a question he'd like to ask or a concern he wants to raise.

4. If no one asks a question, you can wrap up the Q-and-A by saying:

    > Since no one has any questions, I'll recap the points of the presentation and we'll proceed to [whatever comes next].

Use the Five-Step Question-and-Answer Method

When a participant asks a question, the five-step question-and-answer method will help you understand the question, think clearly about it, and respond effectively to it. Here are the steps:

1. Attend to the questioner.
2. Paraphrase the question, speaking directly to the questioner.
3. Pause briefly while still attending to the questioner.
4. Turn to face the group, and invite or give an answer to the question.
5. Transition back to the presentation.

Step 1: Attend to the Questioner

One of the most effective things you can do when receiving a question is to attend to the questioner. Turn your body toward her, square your shoulders to hers, and maintain eye contact as you take in her question. Don't move closer to the questioner as that tends to exclude the rest of the group. And it could make the questioner uncomfortable. Attending to the questioner in this way communicates that you are taking her seriously, are trying to understand her question, and that you want to respond helpfully. To recall how to use the skill of attending, review Chapter 12.

Step 2: Paraphrase the Question, Speaking Directly to the Questioner

It can be as challenging to understand a question as it is to respond effectively to it. Sometimes the words of a question don't match what the participant intended to say. A person may be confused about what he's learning and may not know how to ask a question that will communicate specifically what he wants to have cleared up. Or the question may be constructed well but the trainer simply misunderstands it. One way or another, misunderstandings sometimes occur when we communicate. So, rather than answer the wrong question, begin your response by paraphrasing the question: boil it down and state your understanding in your own words. The previous chapter on listening provided instruction on how to paraphrase what someone says to you. Later in this chapter you'll find examples of paraphrasing in Q-and-A situations.

Paraphrasing a question is the quickest and most effective way of doing an accuracy check on what the questioner really wants to know. It focuses the questioner's, the participants', and your attention on the heart of the matter. It's often said that a good definition of a problem gets you halfway to the solution. In a somewhat similar way, an effective paraphrase of a question often brings you halfway to the answer.

While listening to the question you were facing the questioner. Continue facing the questioner as you paraphrase the question.

Question:

Do you think it's possible that a person with very high flexibility may come across as insincere and lose credibility? You know, pretending to be someone he's not.

Paraphrase:

You're concerned that highly flexible people might be perceived as phonies.

Step 3: Pause Briefly While Still Attending to the Questioner

When you've paraphrased the question, pause for four or five seconds. Maintain eye contact during the silence. The pause will allow the questioner to elaborate or add to her question if she chooses to. The questioner will often add, "The reason I'm asking is . . ." or words to that effect. The refinement of the question that frequently occurs during the pause often narrows the question's focus or otherwise elaborates on what is being asked, which generally enables you to give a more succinct and useful answer. The pause also gives you a bit of time to think about both the issue being raised and the approach you'll take when responding.

It's more challenging than one might think to pause after being asked a question. When being queried regarding something we're knowledgeable about the mind seems to instinctively begin developing an answer. And that tendency often escalates when giving a presentation. As William Steele says, "There is something about public speaking that causes even the most careful people to be in a hurry to give answers. They will begin answering the second a questioner stops talking, even if the question was vague and confusing. They guess at what was being asked and then start talking."[5]

You'll find that you are more comfortable pausing when you learn to use these brief moments of time constructively. As you'll soon see, there are at least nine methods of responding to a participant's question. One pragmatic way of employing these pauses is to use this brief time to decide which of the nine methods you'll use in this interaction.

Step 4: Turn to Face the Group, and Invite or Give an Answer to the Question

It's important to disengage from the one-to-one interaction and respond to the whole group. Note that this step is *generate an answer* rather than *answer the question*. Some trainers answer every question themselves:

Participant question	➡	Trainer answer.
Participant question	➡	Trainer answer.
Participant question	➡	Trainer answer.

How limiting and how boring to use the same approach for responding to every question. Fortunately, in addition to the trainer answering participants' questions, there are at least eight other methods for responding to questions, most of which foster increased participation. Dynamic trainers use the full spectrum of the following options for responding to questions.

Nine Methods for Responding to Participants' Questions

1. The Trainer Answers the Question When you answer the question yourself, turn away from the questioner and address the whole group. Keep your answer as short and as simple as possible—without oversimplifying. Consider stating the gist of your response first and follow it with a fuller, but still very brief, explanation—between thirty seconds and one minute in length.

Answer in one sentence; amplify in a paragraph.

Question: "Sometimes I wonder about people styles and flexibility—like which do you think is more important—someone's interpersonal style or their interpersonal flexibility?"

Paraphrase: "You're wondering which is key—style or flexibility."

Answer in a sentence: "For practical purposes, a person's interpersonal flexibility is most important."

Amplify in a paragraph: "A person's interpersonal style is an enduring pattern of interpersonal behavior. It's a given—a permanent aspect of a person's life. None of us can change our style. But each of us can increase our interpersonal flexibility. In fact, that's a major goal of this course. Since we can't alter our style, it's important to become proficient at interpersonal flexibility, which enables us to relate well and work productively with all types of people."

2. The Trainer Refers the Question to the Group

> Anyone have any thoughts about that?

There are a couple of benefits of referring the question to the group. It allows participants to see the reaction of other members of the group. And it takes you out of the lecture mode which tends to be good for group process.

3. The Trainer Sends the Question Back to the Asker

> Sounds like you've been thinking about this for a while. What's your take on this, Joanne?

4. The Trainer Refers the Question to a Knowledgeable Participant

> Mike, I believe you've had some experience with this. Do you have any comments?

5. The Trainer Invites Contrasting Opinions

> Some people think differently about this. Anyone here think this may not work?

6. The Trainer Does a Mini-Demonstration of How the Situation Might Be Handled   When doing a mini-demonstration, the trainer typically role plays the answer. For example, in a Train-the-Trainer workshop, the trainer might say:

> I'd like to act out my response to your question. Would you mind bringing your chair opposite mine? Then, say something about the course content not being practical and I'll demonstrate one way you might handle the situation.

It's usually more convincing to see a role-played response than merely hear a verbalized answer. Besides, the brief role play brings a welcome change of pace to the workshop.

This is a good approach to take with questions that begin with, "What if."

7. The Trainer Refers the Questioner to a Resource   To avoid a time-consuming theoretical discussion, during which you may lose the attention of the group, you can refer the questioner to the course text, workbook, or other resource. A few participants may enjoy class time spent in long theoretical discussions. Most don't.

8. The Trainer Negotiates to Respond Later   Collecting questions on a Question Parking Lot Chart is a commonly used way of postponing a response to a later time. You might say something like this to the questioner:

> Danni, I'll write your question on this Question Parking Lot Chart and respond to it before the day (or module or course) is over. I'll put your name by your question as a reminder to me to be sure I provide you with the information you want.

Then, when you feel it's appropriate, refer back to the question, respond to it, and when it's been covered check it off the Question Parking Lot Chart.

Or you could say, "Let's talk on break and I'll see if I can clarify this for you."

9. The Trainer Doesn't Know the Answer and Says So You can be very knowledgeable about a subject and yet not be able to answer every possible question about it. When asked a question that you don't have a good answer for, the best policy is to say so. Regarding a question that he had been asked, Mark Twain said, "I was gratified to be able to answer promptly, and I did. I said I didn't know."[6] Samuel Johnson, who was probably the most distinguished man of letters in English history, was asked why, in his dictionary, he had defined *pastern* as a *horse's knee*. Johnson replied, "Ignorance, Madam, pure ignorance."[7]

In training, if the issue is relevant and you don't know the answer and you doubt that anyone else in the room does, you might say:

> I've never thought about that. Thanks for raising the issue. Although I don't know the answer, I'll find out and get back to you with some information before the close of the workshop.

If that time frame is unrealistic, state a time that is feasible. Most, if not all, participants will respect you for admitting that there are some questions you can't answer.

When using any of these methods for responding to questions keep in mind the Italian proverb:

> It's a good answer that knows when to stop.

Step 5. Transition Back to the Presentation

When transitioning out of a Q-and-A, if time permits ask if there are more questions. If any are raised, handle them. But don't let the Q-and-A Period just peter out. Close by energetically summarizing the points of your presentation. Add important points that were raised in the Q-and-A period. Then, in thirty to forty seconds, briefly indicate what's coming next.

Integrate Material from Your Responses into the Course Design

As indicated earlier, many of the questions participants ask have been raised in previous workshops and therefore are predictable. But a new issue may surface that calls for new information that belongs in the workshop design.

From time to time consider doing a minor revamp of the course based on the salient questions that are asked and your responses to them. The goal in including material generated by these questions is not to sidestep all questions, but to be sure you have included in the content of your course the material that provides learners with the most insight into the subject matter.

Avoid Two Commonly Made Mistakes When Handling Questions

There are two frequently made mistakes to avoid when responding to questions: (1) saying, "That's a good question"; and (2) asking, "Did I answer your question?"

In the first mistake, the trainer's intent is usually constructive when making this type of statement—he wants to support the questioner and encourage the asking of questions in the group. However, when someone says, "That's a good question," whether he means to or not, he is voicing a judgment on the quality of the question. In this case it's a positive judgment. But when the trainer responds to subsequent questions with, "That's a good question," he'll soon sound repetitive. And, of course, if some questions don't get the "Good question" response, people are likely to assume that the trainer thinks those are *not* good questions. Furthermore, although we've heard presenters say, "There's no such thing as a dumb question," we've fielded more than a few questions that were irrelevant to the module of the workshop or very difficult to unscramble. It would be false and inappropriate to respond to them with the compliment, "Good question."

The second mistake, asking, "Did I answer your question?" has been called the "masochistic question" because it often prompts a mini-speech by the participant, which is often rather boring and typically is a workshop timewaster.

If you have the skills for responding to questions, comments, and objections and feel confident in your ability to do so, you will succeed in moving the workshop along without a lot of bumps in the road, and your life as a trainer will be much more relaxed and enjoyable.

14

Making Presentations Interactive

Learning is not a spectator sport.

——John Newstrom

Picture a good conversation among people you know; their body language demonstrates their engagement, thoughtful comments are made, one idea stimulates another, humor pops up unexpectedly, energy flows, and time flies for those involved. That positive and memorable communication experience is the kind of participant involvement we imagine when we talk about interactive presenting. This chapter emphasizes the importance of making presentations interactive and discusses how to increase participants' verbal involvement in your training talks. The chapter closes with a description of three additional methods for generating increased participant involvement.

Interactive Presenting

Dynamic trainers are not only good at presenting; they also excel in making their presentations interactive. Effective speaking isn't only about the content of your message and your mastery of delivery; it's also about the invitation that participants feel to respond to the message.

In training we use the phrase *interactive presenting* to refer to a type of delivery that generates discussion between the trainer and the participants as well as among the participants themselves. It transforms a presentation from monologue to dialogue. Interactive presenting involves an appropriate balance of the trainer's speaking, questioning, and listening, which creates give-and-take in a workshop and transforms a presentation from a monologue to a dialogue. Dynamic trainers are good at present-ing *and* they excel at getting participants to talk. As Ken Bain, president of Best Teachers Institute, says, "Good teachers know how to talk well, but they also can get students talking."[1]

The Benefits of Making Presentations Interactive

Most trainers are good talkers—not only good talkers but BIG TALKERS. Words typically come easily to them. Not infrequently this results in the occupational hazard of over-talking—often to the point of making one-way communication the trainer's primary leadership style. What's sometimes called the "pour and snore" method puts the learner in a passive role. When you monopolize the conversation, you can be sure the other person's mind will soon be drifing off.

Interactive presenting provides a good remedy for the problem of excessive talking by the trainer. Two–way interplay is far more energizing than the typical one-way presentation. Two-way communication injects a shot of dynamism into the workshop. The participant who responds becomes more alert and others perk up because they're hearing from one of their own.

Adult learners have built up a storehouse of knowledge and experience about a wide variety of subjects. When a trainer uses interactive presenting, he's showing respect for that knowledge and experience. He makes use of the class's fund of knowledge throughout his presentations by inviting people to share their experi-ence, their point of view, or information they have on the topic. Interactive present-ing also provides the trainer with a way of finding out whether or not the ideas, attitudes, and skills being taught are clearly understood by the participants. And when learning is interactive it tends to be more satisfying, which enhances people's motivation to learn. Furthermore, when you ask participants to recall their experi-ences and apply the material to their situations you are inviting them to link what you are teaching to their world so the training becomes more meaningful and more rooted in their lives.

Interactive speaking can also be used in other modules of your courses besides presenting. For example, debriefing (discussed in Chapter 6) expands your opportu-nities for back-and-forth communication when you use interactive speaking in the debriefing. You'll also find this method of teaching useful in your coaching of par-ticipants, especially when giving feedback. And when interactive speaking is inte-grated into your communication style, it generates more participation in other parts of your workshops.

Finally, and perhaps most important, interactive presenting increases learning. Research has shown that when a presenter engages the audience in some form of participation, their recall and use of the content increases dramatically. Classroom discourse researcher Martin Nystrand and his colleagues found that dialogically organized instruction had a strong, positive effect on learning.[2] And that, after all, is what we trainers are after.

How to Make Presentations Interactive

Here are four steps for making presentations more of a dialogue than a monologue:

1. Plan for interaction.
2. "Read" the group while you speak.
3. Involve participants early and often.
4. Ask checking questions.

1. Plan for Interaction

Look for places in each presentation where you think participants might have a reaction to what's being said. Judging from the nature of the content you'll be teaching or from your previous experience of teaching the material, you'll be able to guess fairly accurately where some participants may be a bit resistant as well as where some probably have had previous experiences that are relevant to what's being taught. Other times that also tend to be fruitful for interaction are at the end of a point or concept that's challenging to understand or an idea or a method that's likely to be met with resistance.

2. "Read" the Group While You Speak

Trainers need to be constantly alert to the signals emanating from the group. This is the case even when the trainer is delivering a presentation. Watching for participants' reactions to what's being said and responding to those reactions when appropriate provides an opportunity to integrate one or more people into partnering in the presentation. For example, a trainer, when presenting, says,

All interpersonal styles can be successful in managing people.

The trainer observes a perplexed look on participant Ben's face, and the following dialogue ensues:

Trainer: Ben, it looks like that sounds a little off to you.

Ben: Yeah, it does.

Trainer: Can you say more about that?

Ben: Sure. When it comes to managing people, it just makes common sense to me that the more assertive styles would be more successful than the less assertive styles.

Trainer: Seems logical to you.

Ben: Yeah.

Trainer: The People Styles workshop developers researched that very issue and, contrary to popular opinion, they found that no particular people style is associated with a greater likelihood of success. Strong interpersonal flexibility is the variable that's associated with higher levels of success.

3. Involve Participants Early and Often

Chapter 4 describes how to involve participants very early in a workshop. Here's how Ferdinand Fournies involves participants in his coaching workshops from the get-go. In his opening remarks he says,

> It appears obvious to me, looking around the room, that the majority of you managers have been managers for quite a long time; therefore, I assume you have been doing that thing called coaching or counseling or appraising for a long time. The question that occurs to me is this: Realizing how important time is to you managers, I wonder why you would want to take a day of your time and spend it on a subject that you obviously have been doing for many years.[3]

Then Fournies tells us, "I shut up."

When Fournies stops talking the participants start speaking and he finds that they tell him the same things that he would have told them—which is far more impactful than if the words had come from him. That's a great way to get a workshop off to a talkative start.

This chapter discusses how to involve participants at numerous points in the workshop. Of course, two of the most natural times to involve participants are during a point or concept that's challenging to understand or when presenting an idea or method that's likely to be met with resistance.

4. Ask Checking Questions

A checking question is a brief question by the trainer that invites participants to respond to what they're hearing. Here's a step-by-step way of generating involvement with checking questions:

1. Create the checking question.
2. Preface some of the questions.
3. Ask the question.
4. Pause.
5. Paraphrase the response.
6. Invite input from others.
7. Resume presenting.

Create the Checking Question

Phrasing the question clearly is a major part of getting it answered thoughtfully. But many trainers tend to ask vague questions that generate humdrum answers. Ruthlessly prune away low-yield questions. Then put forth the time and effort to create thought-provoking inquiries.

Checking questions are open-ended rather than closed-ended. Open-ended questions (often called "open questions") are the tools of choice when you want to get people thinking and talking. They typically begin with one of these words or phrases:

How

What

Why

In what way(s)

Here are some examples of open-ended questions:

How well do you think you did using the skill in this practice?

What stands out as important to you?

Why do you think it won't work in your situation?

In what way(s) could you have handled that better?

Here are some additional open-ended checking questions:

How does this sound to you?

How practical does that seem to you?

How does this measure on your "makes sense" meter?

In what way does this fit with your experience?

What are your reactions to what you've heard so far?

What have we learned here?

What stands out to you as important?

What would you add to what I've said about_____?

What specifically do you need more detail on?

These kinds of questions often elicit support for what you've said and enrich the ideas presented. Just as beneficial are the times when an open question elicits disagreement with what's been taught. This red alert provides a chance for the trainer to work through problem areas rather than face a gradual buildup of resistance, which tends to become stronger the longer the disagreements remain buried and unaddressed.

Notice that no closed questions are listed above. Closed questions usually begin with words such as *Are, Can, Could, Did, Do, Does, Have, Is, May, Might, Should, Were,* and *Will.* These questions tend to produce a yes or no response, and although they have valuable uses, they tend to limit rather than encourage interaction.

When people respond to checking questions they're giving their own reaction to what you've said or telling about their own experience. And they are the best authorities in the room about those things. So, responding to this type of question tends to feel less risky than many other types of participation. Once participants speak and experience their contributions being accepted and valued, they'll feel more comfortable about talking in the large group in the future.

Preface Some of the Questions

A preface creates a context that provides the listener with a clearer understanding of your question and why you are asking it. In training, the part of the presentation that preceded the question often provides a context for understanding the question. In such cases there's no need for a preface.

When a preface is needed, here's an easy way to create one. Once you have your question in mind, mentally complete this sentence:

The reason I ask is . . .

When you finish this sentence, you have the essence of the preface.
For example, a preface to the question "What would you add to what I've said?" might sound something like this:

Preface: "I know many of you have years of experience and could build on what I've presented."

Question: "What would you add to what I've said?"

Ask the Question

When you come to a natural break in your presentation, ask a checking question to elicit participants' reactions. Address your checking question to the entire group instead of calling on someone by name. Don't say, "Jim, what are your thoughts about the contrast between leadership and management?" Just let the question float around the group and see who wants to contribute.

Pause

What's your best guess about how long it takes people to respond to a question? Are you thinking about the question you just read? Is it taking you some time to come up with your best guess? It will take your participants some time to respond to your questions, too. So leave five to ten seconds for participants to think about the question. (At first you may need to count the seconds off in your head.) It may seem like an eternity to you, but participants will be busy thinking of a response and then deciding whether or not they want to volunteer an answer. Don't interrupt that process by answering the question yourself.

When leading a group, many trainers experience silence as being very stressful. That's a fear that needs to be overcome. In a well-functioning learning environment, silence is not a vacuum. It provides a reflective interlude for people to absorb what's been said and done. So let the pause linger a bit.

Assume that many participants want to be involved. They just may not be ready yet or may be holding back for some other reason.

If no one answers, rephrase your question and pause again. People may need a bit more time to mull it over. The pause will put a little pressure on the participants to respond.

During the pause, pay close attention to the participants: read their faces and their other body language. Nonverbal indicators can provide as many clues about people's involvement as their verbal responses do.

In the unlikely event that no one speaks up, there's a very simple and easy way of handling the situation which we describe later in the chapter.

Paraphrase the Response

As participants begin to open up and respond to your checking questions, the most encouraging thing you can do to support a fruitful dialogue is to use the paraphrasing skills that were discussed in Chapter 12. Your paraphrase will let the speaker know that you are taking her input seriously. And it will contribute to creating a safe and positive learning climate. As mentioned earlier, many participants bring with them memories of some negative school experiences and may need proof that this educational experience is different; no embarrassments will occur and no negative judgments will be passed on their contributions.

Respond acceptingly. Put a bit of variety into your responses:

"Thanks for that."

"Mm-hmm."

Or just nod your head.

Then look to another section of the room for more responses.

Invite Input from Others

When someone has replied to your checking question and you have reflected her response, sometimes it's desirable to ask a follow-up question:

"Reactions?"

"Anyone else?"

"Other thoughts?"

"Anyone feel the same or different about that?"

"What are some other opinions?"

Occasionally ask the respondent a follow-up question:

"Would you elaborate on that?"

"What examples of that come to mind?"

"How did that work out?"

Resume Presenting

When the input is drying up or when the time allotted to this part of the presentation is over, transition to the next part of the workshop. Timing is important. You can't allow the participants' discussions to go on so long that the workshop schedule is negatively affected. So keep an eye on the time. And make a smooth transition from the discussion to what comes next.

The transition can include something of what you've learned about the participants' points of view along with a smooth segue back into your presentation. Here are some examples of a transition:

"The next part of this presentation considers that very point."

"Pat's concern is addressed in the next section of this material, so let's move on."

"You've expressed interest in learning more about dealing with difficult customers; I'd like to present some ideas about that."

The more you use interactive presenting in your class, the more smoothly the process will go. People will get used to it. They'll like it. They'll feel valued and respected. There will be times when participants no longer wait for your questions, but will jump in when they have a comment or question.

What If You Invite Participation and No One Responds?

Many novice trainers are afraid that they will ask a question and no one will respond to it and that a dark and awful silence will fill the room. However, if you patiently wait about fifteen seconds, someone will usually respond. If no one speaks up, you can say,

When anyone feels like saying something just jump in.

And again pause for another five to ten seconds. If no one rises to the occasion, you can matter-of-factly say,

Looks like you're all set on this so we'll move on.

Additional Involvement Methods

There are three additional ways to make your workshops more interactive:

1. Prime the Pump

When a group is slow to respond to checking questions, you may want to prime the pump. With this method you plant the seed of a question or a comment in the minds of participants by saying things like:

> In an objective-setting course: "Some people aren't sure about how accountability is integrated into objective setting. Is that something you're interested in hearing more about?"
>
> In a presentation-skills course: "Being centered in a home base from which most of your presentation will be given will help members of the group stay focused on you and will contribute to your success in employing the body language of presenting. What's your reaction to that?"
>
> In a communication-skills course: "Remaining yourself while incorporating a variety of new ways of communicating into your repertoire can be a challenge. What are your thoughts about that?"

Often a participant will speak up on the issue you mention. If not, you can encourage conversation by responding to the nodding or shaking of heads that you observe. You might ask,

> Several heads are nodding; would someone put their thoughts into words?

Technically, this is a closed question. But it functions as an open question since it invites a broad response rather than a one- or two-word answer.

2. Set Up Buzz Groups

There are some groups that just don't do much interacting with the trainer. You can use open-ended questions, preface them, prime the pump, and still get little or nothing back. In this type of situation, you might consider using buzz groups—subgroups of three, four, or five persons.

Then you ask the subgroups to decide who will report their ideas to the large group at the end of their discussion.

You give an assignment, such as, "Come up with three questions you would like addressed about the methods you've just practiced." Or, "Develop two or three on-the-job applications of the skills you've just learned."

At the end of the time given for that discussion, the subgroups return to the large group and each reporter summarizes what transpired in their subgroup. This may elicit questions from others or from you. The best-case scenario is that a good discussion that started in the subgroup will carry over into the large group. Valuable ideas may surface that would not have been discussed through questioning the large group.

At the appropriate time, you transition out of the subgroups and back into your presentation or the next part of the workshop.

Of course, buzz groups can serve very different but equally useful functions in workshops where the trainees are highly participative.

3. Poll the Group

Polling is another method for making presentations interactive. It's a good way of generating interaction in its own right and it's also a useful fallback when a group isn't responding to checking questions. It's also a technique that can be used at various points during training. We referred to it in Chapter 4 as a way of breaking the ice when participants are first meeting each other. Polling can also be used for the double purpose of

- checking for learning, and
- increasing the interactivity of the workshop.

Polling is one of the easiest and least risky ways for shy people to participate in a workshop. There's no need for participants to speak since a nonverbal response is all that's called for. And there will be safety in numbers—several other people will almost certainly be voting on the topic the same way any given participant is voting. This type of nonverbal participation can be a way of easing participants into verbal participation in the large group a bit later.

Some examples of polling:

"Raise your hand to give us a sense of how many of you face this in your day-to-day work life."

"Let's have a show of hands if you still have questions about X. About Y."

"Thumbs up if this is really clear to you and thumbs down if you still have questions about how to do this."

"Raise your hand if this is something you want to hear more about."

You take in the nonverbal information and report what you see to the group. If you choose, you may then ask a checking question about a specific part of what was shared nonverbally, thus inviting some verbal interaction. When it's time to end the interaction, transition from the discussion back to your presentation.

Polling can give you a quick check on where the group is and often provides you with course-correcting information. After polling you may decide to slow down, speed up, take more—or less—time for questions, etc.

We've gone into considerable detail on how to make your presentations interactive because when used well this ability has such positive impact on workshop climate and outcome. Some of the skills can be useful in one-to-one situations, too.

15

Managing the Tough Moments

When dealing with a confrontational question, separate the attitude of the questionnaire from the content of the question.

——Andrew Bryant

This chapter discusses how to graciously manage three kinds of participant-trainer challenges that sometimes surface in a workshop:

1. How to respond to disruptive questions and comments.
2. How to manage a monopolizer.
3. How to disagree with a participant's comment that you think is inaccurate.

If difficult questions or statements are handled ineptly, it's likely to waste workshop time and undermine the effectiveness of the training. For example, if a person says, "When are you going to stop pussyfooting around the basic issues?" you could say, "In about five minutes," and probably get a laugh. However, if you want to maintain a positive workshop climate, you could use the following method for responding to disruptive comments.

Responding to Disruptive Questions and Comments

When handling disruptive questions or statements, follow these four steps:

1. Attend to the questioner.
2. Paraphrase the question or comment.
3. Respond to the question or comment.
4. Transition back to the presentation.

Mastering this four-step method will enable you to relate constructively to virtually any disruptive participant. So the bulk of this section of the chapter focuses on the way you do these steps.

Step 1: Attend to the Questioner

Use good attending to demonstrate respect for the questioner. No matter how negative the questioner is, your respectful responses to him should never waver.

Step 2: Paraphrase the Question or Comment

When you paraphrase the question or comment, rather than direct your paraphrase to the questioner/speaker, break eye contact with the questioner, turn to face a different section of the group, and paraphrase the question or comment using neutral language.

Break Eye Contact with the Questioner

Perhaps you recall from the Chapter 12 that under normal circumstances you would continue facing the questioner during your paraphrase of his question. But when interacting with someone who tends to be overly talkative or disruptive, continued attending could prolong an already verbose or otherwise troublesome interaction.

Breaking eye contact signals that the question has been received and it's now time for the response. The questioner may or may not heed the signal, but at least the rest of the group will get the picture and will appreciate your constructive effort to move the group along while still treating the participant with respect.

Turn and Face the Group

Turning to the group sends a nonverbal message to everyone in the room that the one-to-one dialogue with the questioner has ended.

Use Impersonal or Neutral Language

When you paraphrase the question, it's important for the wording to be impersonal. To avoid a you-versus-me situation, use impersonal language when restating what was said.

Instead of saying something like:	Say something like:
"**Your** issue is. . . ." or	"**The** issue is that . . . ." or
"**You're** wondering . . . ." or	"**It** seems like . . . ." or
"**You** think . . . ,"	"**The** concern is . . . ."

The slight change in the wording helps depersonalize the interaction and may prevent the escalation of a tense situation.

When a question contains loaded language, restate it using neutral language:

Participant's loaded question: "When are you going to stop pussyfooting around the basic issues?"

Neutral language paraphrase: "The concern is that I'm not being forthright with this group."

Step 3: Respond to the Question or Comment

Continue facing the group as you give a response using one of these options:

- Answer the question.
- Refer the question to the group.
- Invite other opinions.
- Do a mini-demonstration of how the situation might be handled.
- Negotiate to respond later.
- Refer the questioner to a resource.
- If you don't know the answer, say so.

Two of the types of responses to genuine questions and well-intentioned comments are not listed here because they would be counterproductive when dealing with participants who tend to be disruptive or who are especially verbose. The responses to avoid in these situations are the following:

- When you receive a question from a person who tends to monopolize, it's unwise to send the question back to the asker.
- When a participant who tends to be disruptive asks a question, it's masochistic to send the question back to the asker and unprofessional to forward it to another participant.

To practice this skill in our Presentation Skills course, we have participants pair up. One person is the questioner, the other the trainer. The questioner is to ask an argumentative question, and is cautioned to be realistic and not to overplay the role. The trainer positions herself facing away from the questioner. When the questioner asks a disruptive question, the trainer uses the method for handling disruptive questions. Then participants reverse roles.

Not until participants stand up and practice the method do they realize how difficult it is to hear the argumentative question accurately, think of which of the seven ways of responding they will select, while at the same time using the suggested body language. (Breaking eye content with the questioner, facing another part of the room, and responding with neutral language.)

When you receive disruptive questions and comments objectively, handle them with respect, and make sure that the questioner's standing in the group is not jeopardized, you will have demonstrated grace under fire and will gain credibility with the group.

Step 4: Transition Back to the Presentation

As mentioned in earlier chapters, transitions connect the content you've been discussing with what is coming next. They link where we've been in the workshop with where we're going. For example:

Say where we've been:
"The last question focused mainly on theoretical underpinnings."
Tell where we're going:
"We're now moving into practical applications."

The Trainer's Body Language

The body language of the trainer is a major factor in handling disruptive questions successfully. Figure 15.1 describes how the trainer's body language supported the process of handling the disruptive question mentioned above.

The manner in which a trainer responds to a disruptive question can affect the climate of the workshop significantly. A heavy-handed reaction can cause a group to split into those who side with the participant and those who side with the trainer. If the trainer assumes a dictatorial stance, the group can turn against him. In either case, the learning climate becomes negative and the trainer becomes the enemy.

In responding to some attacks, whether in the form of a disruptive question or a negative comment, it helps if the trainer is relatively nondefensive and has a good sense of humor. As an example, a few minutes into a workshop a trainer mentioned her children during her self-introduction. A male participant interrupted the trainer

Figure 15-1. The trainer's body language when dealing with disruptive questions.

Dialogue	Trainer's Body Language
Questioner: "When are you going to stop pussyfooting around the basic issue, which is the lack of management support for what you are teaching?"	**While listening,** the trainer turns her whole body to **face the questioner.** Body and face are relaxed as she makes eye contact with the questioner.
Trainer: "The concern is that I'm not being forthright with this group." (Pauses)	Then, **when paraphrasing the question,** the trainer turns her whole body away from the questioner and faces the group.
The trainer responds. Whatever is appropriate to the particular group's situation.	The trainer continues facing the group during her response to the question.

by calling out, "Who's with your children while you're traveling all over the country doing training?" The trainer with a big smile said, "This is great! Ten minutes into the workshop and we've already got something going. [To the questioner] Let's discuss it at lunch." And she continued introducing the workshop. At lunch, the questioner revealed the problems he was having with his wife who traveled as part of her work while his preference was that she switch to a job that didn't require travel. In class he settled down and worked successfully at learning what was taught.

Attacks on a trainer or the course material often have little to do with the trainer or the material and much to do with what's going on in the disgruntled participant's life. When trainers realize that, it makes it easier to remain nondefensive. Also, there's a proverb in many societies that you can often learn more from your critics than from your friends. So when dealing with a disgruntled participant, look for the silver lining—search for what you can learn from his dissatisfaction.

How to Manage a Monopolizer

In workshops that we've conducted, we encountered more monopolizers than disruptive questioners. Monopolizers tend to lack self-awareness and sensitivity to social situations. The participation of monopolizers is unbalanced: they speak too often and too long. So it's useful, before beginning a workshop to mentally establish a time limit for how long you will let a person hold forth before intervening.

Here's one way to figure out a reasonable time limit for questions and comments. Twenty to thirty seconds is enough time for asking most questions. After forty-five seconds, other participants are likely to be getting impatient. If a person prefaces a question for sixty seconds, it's probably time for the trainer to break in. You don't want to seem rude or impolite but it is your job to manage workshop time. And monopolizers tend to engage frequently in their overly talkative behavior, so you want to establish parameters early. Therefore, when a participant who is generally over-talkative in the group continues to elaborate his point of view yet again:

1. Look to another part of the room.
2. Cut in and say, "Let's see if I have the drift of the concern."
3. Succinctly paraphrase the point being made.

Here are some additional options for managing someone's over-participation:

- If a loquacious participant starts giving an extended comment or a wordy preface to a question, consider breaking in with a statement such as, "You've given us a lot to digest. Let's see if I've got the point," and turn toward another part of the room as you paraphrase what was said and give a brief reply. While facing the other part of the room you might ask if there are other questions or comments.

- Continue looking at the other part of the room and say, "This could take more time than we have right now. I'll stay after class for more discussion with anyone who wishes to pursue this." While the invitation is sincere, it's interesting that many questions lose their urgency when deferred to the end of the day.
- When it's clear that you are dealing with a confirmed monopolizer and you sense that he's about to begin another overly long statement, turn to face a different section of the room and *quickly* call on another questioner or direct a question to people in that part of the room.

For information on stronger measures for managing participant behavior that's undermining a workshop, see Chapter 23. Although that chapter doesn't deal specifically with monologuing, it provides information that could be very useful in dealing with this type of behavior.

How to Disagree with a Participant's Comment

If the issue is unimportant, just let it pass. An "Um-hmm" or "I see" is all that's needed. However, when you disagree with a comment that's related to an important workshop concept or method, you can do the following:

1. Paraphrase the comment until the speaker affirms the accuracy of your reflection by
   a. saying yes,
   b. nodding affirmatively,
   c. saying "Mm-hmm," or
   d. signaling that your paraphrase was on the mark.
2. Now that the person has indicated that you accurately understand her position, briefly state your point of view. For example, this interaction occurred during a day-long Listening for the Sale workshop:

Participant: As a salesperson, my job is to convince the prospect to buy. I don't get that done by listening to her. I need to control the sales call with strong presentations.

Trainer: Your sense of what's effective on a sales call is to keep the focus on what you want to say.

Participant: Right.

Trainer: A strong, well thought-out presentation is essential to an effective sales call. Balanced with that is discovering the customer's need by listening to what he's telling you. Listening well will help you learn what benefits to emphasize in your presentation.

The methods for handling disruptive questions, managing a monopolizer, and for disagreeing with a participant's comment presented in this chapter will help you make your way through many challenging situations that trainers are apt to encounter in any workshop. When the going gets tough, having a go-to set of methods gives you the confidence and the ability to manage the situation in a way that's constructive for you, the participant, and the group. Everybody wins when the trainer handles a challenging situation well.

16

Demonstrating What You Teach

A picture is worth a thousand words.

——Fredrick Barnard

When you want to teach someone a new ability, it's seldom enough to simply *tell* them what to do. Even the most specific wording can be misunderstood. Edward Thorndike, the noted educational psychologist, found that the five hundred most frequently used words in the English language have an average of twenty-four separate and distinct meanings. So, when you tell someone how to do something, there can be plenty of room for misunderstanding. This is especially the case when teaching someone how to do a complex skill or a familiar behavior in a more proficient way. *Skills are concrete but words are abstract.* A good demonstration—since it is concrete—tends to clear up misunderstandings that remain from the useful but the more abstract Tell How. Think of a demonstration as a movie of the desired performance.

An additional benefit of a well-done demonstration is that it highlights the viability of the course content since participants can see that what's being taught works.

Trainers Must Be Competent at Doing What They Teach

A number of research studies by Robert Carkhuff and other behavioral scientists found that trainees rarely surpass the skill proficiency of their teachers in the subject matter being taught.[1] A good Tell How is a plus, but in and of itself, it's usually insufficient for teaching someone a skill. If the teacher isn't sufficiently capable at actually doing what's being taught, the pupil's skill development will be stunted. It's unfortunate that few train-the-trainer programs for skill development courses are designed to foster sufficient skill development for the trainer to do proficient live demos or use the skill well in the workshop or in their civilian life. Responsibility for becoming adept with the course skills often rests squarely on the trainer's shoulders. One option is for the trainer to find someone who can do the skill well, enlist him as a coach, and then practice the skill until capable of doing an effective demonstration, and when applicable, of using the skill effectively in daily life.

In dynamic training, a demonstration generally precedes a practice as diagrammed below. The demonstration's main purpose is to provide a roadmap of what participants are to do in the practice, which follows immediately after it. Demonstrations are sometimes called "demos" and are also referred to as "behavioral modeling."

Chapter 3 described a six-component process for skill-building instruction:

Involve ➡ Tell How ➡ Demonstrate ➡ Practice ➡ Feedback ➡ Apply

Chapter 4 showed how to cover all the bases efficiently when opening a workshop. Chapter 5 discussed using activities to connect participants to the content and to one another. Chapter 6 showed you how to maximize learnings by skillful debriefing. Now its showtime, and this chapter teaches you how to excel when you demonstrate how to do the ability that you are teaching.

Develop a Sequence of Demonstrations

When teaching any fairly demanding skill, a sequence of three cycles of the middle four components of the skill-building process is usually required. Of course, the Tell How that precedes each of the demos is geared to the level of the skill that's required for the particular practice. In the third cycle, the Tell How and Show How components are printed in gray to indicate that in some workshops where participants are learning exceptionally well, these steps often can be greatly compressed or even eliminated.

Figure 16-1. Three cycles through the relevant components of the skill building process are usually required to learn a somewhat complex skill.

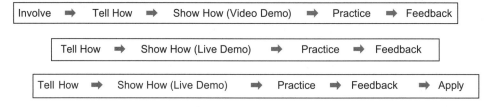

The Benefits and the Drawbacks of Video Demonstrations

It's often desirable to use a video example for the first demonstration. Video demos have a lot going for them—especially for the initial demo. They're predictable; you know that the skill user will be in top form. The length of the demo is predetermined. The brief video provides a change from the teaching modality you've been using. You can zoom in and out to emphasize something that's a key to success in doing what you are teaching. Instructive captions or voiceover can be used to drive home a key point. You also have useful options in playback mode; you can freeze frame, fast forward, or replay a key part.

There are, however, some downsides to video demos. Although the methods or skills being demonstrated may be relevant to what's being taught it's unlikely that the actors will be depicting the type of industry the participants are in or the viewers' vocational profile. Participants may question the viability of the script. They're aware that neither the script writer nor the producer would allow the skill user to fail in what's intended to be a positive demonstration. Furthermore, video demos lack the dynamic, engaging quality of a live demonstration. Despite these drawbacks, video demos can be incredibly useful training tools.

A point that most trainers would probably agree on is that many training videos are far from a perfect fit for the age, vocational profile, or other attributes of the group viewing it. So a disclaimer typically is useful for heading off criticisms that participants are apt to make that would consume workshop time and add little or nothing to learning the skill being taught. (Refer back to Chapter 11.)

The Benefits of Live Demonstrations

Live demos avoid most of the disadvantages of video demos. And, as you'll see later in this chapter, informal live demonstrations are especially useful for addressing issues raised by participants. Live demos sometimes generate suspense, as participants wonder whether the trainer will be able to achieve the desired outcome. And live demos have the additional benefit of showcasing the trainer's mastery of the skill, which adds to her credibility.

The biggest challenge of live demos is their unpredictability. In all likelihood the trainer's demo partner will be a volunteer from the group. Our experience has been that you often get a fairly good volunteer, but every once in a while a volunteer plays the role ineptly and doesn't give you much to work with. Occasionally, a volunteer will be "harder than life"—playing the role in a much more difficult manner than one would expect to encounter in the real world.

Despite these potential problems, we love live demos. When you've mastered the skills of dynamic training and the material of the course you are teaching, you'll be able to handle virtually any harder-than-life situations that skeptical participants bring up. In fact, these challenging situations add interest and energy to the workshop. And your ability to handle these difficult interactions will strengthen participants' motivation to master what you are teaching.

When Possible, Use Both Video and Live Demonstrations

When teaching a major skill, it's often advisable to use a video demo first because of its predictability—you know the skill will be demonstrated effectively as well as some of the other advantages mentioned earlier. Later, when participants are more knowledgeable about and competent in using the skills, they'll undoubtedly get more out of live demonstrations. And the likelihood of a live demo being much more credible is a significant additional benefit.

Tips for Leading Video Demonstrations

It's essential that the video equipment be ready and that the trainer can operate the system. It's usually best to begin by playing the whole demonstration, so participants get an overview of what they will be doing. Stopping and starting makes the viewing disjointed, and viewers are unlikely to see how the whole demonstration hangs together. So, before beginning the video, ask people to hold their questions. Then play the video.

Depending on the situation, you may decide to replay the video in whole or in part. Sometimes it's useful to stop in places that are especially important for succeeding in the upcoming practice or that were of particular interest or concern to the participants.

Planning Live Demonstrations

Live demonstrations, in contrast to video demonstrations, can be used for the following:

- Using an interpersonal skill
- Operating a piece of equipment/using materials

Planning a Live Demonstration of Using an Interpersonal Skill

In a live demonstration of an interpersonal skill you don't know exactly how the receiver of the skills is going to respond, so it's not possible to do a step-by-step plan of the demonstration, as is appropriate when preparing to do demonstrate how to operate a piece of equipment.

The first step in preparing to do a live demonstration of an interpersonal skill is to achieve excellence in performing the skill. If you are demonstrating the skill of listening, you need to be able to use the body language of listening and reflect the essence of the message in a conversational manner. If you demonstrate handling a complaint, you must be able to defuse the customer's negative feelings to the extent that effective problem solving can be done. When the demo is on giving feedback, the trainer needs to be able to use objective, behavioral descriptions and handle any defensive responses that may be triggered.

Live interpersonal skills demonstrations have a spontaneous, even risky element that tends to heighten the interest of participants. When done well, they're often among the highlights of a workshop. To help guide your preparation for this type of demo, you'll find a sample Interpersonal Skills Demonstration Worksheet in Appendix I.

Planning a Live Demonstration of Operating a Piece of Equipment

Detailed planning of the body of an equipment demonstration (step 6 below) will go a long way toward assuring success. In the planning stage, actually do the demonstration and write the steps as you proceed.

Regarding the written steps, do the demonstration again and edit the written directions for clarity and brevity. Once you're clear on the steps, practice the demo until its second nature to you.

How to Do Effective Demonstrations

Following these steps will help you effectively demonstrate what you are teaching:

1. Introduce the demonstration.
2. Give the directions.
3. Ask for a volunteer or volunteers (when needed).
4. Mention the specific things to watch for and/or listen for.
5. Use a disclaimer (when appropriate).
6. Do the demonstration.
7. Debrief the demonstration.
8. Conclude the demonstration.

1. Introduce the Demonstration

The introduction to a demonstration is similar to the introduction to leading an activity, which was discussed in Chapter 5:

- Transition in: link the component that was just covered (usually a Tell How) with the upcoming demonstration.

- State the purpose: explain that this demo models the ability that was described in the Tell How and shows what they will be doing in their upcoming practice.
- Preview: briefly preview what the demo will cover.

2. Give the Directions

When giving directions, start by setting the stage. Describe the following:

- What the situation is
- The role you'll be taking
- The role the other person will be taking
- If equipment and/or materials are involved, explain what they are and how
  they'll be used.

3. Ask for a Volunteer (or Volunteers)

If one or more volunteers are needed, first describe exactly what they will be asked
to do. Then ask for volunteers. People may be slow to volunteer, especially at the
beginning of a workshop. Don't try to rush the situation. Sometimes it's useful to
repeat what the volunteers will do in the demo and invite again. Wait. Expect someone to volunteer. Be patient.

4. Mention Specific Things to Watch for and/or Listen for

Set the stage:

- The situation
- The people
- Moments of special importance. This often is a very brief reference to
  points that were made in the Tell How. In a video demo, these may highlight crucial moments in the film.

Some trainers like to use Observer worksheets. Observer's Worksheets are developed
by the trainer to fit each unique demonstration. The worksheet indicates specific
parts of the demonstration that participants can look for to get the most out of observing a demonstration. If you are using observer's worksheets, distribute them now.
You should start developing the worksheets when you are planning the demonstration. That way you can easily match the items on the worksheet with the material
that you'll be teaching.

5. Use a Disclaimer

Using a disclaimer generally is an important part of leading a demonstration—and it's one that's often omitted. While disclaimers are important in many parts of a workshop, they're especially important prior to viewing most demonstrations. A demo can't show every problem that's likely to come up in the situation portrayed, and participants typically can raise a number of potential problems that were not addressed in the demonstration. And live demonstrations rarely are completely flawless. So rely on disclaimers to create more realistic expectations.

A disclaimer relating to a demo might sound like this:

The concern: "When this video was made last year, it was made using XYZ software which, as you know, we're not using any more."

The not-to-worry: "Although the software we are using is different from the software used in the video, the steps for handling this aspect of the software are identical to the ones you will be viewing in the film."

Sometimes both parts of a disclaimer can be stated in one short sentence:

The concern: "Don't expect any problems to be solved in this demo."

The not-to-worry: "We'll only be viewing a brief slice of a longer interaction."

With an effective disclaimer, the trainer can head off much irrelevant discussion that might otherwise occur and keep the focus on what participants need to watch and/or listen for to be well prepared for the coming practice.

6. Do the Demonstration

All the time you've spent preparing your presentations, practicing their delivery, and developing the skills needed to do demonstrations have brought you to this moment of actually doing the demonstration. When done well, this can be an "Aha" moment for learners. All your efforts prior to this will have been worth it when you see participants' reactions:

"Yeah, I get it now."

"I can see how this skill will be really useful."

7. Debrief the Demonstration

Ask questions that prompt participants to react to what they've seen and heard. Respond with a reflection of what was said, or simply say, "Thank you." For more information on debriefing refer to Chapter 6.

8. Conclude the Demonstration

To wrap up the demo, briefly review the steps of the demonstration and perhaps mention a highlight or two if there were some standout moments. Then transition to what's next on the agenda. Bridging to the next part of the workshop avoids the disjointed endings and beginnings that people experience in workshops that lack smooth transitions.

What to Do if No One Volunteers to Participate

This issue comes up a lot in Train the Trainer workshops. However, in dynamic workshops lack of volunteers has not been an issue because of the highly participative workshop designs. While we've never had the experience of no one volunteering, it probably could happen. And it's wise to be prepared for that possibility.

In the unlikely event that no one volunteers, here's a way of responding to the situation:

- Manage your mindset. Remind yourself that you've mastered the skills of dynamic training and therefore have the skills to handle the situation. And whenever a trainer manages a difficult workshop situation effectively both she and what she is teaching gain increased credibility.
- If you think the demonstration is crucial to learning the ability you are teaching, consider doing the demo solo—taking both roles yourself.

A listening skills demo without the needed volunteer could be done as follows: The trainer arranges two chairs facing each other and says, "Since no one is ready to volunteer yet, I'll play both roles, the role of the participant and the role of the trainer. The participant has chosen to talk about a problem she's having at work."

The trainer sits in the participant's chair and begins: "I'm now sitting in the participant's chair. When I role play myself, I'll sit in that chair [pointing], which is the trainer's chair. Speaking now as the participant, I say, 'It gets harder and harder to keep my team motivated at work because of all the downsizing. When people see their friends leaving, one after another, they begin to wonder if they'll be next and if so why are they breaking their backs working so hard for a company that doesn't value them.'"

The trainer moves to the trainer's chair and reflects, "You can sense their discouragement."

The trainer moves to the participant's chair and says, "Yeah, I know where they're coming from, and, frankly, I feel a little like that myself."

The trainer moves to the trainer's chair and reflects, "You understand because you share some of those feelings."

The trainer moves to the participant's chair and replies, "You've got that right."

The trainer then steps out of the demonstration saying, "I'll cut the demo here." She debriefs the demonstration with the group and transitions to giving directions for the practice.

Assess the Learning Climate of the Workshop

If you ask for volunteers and no one offers to be part of the demonstration, you probably should begin to wonder about the learning climate you've established and increase your efforts to build a safe and supportive environment in which volunteering won't be perceived as too risky.

Guidelines for Doing Negative Demonstrations

Sometimes it's useful to compare the behavior that's being taught with less desirable behaviors that are commonly employed. Negative demonstrations can be used to contrast the undesirable effects of people's typical ways of behaving with the benefits obtained from using the course skills in the same situation.

When a negative demonstration is used, it should

- depict a frequently made mistake or a recurring problem in participants' efforts to master what's being taught,
- follow a positive demonstration, and
- repeat the exact situation that was depicted in the positive demo (but without using the skills that were used in the positive demonstration).

When doing negative demonstrations, many trainers are tempted to overplay the negative behaviors since doing so often brings laughs. While that may provide a few minutes of fun for everyone, it defeats the purpose of the negative demo, which is to provide a fair, objective, and realistic example of a commonplace but less desirable alternative to what you are teaching. Steer clear of the tendency to overdo negative demonstrations.

Informal Demonstrations

Two types of informal demonstrations contribute significantly to participant learning:

- Responding to a how-to question
- Walking the talk

Responding to a How-to Question

An important use of informal demonstrations in a workshop occurs when responding to participants' how-to questions. Chapter 13 discussed how to respond to this type of question with a mini-demonstration rather than by giving a strictly verbal answer. Another option is to respond with a succinct Tell How followed by a brief Show How.

Walking the Talk

Walking the talk is behaving and generally living in line with what you are teaching. The research is clear: when teachers don't proficiently practice what they teach, the training they lead will be mediocre at best and at worst a waste of the participants' time and the organization's money.

Walking the talk occurs when the trainer uses the skills and abilities being taught when he's not in the Show How component of a workshop. If listening is being taught, the trainer needs to listen effectively whenever he interacts with participants. If the course teaches setting objectives, the course objectives should be written in the same objective-setting format that's taught in the course. If the course teaches decision making, the trainer's decisions in the classroom should embody as much of what is being taught that is pertinent to the course. In other words the trainer "walks the talk"—in all facets of the workshop as well as in his "civilian" life. As St. Jerome counseled his fellow fourth-century Christians, "Do not let your deeds belie your words, lest when you speak in church someone may say to himself, 'Why do you not practice what you preach?'"

Like everyone else, trainers are human; we have feet of clay. So we are not going to perfectly embody what we teach. But when a trainer doesn't walk the talk reasonably well, he or she is soon recognized as a phony and what's being taught will be seriously undermined if not totally negated.

17

Leading Practices:
Dress Rehearsals for the Real Thing

It's a funny thing, the more I practice the luckier I get.

——Arnold Palmer

With few exceptions the ability to learn how to do new things will only occur if one actually practices what's being taught. That's true whether the activity playing the violin, golfing, bike riding, or shooting free throws. To simply read a book, hear someone speak on one of these subjects, or do paper and pencil activities won't do the trick. As Japan's greatest ever baseball player, Sadaharu Oh, said, "Skill is improved by repetition. There's no avoiding it."[1] That learning principle underlies sayings such as "Practice makes perfect" and "You learn by doing." The power of this principle is why swimming coaches get swimmers into the water and why football coaches don't stop with chalk talks in the locker room. To successfully teach skills like these you need to build plenty of practice into the learning. Similarly, to help people develop skills like listening, cooperative problem solving, coaching, giving feedback, delivering impactful presentations, and selling, you need to provide opportunities for practice. In the first century BC, Publilius Syrus noted that, "practice is the best of all instructors."[2]

Everything in dynamic training builds up to a practice or flows from it. The involvement activities, presentations, and demonstrations showing how to do what you are teaching are all preface. As noted in previous chapters, Components are the basic building blocks of dynamic training and the components of each skill development module are taught in the following sequence:

Involve ➡ Tell How ➡ Show How ➡ Practice ➡
Feedback ➡ Apply ➡ Evaluate

The first three components in this sequence, Involve, Tell How, and Show How, prepare the way for success in the fourth component, Practice. The sixth component, Apply, focuses on the transfer of learning—how to make good use of what was just practiced. The final component, Evaluate, enables the participant to judge how well (or how poorly) she mastered the skill being taught. Thus, Practice is the primary component of a skill-building module; every other component either builds up to it or flows from it.

Distinguishing Between Practices and Activities

Strange as it may seem, some people who are reasonably knowledgeable about training don't differentiate between activities and practices. Tim, a training director who was savvy about the distinction, considered purchasing a training program and asked the person who recommended the program if skill practices were part of the course. The person responded, "Sure, more than 30 percent of the class time is spent in practices." When studying the material, however, Tim realized that there were no skill practices in the workshop—the 30 percent of the so-called practice time was devoted to activities that generated interest in or knowledge about the topic but otherwise made no contribution to acquiring the skill. But the person recommending the course wasn't being deceptive; he just thought that *practices* and *activities* were the same thing. It's a fairly common misunderstanding, so we'll take a moment to look at the similarities and the differences between activities and practices. Then we'll describe a three-step process for leading practices effectively.

Similarities Between Practices and Activities

When led effectively, practices and activities have several characteristics in common:

- They have a specific purpose.
- They typically divide the whole group into subgroups.
- They have definite steps to be followed.
- They generate information for discussion.
- They employ debriefing to enhance learning.

When people who have not experienced skill training participate in a workshop where the actionable aspects of the class have the above characteristics, they assume they are in a skill development workshop. They *may* be in a skill development workshop—but they may be in a workshop with activities but no practices. The difference in the potential for learning is enormous. Despite some similarities, there's a major functional difference between activities and practices as well as some less weighty distinctions.

Differences between Practices and Activities

Activities are used to accomplish a variety of purposes within the workshop; by contrast, practices help participants develop a skill or other ability for use in their daily environment.

Many activities are primarily stimulants that can put more oomph into a low-energy period of a training event. Some activities are designed to increase participants' motivation for learning what's about to be taught. Others are designed to increase the understanding of a concept, or to provide an energizer when needed.

In stark contrast to practices, activities do not develop specific skills or abilities for use in daily situations. They don't contribute directly to improving daily performance. There are other distinctions between practices and activities. Leading a skill practice normally requires giving more complex directions and providing for feedback in practices. Also, leading a practice usually requires considerably more time than leading an activity.

Dynamic workshop leaders use activities very selectively and very purposefully to advance the objectives of the workshop. Practices, by contrast, are the workhorses of every dynamic workshop. The following factors are involved in learning a new ability:

1. Cognitively understanding the new way of doing things
2. Breaking the current accustomed way
3. Developing the new ability or way of doing things

Three Characteristics of Successful Practices

For learning somewhat demanding abilities, there needs to be

- a *sufficient amount* of practice,
- *deliberate* practice, and
- a *supportive* learning environment.

A Sufficient Amount of Practice

It's crucial for learning to include a sufficient number of practices in the workshop design as well as sufficient time for each practice. In a successful skill practice, learners not only develop the skill but also gain sufficient confidence to use it in their work situations. To use Mel Silberman and Carol Auerbach's analogy, "Skill mastery is like the process of breaking in new shoes. At first it feels unnatural but, with enough wear, the shoes begin to feel comfortable. Confidence grows even more when participants master practices of increasing difficulty. Eventually they feel that they truly own the skill."[3]

> When learning a somewhat complex skill, in addition to proficient verbal instructions and competent demonstration of the skill, participants usually need to practice a skill and receive feedback on their performance three or more times as part of their supervised learning plus continued practice after completion of the instruction.

In our admittedly limited survey of skill development training programs, we find that frequently there's insufficient time allocated to practice what's being taught.

Avoid the Erosion of Practice Time

Even when sufficient time is allotted to practices in a workshop design, some of the time that is allotted for practice often gets chipped away in the course of a workshop day. As you've probably experienced, innumerable things can happen that can cause a workshop to fall behind schedule. Practices typically occur after the Involve, Tell How, and Show How components of a workshop; if the trainer's time management is not highly disciplined during those components, she could be running behind schedule before getting to the practice components, and long-winded participants may have eaten up valuable time. Trainers often gain the time back by shortening or even totally eliminating one or more practices. The probable consequence of cutting practice time is that participants will not develop sufficient competence at what's being taught to implement it in their everyday life, in which case the training is pointless. So one of the trainer's most important contributions to effective learning is to prevent the erosion of practice time.

Here's a good rule of thumb for trainers:

No matter how pressed you are for time, don't trim a practice and don't even think of eliminating one.

To prevent the erosion of practice time, it is helpful to establish milestones—key places in the workshop where you will arrive by a certain time. Furthermore, decide in advance where and how you can make up lost time if you get behind schedule.

Look for Optional Way to Gain Back Lost Time

Rather than invade practice time, you can often regain time with the least negative effect by condensing what's said and done in the Involve and Tell How components of the next module (assuming you are not currently teaching the last module of the course).

Deliberate Practices

Repetition is a critical aspect of practice. For some people, however, practice sessions are a matter of rote repetition—they go through the motions of a practice but their minds are not fully engaged in the process. However, unthinking repetition rarely fosters improvement. Biologist Carla Hannaford reports that "mere repetition of a behavior doesn't determine whether you learn it. Neural connections can be altered and grown only if there is full attention, focused interest on what we do."[4]

The kind of practice that promotes learning is *deliberate practice*. (Deliberate practice is *mindful* of what it is doing.) It's highly focused. Your attention is completely concentrated on what you are doing.

A Supportive Learning Environment

Making mistakes and learning from them is an integral part of developing new competences or improving existing ones. Learning flourishes when participants feel they're in an accepting environment and that errors made while learning are a natural part of the improvement process.

A Sequence of Three Types of Practice

The following sequence of three types of practice enables participants to develop proficiency in an ability that's somewhat challenging to learn:

Wagon Wheel ➡ Role Play ➡ Real Play

Our colleagues have found this to be an especially effective sequence of practices for skills training. The last of the three practices is a dry run for applying what's being learned to a real situation in each participant's work or personal life and has proven to be a powerful stimulus to transfer of learning.

Wagon Wheel Practices

Of the three types of practice, wagon wheel practices require the lowest level of skill use, and for that reason it is used first in this hierarchy of easiest to most challenging of these three types of skill practice. It can be used to teach just one part of a somewhat complex ability or a simple version of a more complicated capability. Even though it's a rather elementary practice, some people struggle in this practice. So, during wagon wheel practices, some trainers display a chart with the reassuring message:

If at first you don't succeed you're running about average.[5]

A wagon wheel practice provides instantaneous feedback at the group level. In this method of practice, participants are seated in a semicircle or full circle—hence the name "wagon wheel." The trainer stands in the middle of the circle and gives the directions for the skill practice. Here's how a wagon wheel practice might go when teaching people how to handle a defensive response. The trainer, giving no context, makes a defensive statement, for example:

"No one told me I was supposed to do that."

The first person in the circle practices using the kind of listening response she has just learned—one that's geared to lowering the person's defensiveness. After a short debriefing, the trainer turns to the next person and gives another defensive statement:

"How can you expect me to meet a deadline when Joe's team didn't provide me with the data I needed to finish the project?"

This participant then tries out the kind of reply that the class learned would usually reduce the other person's defensiveness. A quick debriefing follows, and the trainer moves to the next person and delivers a third totally different defensive statement. And so on around the circle.

There are several benefits to having a wagon wheel practice prior to doing a role play or a real play:

- It's a very efficient and effective learning tool. Participants observe a lot of ways of doing the skill reasonably correctly and they witness a number of mistakes to avoid.
- There's a good likelihood that participants will succeed since, rather than use the skill for a whole conversation, they only have to concentrate on using it once.
- Participants are usually highly motivated to succeed since everyone else in the group will be watching them when it's their turn.

When a response is way off target, the trainer can do a brief coaching intervention. However, if the trainer senses that the participant may be nervous about being taught in front of the group, she might provide a very brief amount of coaching and move on without asking the participant to give it another try. If the trainer thinks the participant is very close to getting it and is generally self-confident, she might decide to have him attempt it again. When everyone has had a turn, the trainer leads a large group debriefing.

Role Plays

Usually designed for dyads or triads, role plays are practice situations that are written prior to the training. They create feasible situations that have been customized to reflect the participants' work lives. Roles are written for each person in the practice group.

The advantage of using a role play prior to using a real play is that role plays are hypothetical situations, removed just enough from the actual life experience of the participant that they are more impersonal and less complex than real life.

Real Plays—Dress Rehearsals

In real play practices, participants come up with an actual situation that they face at work or in some other aspect of their life in which it would be appropriate to use the ability being taught. Nothing is written except a summary on an easel pad of the steps that the skill user is to employ.

In the practice group (usually a dyad or triad) the skill user succinctly describes the real play situation. For example, the skill user has a difficult employee with whom she wants to have a performance improvement discussion. To help her partner in the real play react similarly to the way her employee would, she describes his concerns about the employee's performance. She also tells her partner how she thinks the employee is likely to react, which provides the real play partner with tips on how to respond during the practice.

Since real plays are the most demanding of these three types of practice, they're usually scheduled after a wagon wheel practice and role play practice. Real play practices provide a dry run for using a newly acquired skill to handle a somewhat challenging situation back at work or in one's personal life. So, real plays make an important contribution to transferring learning from the workshop to the work-place. And a successful real play can be very motivational for applying the skill being taught.

How to Set Up Role Plays and Real Plays

You generally have two options regarding the number of people in a role play or real play—dyads (twosomes) or triads (threesomes).

When you set up practices using dyads, have each twosome decide who will be the skill user and who will be the receiver of the skills in the first of two role plays. The skill receiver will respond to the skill user and after the practice will pro-vide feedback to the skill user. Then the trainer asks the dyad partners to switch roles for the next practice.

Triads are set up like dyads with the addition of an observer who, along with the receiver of the skills, provides feedback to the skill user. Triads often generate more learning than dyads but require considerably more time.

The Observer's Role

The observer in a triad practice typically has four functions to perform:

1. Observe
    a. The skill user's use of the ability being taught
    b. How the skill receiver is impacted by the way the ability is being used.
2. Write down what you observe. It's difficult to provide accurate feedback if written notes haven't been made. Most well designed workshops provide observer's feedback worksheets.
3. Direct the feedback. Triad members generally are asked to give feedback in the following order:
    a. Skill user
    b. Skill receiver
    c. Observer
4. Serve as time keeper.

An observer's feedback worksheet should indicate the timing of the practice and the feedback sessions.

As an example, the following positioning and practice chart for a listening skills practice helps participants quickly see how to position themselves for the practice as well as who is to do what in each round of the practice.

Figure 17-1. Positioning, roles, and timing chart for a listening skills practice.

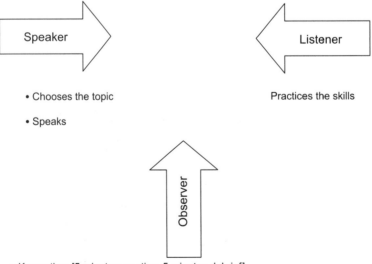

• Chooses the topic

• Speaks

Practices the skills

• Keeps time [5 minutes practice, 5 minutes debrief]

• Makes notes on the observer's worksheet during the practice

• Leads debriefing

A Step-by-Step Process for Leading Role Plays and Real Plays

The steps for leading a skill practice are similar to those that we recommended for leading an activity. So this chapter will repeat some of what you learned in Chapter 5. We consider the repetition of these steps to be a plus since learning to effectively lead skill practices and activities is essential to successful training. And repetition provides a good assist to learning.

The major differences between leading activities and leading practices are in giving the directions and in providing targeted feedback in skill practices.

The following steps are used when leading either a role play or a real play:

1. Transition In
   Very briefly bridge from what the group was doing to what they are about to do. For example:
   > You've heard a presentation on how to handle defensive responses and you've had a brief practice in which you gave one reflection to a defensive response. Now you'll have an opportunity to do a longer, more challenging practice using a role play with a partner.

2. Purpose
   Explain what people will get out of this practice. For example:
   > This practice is designed to increase your ability to keep your cool while handling argumentative or defensive responses that an individual might give when he's receiving corrective feedback.

3. Preview
   Give a succinct summary of what participants will be doing in the practice. For example:
   > You'll be working in pairs for a total of twenty minutes during which you'd each get a chance to practice and receive feedback.

4. Directions
   When engaging in a practice, participants usually need to know the following information in this order:
   a. What they will be doing in the subgroups
   b. The practice locations where they will do the practice
   c. Who they will be doing it with
   d. How they will do it
   e. How much time they have
   f. What materials (if any) they will use
   g. The trainer's role
   When the directions for a skill practice are lengthy or complex it's advisable to post a prepared chart or distribute a handout with a summary of the instructions.

5. Observe/Guide
   Let the group know that you'll be walking around observing successes and difficulties and that you will not interrupt their work unless they absolutely need help.

6. Debriefing
   Debriefing maximizes the learnings obtained from the practice. We recommend rereading Chapter 6 to help you heighten the learning that accrues from the practices you lead.

7. Conclude
   This transition provides a summary of what was practiced and tells where we're headed.

How to Give Directions for Role Plays and Real Plays

Here is an example of how to do step 4—giving directions when leading a skill practice using role plays or real plays (you present the same type of information when giving directions for either a role play or a real play).

> *Note to the trainer:* Each time you see "Ask a Checking Question" written after a segment of directions, it refers to using a question like one of the following to be sure participants understand what you just said:
>
> - "What questions do you have?
> - "Does anyone need clarification?"
> - "Are you with me so far?"

Directions

What they'll be doing: "You're about to do a practice in which you will use interactive speaking in a performance improvement discussion."

Where: "You'll be in this room in groups as far away from other groups as you can manage."

With whom: "Please count off in three's for this practice."

   (Pause while they count off.)

How to do it: "There will be three rounds in this practice. In each round there will be a skill user, a skill receiver, and an observer. Decide who will take each role in the first round."

   (Ask a checking question and pause for possible responses.)

Timing: "Each round will be fifteen minutes: five minutes for the skill user to practice, followed by whatever the skill user wants to say about his performance. Then the skill receiver and the observer add their feedback in that order. I will give a four-minute alert and then call for the end of the practice in five minutes. The feedback period will have the same timing—a four-minute alert and after one more minute I'll announce the end of the feedback session. We'll have a large group debrief at the end of each round."

(Ask a checking question and pause for possible responses.)

Materials: "For the first round you'll see three stacks of handouts on the table: First, here on your left, is a Skill User Role [hold it up]. This will give you information about what the situation is and who you are. Second, a Skill Receiver Role [hold it up]. This will tell you what the situation is and who you are portraying along with tips about how to react in your role. Third, an Observer Worksheet [hold it up]. The Observer Worksheet has a list of some important things to focus on when observing this practice. The list consists of the points covered in the last presentation."

> *Note to the trainer:* Read aloud each item on the Observer's list. That will help the Observers understand their role and will also remind the Skill User of what she is to do.

(Ask a checking question and pause for possible responses.)

"The first round Skill Users please come up and take a Skill User Role, a Skill Receiver Role, and an Observer Work Sheet to distribute to your subgroup."

(Pause)

"Everyone take a few minutes to read and think about your role."

(Ask a checking question and pause for possible responses.)

"OK, go ahead and begin."

> *Note to the trainer:* Keep time and observe.

Debrief in the large group for five minutes after each round.

Further Directions for Practices Using Real Plays

There are no written roles for real plays because the content of the real play comes from an actual life experience of the skill user. To set up a successful practice, it is important to provide the skill user with some guidance about the kinds of situations that would work well in this practice. When doing a real play, participants often think of the most difficult person, situation, or problem in their lives to use in this practice. But participants who are just beginning to learn these skills need to work with less challenging situations in order to be successful in their practice.

Here are some guidelines for selecting a real play situation that's suitable for this type of practice:

- The situation should be of low to moderate difficulty.
- It should not involve anyone whom the skill user perceives as especially difficult to work with.
- It should be a current situation, not one from the past.
- It should not relate to a current or potential future interaction with a participant in this workshop.

Manage Feedback When Leading a Practice

After a role play or real play, feedback is given by the receiver of the skills and, when there is an observer, by the observer of the practice. Since a number of participants may not have well-developed feedback skills, it helps to provide some guidance before they jump into a feedback session. The main purpose of the guidance is to prevent an overload of criticism being dumped on someone who is just beginning to learn the skill she is practicing.

For this feedback you might ask the receiver of the skills to use objective, behavioral language to pinpoint:

- Two things the skill user did well
- One thing she could improve

If an observation checklist has been provided, feedback can be based on how the skill user did in relation to the items on the list.

Because giving specific feedback is so crucial to effective training, Chapter 18 provides more information on how to use this important tool during a workshop.

Practice Preparation Worksheets

In Appendix I you'll find a Practice Worksheet to aid you in planning an effective practice session.

18

Providing In-the-Moment Feedback

Feedback is the breakfast of champions.

—Ken Blanchard and Spencer Johnson

To be able to give feedback sensitively and skillfully is a fundamental training ability—like the ability to sauté is to a chef, like the ability to score points is to a basketball player, and like having sensitivity to color is to an artist. You may think we're going a bit overboard here, but the skill of giving feedback is such a basic trainer competency that a trainer shouldn't leave home without it. Noted social scientist Richard Thaler and scholar Cass Sunstein state:

> The best way to help humans improve their performance is to provide feedback.[1]

And top ranked leadership thinker[2] Marshall Goldsmith adds, "We all need feedback to see where we are, where we need to go, and to measure our progress."[3]

In this chapter we focus on the importance of feedback in training and describe the unique ability of giving feedback in the exceedingly limited time available during workshop practices.

Feedback Enhances Learning

Why is such a simple procedure as telling people how they're doing so powerful? Feedback's effectiveness stems from its function as a guidance system. In rocketry, feedback enables a missile to correct its course; in training, feedback provides people with information they need to maintain what they're doing or to improve in areas where enhanced performance is desired. On-target feedback lets a person know exactly what's good and what's not so good about what he's doing. That knowledge leads to more accurate and more rapid learning.

However, not all feedback is effective. In this chapter you'll learn how to give feedback that works. Feedback can take a number of forms, depending on the situation. As the chapter title suggests, we'll be focusing on how to give feedback during workshop practice sessions.

In a training practice, feedback is information about current performance that helps a person maintain or achieve the desired level of performance.

Managing Feedback During Practices with Tight Time Constraints

The brevity of coaching interactions during a workshop practice period puts severe time limitations on the feedback process. For example, a thirty-five-minute practice will be divided as follows:

> Five minutes to give an overview of what people will be doing and to have people subgroup into pairs or threesomes
>
> Fifteen minutes for the practice
>
> Five minutes to debrief in subgroups
>
> Ten minutes for a large group debriefing and a transition out

Assuming the above timing, in a twenty-person training group a fifteen-minute role play allows only an average of one and one half minutes per dyad for the trainer to do the following:

- Observe part of the dyad's practice.
- Give feedback *if appropriate*. (There'll only be time enough for a few dyads to receive feedback.)
- Move to observe another targeted dyad.

So, the time constraints are very tight.

Fortunately, when done well, even very brief feedback can be helpful. Coach John Wooden, who led the UCLA Bruins to ten NCAA basketball championships in twelve years, gave remarkably effective and extremely brief feedback during practices. His feedback usually took less than five seconds. The point is not that your feedback should be limited to five seconds or less; coaching in basketball is very different from coaching a workshop practice. But in either situation, when you work effectively it's possible to offer helpful feedback very quickly.

Know What to Observe

Good athletic coaches know what they are looking for when they observe their players in action. They know what excellence looks like and what it takes to achieve it. Likewise, a trainer–coach knows in advance what behaviors are important to observe. In fact, she's already spelled them out in the Tell How, demonstrated them in the Show How, and summarized them in a checklist describing what the person using the skill is to do and on which the trainer and the observer (when there is an observer) should focus.

The Standard-Behavior-Effect (S-B-E) Feedback Format

When it's time to let the skill user know how he's doing, the S–B–E feedback format enables you to cover all the feedback bases with few words, which makes it easier for the recipient to receive the information accurately.

There are three parts to the S–B–E feedback format:

1. *Standard:* s specified level of proficiency
2. *Behavior:* What the person did
   - to improve her performance, or
   - to maintain an already effective performance
3. Effect: How the behavior impacted what the sender was trying to achieve

Using this format enables participants to see how well they're doing in comparison to the standard.

Here's an example of a feedback message using the S–B–E format:

Standard: "When giving a sales presentation, begin with an attention getter."

Behavior: "You began with a series of tantalizing questions."

Effect: "The effect was that the prospect was with you from the start."

When sending an S–B–E message, take care that your body language and tone of voice support the nonjudgmental wording of your feedback.

Phrase Your Message in Specific, Behavioral Language

Effective trainers avoid giving feedback in vague language, such as, "Great job," when a participant does exceptionally well in a practice session. Instead they give specific descriptive feedback. Participants have to be convinced that our affirmative feedback is genuine. The following interactions between Pablo Casals, the world-famous cellist, and the younger upcoming cellist, Gregor Piatigorsky, demonstrate how global feedback can be misunderstood and even backfire, whereas specific descriptive feedback results in much more accurate communication.

When the two cellists first met, Casals asked the younger musician to play. Piatigorsky was nervous and gave what he thought was a terrible performance—so bad that he stopped playing in the middle of the piece.

However, Casals applauded as he gave his lavish, but very nonspecific praise: "Bravo! Wonderful!"

Piatigorsky later noted that he felt bewildered at the compliment since he felt he had played very poorly.

Years later, when the two cellists were together again, Piatigorsky told Casals how he felt about the praise Casals had expressed a few years earlier. In response, Casals rushed to his cello:

"Listen!" He said as he played a phrase from the Beethoven sonata. "Didn't you play this fingering? It was novel to me. And didn't you attack that passage with up-bow like this?" The master went through the music emphasizing all he liked that Piatigorsky had done.

The younger cellist said of the evening when he had been given the highly specific feedback, "I left with the feeling of having been with a great artist and a friend."

Casals had the same goal on both evenings—to express admiration for his younger colleague's virtuosity. But on the first occasion Casals used evaluative praise, which was confusing to the recipient and counterproductive. In the later conversation, however, Casals's specific behavioral feedback was very meaningful to the younger musician who, by the way, went on to become one of the world's great cellists.

Two Types of Feedback

Trainers typically offer two types of feedback during workshop practices: reinforcing feedback and developmental feedback. (We prefer these terms although they're sometimes given other labels. Reinforcing feedback is sometimes termed "positive feedback," and developmental feedback is sometimes termed "negative feedback" or "corrective feedback.") When well targeted, appropriately timed, phrased well, and delivered effectively, both types of feedback are positive for the person and for the organization. So we avoid the use of the adjectives *positive* or *negative* when describing the two types of feedback. And giving "corrective feedback" sounds a bit judgmental. We think this is not mere quibbling about semantics—an endeavor to usefully and accurately label the two types of feedback.

Here's an example of each type of feedback:

Reinforcing Feedback
Standard: "When making a statement, it's effective for your facial expression to support your words."

Behavior: "When you said, 'That was the toughest challenge I ever had,' your facial expression was determined and strong."

Effect: "The effect was that your message came through as believable."

Developmental Feedback
Standard: "When making a statement, it's effective for your facial expression to support your words."

Behavior: "You smiled when you said, 'That was the toughest challenge I ever had.'"

Effect: "The result was that you sent a mixed message that weakened your credibility."

Determine Which Subgroups Could Profit Most from Feedback

Break the group into dyads or triads to practice sending reinforcing feedback and managing the recipient's response. While the trainees practice using the three-part feedback message, walk slowly and quietly around the room to see how the various subgroups are doing. As you pause to observe a subgroup's practice:

- Sit, kneel, or stand out of the line of vision of the people practicing yet close enough so you can see and hear the practice.
- Refrain from making eye contact unless you are intervening with feedback.
- Resume moving about the room to view other groups.

You'll typically find that the various subgroups are having different levels of success in the practice. Notice which groups:

- Need help: One or more subgroup may be struggling or perhaps they're even chatting instead of practicing. They definitely need the trainer's guidance.
- Are practicing fairly well but could benefit from further instruction. Reinforce the most important things they are doing well and give brief developmental feedback on the most serious or most easily correctable error.
- Are having a successful practice. Even though these groups are experiencing a successful practice, they may not realize how well they are doing. Or they may not know specifically what they are doing that's making this practice succeed. So try to reserve time to briefly and explicitly reinforce what people in these groups are doing well.

Tips for Delivering Feedback

Here are some things to consider when deciding whether to offer feedback to an individual participant or to a subgroup.

Determine the Right Amount of Feedback

- It's often better to err on the side of giving too little feedback rather than too much.

- During a practice skill, users sometimes correct themselves. Too much developmental feedback can deflate the learner's confidence and motivation.
- On the other hand, an unsuccessful practice can puncture a learner's confidence and motivation. So make sure you give participants sufficient feedback to succeed at the practice.

Target a Behavior for Feedback

Once you've decided that feedback is called for, ask yourself questions like the following to help you determine what to focus on for improvement:

- What single change is likely to trigger the greatest improvement?
- What change is likely to be easiest for the participant to make?
- What change is this person likely to be most open to and motivated to work on?

Ask yourself the questions in the context of the behavior or skill you are teaching as well as your assessment of how the person you are teaching would answer them. When a person is learning reasonably well in the workshop, you'll probably want to focus on the first question, "What single change is likely to trigger the greatest improvement?"

In a presentation skills workshop, for example, you will have taught and demonstrated the behaviors that participants need to do to present well. As you observe a presentation practice, you are looking for those behaviors. For instance, when teaching the body language of presenting, the presentation stance is one of the sets of behavior that's important for participants to master. You've already taught the presentation stance, which involves placing the feet under the shoulders. If the feet are placed much further apart, the speaker looks like an athlete ready to charge; if they're placed much closer, the speaker appears unstable. You're looking for the behavior of feet placed under the shoulders. Are Bert's feet under his shoulders or are they not? If they are, that part is okay; you may briefly reinforce it and move on to observe other dyads. If Bert's feet are not under the shoulders, you provide brief developmental feedback.

Embody a Helpful Spirit

The above heading seems a bit amorphous but the spirit behind what a trainer says is very real and can be picked up by participants through their observation of his body language. The spirit behind the feedback is conveyed through the trainer's facial expression, eye contact, tone of voice, and energy level. When those are positive, participants feel that the trainer is in their corner and they're more open to his feedback. But when the helpful spirit is weak or seems to be missing, the participant's acceptance of the feedback diminishes.

Use Video Feedback to Escalate Learnings

Video feedback is the most specific and convincing feedback you can use because the recipient of the feedback can see and hear the behaviors you are describing while you are discussing them. However, to videotape practices and review them with participants during class is enormously time-consuming and is an extreme rarity in today's time-pressured organizations. However, there are special circumstances—like teaching presentation skills or some high-level coaching assignments—where it may be realistic to offer playback of a videotaped practice with the trainer offering coaching comments.

Receiving Feedback Nondefensively

During a workshop you will not only be giving feedback; you'll be the recipient of it in evaluations, some debriefings, and perhaps at other times in the training. Treat the feedback as an important learning experience. Take the feedback in, reflect it to be sure that you've understood it, and say, "Thanks for the feedback." (How to reflect what you hear is taught in Chapter 12.) Try to find something in the feedback that you can use to improve your training. Then apply the learning as soon as possible and as often as appropriate. If the feedback seems to you to be only partially correct, work on integrating that part into your training. Receiving feedback nondefensively is an important way to keep growing as a trainer. And it's a crucial part of what it takes to "earn the right" to give feedback to others.

19

Evaluating the Workshop

Conducting training without evaluation is like flying without instruments.

———Ronald Meyer

While some companies have moved toward on-line forms of evaluation, a common scenario regarding the evaluation of workshops is that the trainer is provided evaluation forms to use at the conclusion of the workshop. Typically, he walks into the classroom and the forms are sitting on a table. He picks one up and glances at it to be sure they are the right evaluations for this particular training. He may study it for a few minutes to see what the participants will be rating. But that's about it. Generally, decisions concerning the level of workshop evaluation and the content and form of the evaluation are made prior to the training and without the involvement of the trainer. So why would we include information about evaluation of training in this book? Trainers need to be knowledgeable about the purpose and value of each of the levels of evaluation of training and be informed contributors if and when they are involved in discussions about evaluation. And being fairly knowledgeable about evaluation enables them to be more effective in their part in administering it.

This chapter presents an overview of the five levels of evaluation of training, an estimate of how frequently each level is used, and a brief discussion of some factors to consider when determining the appropriate level to use for a given training program. Due to limitations of space and the infrequency of use of evaluation levels 2 to 5, this chapter focuses primarily on the universally used level 1: evaluation of satisfaction. We also note the important but seldom employed contribution that participants' spoken assessments can add to the evaluation process. If you want to learn about evaluation levels 2 to 5—or delve deeper into level 1—consider supplementing what you read in this chapter with a book-long treatment of the evaluation of training, such as *How to Measure Training Results* by J.J. Phillips and R.S. Stone.

The Five Levels of Training Evaluation

Nearly a half century ago, Donald Kirkpatrick developed a four-level approach to the evaluation of training that attained worldwide acceptance. A bit later, Jack Phillips added a fifth level of evaluation, return on investment (ROI), that's been greeted with general favor for highly selective applications.

The levels of evaluation are sequential. Doing a level-1 evaluation is prerequisite to doing a level-2 evaluation and evaluating at level-2 is necessary before doing a level-3 evaluation, and so on. In other words, each successive level of evaluation includes the previous level(s). And each successive level of evaluation provides a different and, from a business perspective, a more valuable type of information.

However, each successive level of evaluation is considerably more time-consuming and expensive to administer than the previous level. Furthermore, administration of the higher levels of evaluation is more disruptive to the organization. Consequently, in most organizations few if any workshops are evaluated at levels 4 and 5.

Here are the five levels of evaluation, when and where each level is conducted, and the fundamental question(s) that each level seeks to answer:

Levels 1 and 2

These levels usually are conducted in the training room during the training and they're often administered by the trainer. Level 1, the evaluation of satisfaction (also called "reaction") addresses the following:

- How did participants react to the experience?
  (Many level 1 evaluations also ask for the following additional information.)
- How confident are participants about doing what was taught?
- How do they plan to use it?
- What obstacles to application of the course content might they encounter?
- What support, if any, will be provided by other stakeholders?

Level 2, the evaluation of learning, includes level 1 and also addresses how well the participants learned what was taught?

Levels 3, 4, and 5

These levels usually are conducted at the participant's place of work three months to a year after the training.

Level 3, the evaluation of job application (often referred to as evaluation of behavior or evaluation of transfer) includes levels 1 and 2 and also addresses how effectively participants are applying their learning on the job?

Level 4, the evaluation of business impact, includes levels 1 to 3 and also addresses how the organization is benefiting from participants' application of their learning.

Level 5, the evaluation of ROI, includes levels 1 to 4 and addresses how profitable the investment in training was, that is, the monetary value of the business impact minus the costs associated with the training

Unless you know a person's pre-workshop degree of competence at what's being taught, it's impossible to determine what was learned in the workshop or applied in the workplace. So pre-workshop assessments are necessary for effective evaluation at levels 2 to 5.

Evaluations at levels 3, 4, and 5 are administered after there's been sufficient time for the desired changes in knowledge, attitude, or behavior to occur and for the anticipated results to accrue. For level 3, people often need time to break long established habits and develop new abilities before being evaluated, and for levels 4 and 5, six to twelve months or more are generally required to determine whether the training is paying off in increased productivity and/or profitability.

The Percentage of Workshops Evaluated at Each Level

Estimates of the percentage of training events that are assessed at each level of evaluation vary considerably from one authority on evaluation to another. There's general agreement, however, that virtually all training programs do level 1, evaluation of satisfaction, and that there's a significantly decreased amount of evaluation from any given level of evaluation to the next level. Here's one set of guestimates of the percent of training programs that are evaluated at each level:

Level 1, evaluation of satisfaction: This level of evaluation is employed in virtually all training events.

Level 2, evaluation of learning: Slightly fewer than 50 percent of organizations check to see if anyone learned what was taught.

Level 3, evaluation of job application: An American Society for Training and Development (ASTD) survey found that a scant 13 percent of organizations evaluate whether participants are using what was learned.

Level 4, evaluation of business impact: A mere 3 percent of organizations assess whether the application of participants' learning contributed to the organization's bottom line.

Level 5, evaluation of ROI: Fewer than 3 percent of organizations calculate the return on investment from any of their training programs.

One would assume when companies are spending millions of dollars on training programs, they would want to evaluate the results. Not so. Few companies actually do any rigorous follow-up evaluation of their training programs.

Complicating matters still further is the fact that even when rigorous evaluations are conducted through levels 4 and 5, it's difficult to trace the source of improvement exclusively to a particular training program. Too many other factors could influence any business improvement, such as a shift in the economy, a change in personnel, seasonal changes in demand, the entry of a new competitor, and any number of other factors can skew the results of level-4 and level-5 evaluations.

Some evaluation experts attempt to isolate the impact of training from other possible influences by factoring in all of the other elements that could have contributed to any change in business performance or ROI. However, detaching the impact of training from other possible influences requires considerable time, effort, and expense. And a number of critics contend that, in many, if not most, applications of levels 4 and 5 evaluation, some subjectivity is involved, which reduces its usefulness.

Level 1: Evaluating Participant Satisfaction

As mentioned earlier, virtually every workshop obtains feedback on user satisfaction. These level-1 evaluations acquire information about factors over which the trainer has considerable influence. And it's a level of evaluation that provides the trainer with useful information for plying her craft skillfully. Also, as we've noted, it's the most frequently used level of evaluation. Furthermore, the evaluation of participant satisfaction is usually administered during workshops conducted by the trainer whose work is being evaluated. So these evaluations can provide her with immediate feedback. For these reasons—plus the limited space in a book-length treatment on training—this chapter focuses on level-1 evaluations.

Level-1 evaluations solicit feedback that's focused primarily (sometimes solely) on satisfaction—how did participants react to the workshop's content and delivery? Some level 1 evaluations also obtain information about participants' confidence in using what was taught, and some additionally ask participants to anticipate how they will apply their learning back on the job as well as inquiring about potential barriers to implementing the course content. In addition to providing the trainer with feedback, these questions—particularly the last two—often get participants thinking more about transferring the learning to their work situation.

As you've probably experienced, level-1 evaluations of satisfaction are often disparaged as "smile sheets" or "whoopee sheets." They do tend to give somewhat rosier feedback than is warranted. However, there are numerous benefits to using level-1 evaluations. Being aware of the benefits will enable you to profit more fully from these simple tools, which will probably be used in every workshop you teach.

Advantages of Level-1 Evaluations

There are at least eight advantages to using level-1 evaluations:

1. A high level of participant satisfaction is an important contributor to a positive learning experience. Although articles and books on the evaluation of training often assert that participant satisfaction does not ensure increased learning, it's also true that the more favorable the reaction to the workshop, the more likely that participants will have learned the material that was taught. And, the more favorable the reaction, the higher the probability that the content will be applied. Conversely, if participants are dissatisfied with the workshop experience, their learning will be adversely affected.

2. Level-1 evaluation often provides useful feedback to the trainer. An effective trainer is a critical factor for success in most training programs. Yet, as we saw in Chapter 1, corporate trainers seldom receive adequate training for their work. So it's imperative that they develop further on the job. Receiving constructive feedback on their performance in every workshop they lead and applying the most useful pointers can set the trainer on a path of continuous improvement. A well-designed level-1 evaluation can provide very useful feedback to the trainer, which can be a big contributor to the trainer's professional development as well as to the ongoing improvement of the course.

3. Level-1 evaluations influence team leaders' decisions regarding whether or not to encourage other employees to experience the workshop.

4. Level-1 evaluations often influence top management's decisions about whether to continue, expand, or discontinue offering the program.

5. A summary of a level-1 evaluation provides a whole-group report of the degree of satisfaction with the training. A whole-group report can counteract the disproportionate amount of adverse information that may be fed back to team leaders and others by a few disgruntled participants who have negative feelings about the training experience. Whole-group evaluation reports can also put into perspective some overly positive assessments by a handful of gung-ho trainees.

6. Level-1 evaluations are a precondition to the effective use of all other levels of evaluation.

7. Group process is enhanced when level-1 spoken evaluations are used in addition to written evaluations.

8. Level-1 evaluations can be used to achieve all the above purposes even though these evaluations are simple to create, inexpensive to produce, and easy to administer.

These are not insignificant benefits! We hope you'll join those in the training community who refuse to denigrate these evaluations as "whoopee sheets" and instead, profit from both the reinforcing and the corrective feedback that they contain.

End-of-Day Level 1: Evaluations of Participant Satisfaction

Our colleagues have found it useful to employ two types of brief evaluations at the end of the day—written evaluations and spoken evaluations.

Written Evaluations

Most trainers use daily level-1 end-of-day written evaluations. These gather information about what the group thinks you've been doing particularly well, so you know what's wise to continue doing. And, despite the reputation that these evaluations have for being overly positive, they often suggest some things to do differently to create an even better training experience tomorrow.

Unless particular modules or other aspects of content are specifically assessed, each day's evaluation form may be identical except for the number of the workshop day. In a four-day workshop, putting the date in the heading of the end-of-day evaluations helps you determine which days' design may need a bit of tweaking. On the last day of the workshop, a final evaluation typically replaces the end-of-day evaluation.

Signed Evaluations Many experts on evaluation recommend having participants sign their evaluation. Others suggest providing the option to sign. Obtaining signatures enables you to follow up and get more specific information about a comment that seems important but is puzzlingly brief probably because it was written in haste.

From our point of view, it's important to get as frank and candid an evaluation as possible. It's likely that at least some participants will be more forthright if they are anonymous. So, to get as unvarnished a picture as possible, we prefer not to ask for a signature or even suggest that signatures are optional.

Spoken Evaluations

At the end of the day in multiday courses, dynamic trainers typically use a brief level-1 written evaluation followed by a spoken evaluation. Then, on the final day there's usually a more extensive written evaluation, which is followed by a final spoken evaluation.

We strongly favor having spoken evaluations as well as written evaluations. The downside, of course, is that spoken evaluations take time and they occur at the close of the workshop when most participants are eager to leave. Despite this, the participants generally enjoy this part of the workshop. Most are curious about how the others in the group felt about the workshop, and spoken feedback fills this need.

Spoken evaluations are also useful to the trainer. People speak far more quickly than they write, so you may get considerably more information from spoken evaluations than from the written ones, although both types of evaluation are useful. And with spoken evaluations, the rich detail of body language can add to your understanding of people's verbal assessment. Also, we've found that spoken evaluations provide data about group engagement as well as about individual struggles and discoveries—matters that are seldom mentioned on written evaluations. Then, too, spoken evaluations usually contain more self-disclosure than written evaluations, so they tend to enhance end-of-workshop group process while contributing to the evaluation of the workshop.

Finally, spoken evaluations provide the best way we know of for bringing closure to a training day.

Here are some sample end-of-day questions for use when asking for spoken evaluations:

- What did you expect from the training? And, so far, what did you get?
- What do you want to remember about today's course content?
- What's your reaction to the day?

Introducing End-of-Day Written and Spoken Evaluations

End-of day written evaluations are filled out when participants are eager to head for home or to the office to do some catch-up work. So keep the daily evaluations brief.

Here's one way of introducing-end-of-day written and spoken evaluations:

It's been a long day. I promise that you'll be on your way five minutes before our agreed upon ending time of 4:30. In these last twenty-five minutes, I need your help by doing a written and spoken evaluation of the day.

I'll use your written feedback to learn what's going well for you as well as what you need that you're not getting. With that information I can adjust the rest of the workshop to be a better match for your needs and expectations. No need to sign your name.

When you complete the written evaluation, please put it face down on the empty chair by the door at the back of the room.

At the beginning of the workshop tomorrow, I'll provide a summary of the evaluations.

The spoken evaluations will give everyone in the group a sense of the various degrees of satisfaction with today's session. To start that off, I'll provide a cue for you to respond to.

Tabulating the Evaluations

The end of day evaluations need to be tabulated—a job that often falls to the trainer. Usually this can be done fairly quickly if the evaluation form is designed well. Also, when the evaluation form provides space for written comments, these need to be summarized.

Reporting the Results of the Written Evaluations

Since most participants appreciate finding out how others in the class feel about the workshop they are experiencing, it makes sense to report a summary of the previous day's evaluations in the introduction to the next day of the workshop. Presenting the numerical feedback on a chart as well as verbally helps participants understand how their fellow participants felt about the previous day of the workshop. After reporting the numerical feedback, give a brief summary of the written comments.

When you report the feedback to the group, do it with a nonjudgmental tone of voice. Whether the feedback is good, bad, or indifferent, the same "these are the facts" tone of voice shows participants that you accept the feedback, are reporting it objectively, and want to learn from it.

If the feedback is good to excellent, you may want to make a brief comment like, "It looks like we're on target, so we'll keep going with the current approach."

If the feedback shows that the workshop isn't going well you might say something like, "Looks like we need to talk over what's missing—what you need that you're not getting—so we can make some adjustments to what we're doing." Then make sure you make observable modifications unless you explain why you've chosen not to.

When you summarize the end-of-day evaluations objectively, you accomplish five things:

- You help build a sense of community by reporting a whole-group assessment of their common experience of the previous day's training.
- You demonstrate the use of a skill that's central to skill training—applying feedback to improve performance.
- You earn participants' respect by modeling transparency and accountability by even-handedly noting what people disliked as well as what they liked.
- You model responding nondefensively to corrective feedback.
- You show the benefits of end-of-day evaluations, which encourages participants to take them more seriously.

End of Workshop Evaluations

Workshops typically close with a level-1 written evaluation of the entire workshop experience. As you might guess, we strongly advocate adding spoken evaluations to the wrap-up of the workshop. It's a heartening way to close the workshop and send people on their way.

Report the Results to Stakeholders

Begin by identifying the stakeholders of this workshop. They are the people who have a vested interest in the results of the workshop—those who will benefit most from a successful outcome. These would typically include the following:

- Whoever nominated, recommended, or sent the participants to the training —the participants' manager, team leader, coach, etc. Management support for training is crucial for success. Providing participants' managers with a summary of the workshop's final evaluation enables them to discuss the workshop and applications of the learnings to the job.
- The trainer and her supervisor and possibly others in the training department.

A Workshop Confidentiality Policy

Sometimes managers who refer an employee to training ask the trainer to report on how the person did in the workshop. This is often a well-intended request from a conscientious team leader. However, we have a firm ground rule for trainers and participants alike—that other participants' experience or behavior in the workshop be treated confidentially. The place for organizations to assess employee performance is on the job—not in the training room. And the person or group that should be responsible for the assessment is the manager he reports to and/or the team he's part of.

A workshop is a place to consider and experiment with new thoughts, attitudes, and behaviors. To do this is to venture into uncomfortable realms, try out new behaviors, and develop new and improved ways of working. Decades of experience have shown that judging a person's performance seriously impedes this type of growth.

20

Ending the Workshop

A strong conclusion is a must for any training program. . . . It is . . . imperative to have a strong wrap-up that drives home the point(s) you've made.

———Robert Pike[1]

You've provided a comfortable setting for the workshop, helped participants get acquainted with each other, led and debriefed energizing activities, worked well with visual aids, nailed your presentations, demonstrated the skills being taught, led practices, and provided solid feedback. Finally, that's all finished and you're done, right? Not quite. You have to tie a bow on the gift you've given to participants. You do that by bringing the workshop to a meaningful close.

When participants leave a workshop with positive feelings about the learning experience and their accomplishments in the workshop, they're more likely to use the new knowledge and skills back on the job. A solid ending provides a bridge from what was learned in the workshop to the work responsibilities and relationships where participants will apply what they learned. Failing to properly bring closure to the workshop tends to leave the group feeling incomplete and is likely to significantly decrease the transfer of learning to the workplace.

Here are ways to facilitate that happening, when you end a workshop:

- Save time for a thoughtful and productive conclusion to the workshop.
- Review the workshop content.
- Lead action planning.
- Generate action triggers.
- Discuss reentry.
- Facilitate evaluation.

- Wrap up the experience.
- Be available until the last person leaves.

And, if you plan to do follow-up with the group or have sign-ups for after the workshop video feedback, these activities belong at the close of the workshop, too.

Save Time for a Thoughtful and Productive Conclusion to the Workshop

A frequent mistake of neophyte and veteran trainers alike is to run short of time toward the end of the workshops they lead. Course designers often cram too much material into the workshop outline, loquacious participants may over-contribute, the trainer may get carried away on a favorite topic, and numerous other factors may chip away at the time. Unless preventive measures are employed, the cumulative effect of these and other potential drains on workshop time can leave the trainer running out of time before he finishes conveying the course content.

A good antidote for the tendency to run out of time is to develop a time-specific outline. Have the allotted times running down the left hand margin of your outline and note what is to be accomplished in each time period. For example:

11:10–11:20 Presentation: "Defensiveness and how it Works"

11:20–11:25 Demonstration: Show and debrief an automatic defensive response.

11:25–11:30 Directions for the practice.

11:30–12:00 Practice with debrief. (This practice needs to happen before lunch (even if lunch is as much as 10 minutes late).

12:00–12:55 Lunch

Review the Workshop Content

The close of a workshop generally begins with a brief review of the course content. This is a big-picture summary, so it's important to skip the detail. If you've made and posted wall charts of the content of each day, now is a time to refer back to the key charts. Using transitions to link content can help participants integrate what could become an overload of review material.

You can enliven the review by asking checking questions along the way, such as, "Remember how after practicing this particular skill many of you could see several ways of applying it?" Or, "On the first day, some of you said you didn't think this skill would work in the real world. What are your thoughts now?" "How comfortable are you with this approach?" With checking questions like these interspersed in the review you'll draw participants into a dialogue instead of boring them with a monologue.

Lead Action Planning

Having just listened to a review of what the workshop covered, it's a good time for participants to plan what they intend to do with what they've learned. The act of planning how they will use what they learned gives participants an extra nudge to apply the course content. An action plan provides a strong impetus for the transfer of learnings from the workshop to the workplace. The action plan can also be used as an agenda that participants can use in a discussion with their team leader or the whole team as part of their reentry from the training program.

When Michael Jordan, the former NBA superstar, was at the peak of his career, he used to say that with eighty-two games in a season his biggest challenge was to motivate himself to play at his best, game after game. Most of us have a similar problem on a smaller scale: how does a person perform at their best day after day all year long? A well-thought-out action plan can serve as a self-motivator on the job. When participants read what they've written about improving their performance and check their plan to see how they're doing, it can encourage them to keep up the good work. They see that they're improving, which motivates them to continue getting better. Their action plan becomes their silent partner.

Three Approaches to Action Planning

There are a variety of ways to approach action planning. Unless you are familiar with a different approach that would be applicable, consider using one of these methods.

The Four-Column Action Plan

Some trainers develop a 12″ by 8½″ handout with four columns:

- The first column lists the major skills taught in the workshop.
- The second column is for the participant to write where, with whom, and when they plan to use the skill or method.
- The third column is a 1 to 5 self-rating scale of how well they did when using the skill in those situations.
- The fourth column is for notes of where and when to use the method again.

Action Plan and Possible Barriers to Success

Other trainers use a form for participants to write three to five actions they will take from the course back to apply at work, followed by possible obstacles that might prevent them from being successful in their attempt to transfer the skills from the workshop.

Least Difficult to Most Difficult Applications

Another option is to use two written mini-activities that focus on transferring skills back to the workplace. The first activity is for each participant to make an assessment of her skill level with each major skill set covered in the workshop. A simple 1 to 5 scale works well.

The second activity is for the participant to develop specific plans for using the skills in major parts of their work starting with the least challenging application and moving gradually to the most important or most difficult application for them. Participants then note potential barriers to the success of their plan along with ways to overcome the obstacles.

Small Group Discussion

The action planning can conclude with a discussion of the plans in dyads or triads to help each person solidify the plans he made and to discuss the possible barriers to success including ways to overcome the potential barriers. Participants learn from each other in these conversations, so be sure to leave a bit of time at the end of the discussion for people to tweak their action plans by including what they learned from the discussion.

You may have a favorite way of doing action plans that's quite different from what's suggested here. The main point is for action plans to be (1) written and (2) doable, and (3) serve as a tool for transferring at least some of the skills and methods of the workshop to the work environment.

Generate Action Triggers

An action trigger is an event or other signal that can remind you to do something that you want to do but might let slide. Psychologist Peter Gollwitzer describes action triggers as "motivators for action." Action triggers can be powerful aids to changing one's behavior.

For example, one of the authors is a kidney transplant patient who needs to take anti-rejection drugs daily. Her action trigger is keeping her daily medicines in a pillbox at the kitchen sink where she inevitably sees them—and takes them—each morning when cleaning up after breakfast.

Here's an example of using an action trigger at work. A very talkative manager wanted to become a better listener. He took a listening skills course and learned how to listen very effectively. However, when he got back to the workplace, he started to fall back into his old talkative habits. Not wanting to backslide, he taped this action trigger to the back of his nameplate which was visible to him but not to others who dropped by to talk with him.

LISTEN!

He said it was amazing how much that one-word message transformed his communication.

Researchers discovered that the probability of change doubles when people establish a consistent practice of reminding themselves of their commitments.

Discussing Reentry

Just as we trainers have to handle resistance in our workshops, some participants will probably have to handle resistance to whatever changes they make when they re-enter the workplace. People sometimes wonder why anyone wouldn't welcome a change for the better in an associate. Of course, some people will welcome the change. But some may not. Other team members may notice that the returning team member is suddenly doing some things differently, and some may anticipate that they soon may be expected to change too. This concern is especially likely if the workshop was on communication skills or interpersonal relationships.

As you end a workshop, it pays to invest time for participants to think about how resistance back at work might look and how to head it off or deal with it if it should arise. To help participants think about this, you can lead them in building a list of Do's and Don'ts for Reentry. Here are some items that appeared on lists of past participants:

Do's:

Tell others about the skills or methods you'll be trying out.

Discuss the benefits to the team.

Ask for their support and feedback as you try to improve.

Review your action plans once a week.

Reinforce yourself when you successfully use what you learned.

Don'ts:

Overdo it.

Begin with the most difficult people or situations at work.

Give up if you're not perfect.

Tell others that they need to take the workshop.

Add that if some team members become resistant to the changes you're making, it's time to put your reflective listening skills to work (Chapter 12). When they've had their say, own the fact that in a recent workshop you learned some different ways of doing some things and that they will see changes in your behavior because you're determined to improve. Tell them about some of the changes you'll be experimenting with and ask them to give you feedback from time to time.

Facilitate Evaluation

You may want to review Chapter 19 to see if there are suggestions that will help you plan the end of the workshop.

Wrap Up the Experience

One of the main things you want to accomplish at the end of a workshop is to help participants achieve a sense of closure regarding the workshop experience. Everything recommended thus far in this chapter should contribute to achieving that sense of closure. Additionally, at the very end of a workshop it's often appropriate to give people an opportunity to say a brief statement to the group.

The act of saying goodbye when leaving a person or an experience is customary in our culture. Still, it can be an awkward moment for people. One way of facilitating closure is to invite participants to respond to a closure cue. The trainer gives the cue and, to avoid influencing other people's comments, is the last person to respond. The cue can be anything the trainer thinks would fit this particular group and workshop. Here are some closure cues we've used:

"I came here wondering. . .; I leave . . ."

"An important thing I learned was . . ."

"A surprise for me as a result of this training. . ."

"Something from this training that I don't want to forget . . ."

"What will you to do differently on the job to apply what you've learned here?"

Notice that each of these cues call for an element of self-disclosure since each of them includes information about what the participant thinks was important to her personally. This sort of sharing provides a moment for the participants to say what's on their minds, learn what others thought and felt about the experience, and achieve a sense of closure. Furthermore, research shows that publicly expressing appreciation for what one has learned strengthens a person's commitment to use that ability.

Be Prepared for Things to Get a Bit Hectic

During the ending of the workshop things can get a little dicey. Someone has a plane to catch and runs off saying she'll mail the evaluation to you. Another keeps eyeing his watch. Someone else is half out of his chair packing his briefcase. Others, while still in their chairs, may have mentally left the workshop.

If things seem to be falling apart at the end of a workshop as participants tend to their own needs, say what you see and ask for what you need. Doing so could sound like this:

> John has a 4:40 plane to catch so he has left the workshop with a promise to mail his evaluation. I notice that some of you are packing up and others may be mentally out the door already. If you can make a new decision and stay with us for the closing activity, we'll be done by 4:15. That's fifteen minutes earlier than the scheduled ending time. How does that sound?

Most participants will honor this kind of a request made by the trainer. But don't test their patience. Keep things moving and end the class by the promised time.

Be Available Until the Last Person Leaves

By now most participants have left, but you haven't. This is the final time to make yourself available to anyone who needs some time with you. Before you start packing up, wait to see if anyone has stayed behind. It may be that someone just has a need to say a special goodbye because of the camaraderie she felt with you. Or someone may have a question they didn't want to ask in the whole group. On a more serious note, someone may be facing a career decision and wants to talk it over with you. Or someone may have a major problem with his boss that he hasn't been able to share with anyone. It's pretty hard, in the face of such requests, to say, "Sorry, I have to get going." Or "Can't stay; I have a plane to catch." Best to be in the habit of keeping yourself available for thirty minutes after the workshop ends.

PART III

THE TRAINER
AS FACILITATOR

21

Understanding Resistance

Resistance is the most important factor in change and the most neglected. . . .Research suggests that resistance is often the main reason change fails.

———Rick Maurer[1]

R esistance to change is a natural part of the learning process, and dealing with it can be one of the more challenging aspects of training. As change management consultant Jerome Jellison says, "Like gravity, resistance is a fact of life."[2]

As you may have experienced, when handled poorly, participant resistance can scuttle a workshop. However, when you have a pragmatic understanding of resistance and know how to deal with it skillfully, resistance will seldom thwart the progress of your training. This chapter discusses the dynamics of resistance. With this knowledge and the methods that are taught in the next three chapters you'll be able to manage even the most persistent resistance that you might encounter in a workshop.

The Prevalence of Resistance to Change

In the year 1513 Niccolo Machiavelli, founder of the "modern" field of political science, wrote *The Prince*, a book that after 500 years is still required reading in many college and graduate-school courses. Machiavelli emphasized the power and the prevalence of people's resistance to change: "There is nothing more difficult to take in hand . . . or more uncertain in its success than to take the lead in the introduction of a new order of things."[3]

History confirmed Machiavelli's dictum. The greatest advances in virtually every field—mathematics, science, medicine, business, etc.—were vehemently opposed by most of the leading authorities in each field. Prominent scholars and researchers repeatedly refused to give new theories and fresh evidence an objective hearing. And, of course, most of the lesser lights were at least as resistant to change as their leaders. As British editor and essayist Walter Bagehot observed, "One of the greatest pains to human nature is the pain of a new idea."[4]

Resistance in Mathematics

Pythagoras, the ancient Greek philosopher, mathematician, and religious reformer, was one of the most brilliant men of his time. He was confident that there was a rational expression for the square root of two. Hippasus, a young student of his, proved that this could not be true. The ancient seer tried to refute his student's conclusion but was unable to do so. He eliminated the problem by ordering Hippasus to be killed by drowning. Fortunately, not all resistance is that extreme.

Resistance in Science

One would think that scientists, who are commonly regarded as being among the most rational of human beings, would welcome new evidence that calls into question established theories. After all, as scientists they're assumed to be committed to the scientific method, which takes empirical data very seriously. But history shows that even these rigorously rational people are apt to be resistant when new evidence challenges their long-established beliefs. In his *Origin of Species*, Charles Darwin accurately predicted the resistance his work would stir up: "Although the evidence the great naturalist presented was fully convincing to him, he forecast that the seasoned naturalists who were steeped in a radically different point of view would not entertain his theories or even view his astonishingly abundant evidence with open minds. His premonition was shockingly accurate." Max Planck, who won the Nobel Prize in physics wrote, "A new scientific truth does not triumph by convincing its opponents and making them see the light, but rather because its opponents eventually die, and a new generation grows up that is familiar with it."[5]

Resistance in Healthcare

Since the time of Dr. Ignaz Semmelweis, (1818–1865), we've known that physicians and other healthcare workers pick up germs from one patient and then inadvertently pass them on to other patients. The solution is simple and incredibly easy to implement: healthcare workers should simply wash their hands after seeing each patient. Despite knowing this, many doctors, nurses, and other healthcare personnel do not always follow this simple and easy to follow rule. The result? Even today, hospitals remain one of the most dangerous places in any community, causing tens of thousands of deaths annually in large part because healthcare workers simply do not consistently wash their hands. In one study researchers found that although 73 percent of doctors said they washed effectively, only 9 percent met the industry standard.

Resistance in Business

You'd think that profit-oriented business organizations would embrace changes that have a high likelihood of making them more productive and profitable. But resistance flourishes in the corporate world, too. One study reported that, according to senior executives in Fortune 500 companies, fewer than half of the change efforts in their corporations were successful. Resistance was the primary reason for the failures.[6]

Resistance in Daily Life

Of course, it's not only mathematicians, scientists, healthcare workers, and business leaders who resist fresh information and innovative improvements that undermine long-established beliefs or ways of doing things. The average person often resists using new methods even when their usefulness is immediately apparent. For instance, in the early decades of the twentieth century, all grocery stores were small and customers had to go to the store frequently because they were only able to make a few handfuls of purchases on each visit. After all there is only so much a person can carry about with their two hands. Then, a grocer named Sylvan Goldman invented the shopping cart. To Goldman's amazement, though, shoppers were reluctant to use the carts; despite their availability customers were still carrying the groceries in their hands! It wasn't until Goldman hired people of both genders and various ages to push carts around the store that shopping carts were finally accepted.

Resistance in Training

Training is an educational form of change management that is conducted to enhance participants' performance by instigating improvements in their knowledge, attitudes, or skills. To paraphrase philosopher Herbert Spencer, effective training "is clearly associated with change, is its pioneer, is the never-sleeping agent of revolution, is always fitting men for higher things, and unfitting them for things as they are."[7]

To phrase it more prosaically, it's the trainer's job to encourage participants to develop some enhancements or outright changes in their knowledge, attitudes, or behaviors. However, some participants may not be receptive to your well-intentioned input. Since the early period of psychoanalysis, therapists have been aware of a "status quo bias" in human beings that militates against a person's likelihood of making changes—even ones that an objective observer would consider to be in the person's best interest. Resistance is the term that trainers and other change agents tend to use in reference to the status quo bias in human nature. Your ability to deal effectively with participants' resistance will greatly affect the outcome of every workshop you lead. And, yes, you can even face resistance when teaching a webinar.

Why Advocating Change May Provoke Resistance

There are at least four reasons why people might resist the trainer's message:

1. Participants may have had negative experiences in previous training sessions.
2. Participants do not believe there is a need to change.
3. Significant change requires participants to adopt new ways of doing things, when the old, habitual ways worked to their satisfaction.
4. Participants are reluctant to make the effort required to master a new skill.

1. Participants May Have Had Negative Experiences in Previous Training Sessions

When you stop to think about it, it's not surprising that a number of people might not approach a training event with optimistic expectations. Many of those attending your workshops have probably observed one major training effort after another that had no staying power and merely distracted people from their normal duties that they were still expected to perform. So it's not unreasonable for some people to wonder why this new approach will be any better.

2. Participants Do Not Believe There Is a Need to Change

Participants may not feel there is a need to improve what they're doing—at least in the areas of the course content. In many courses, participants will already have their own way of doing the things that are being taught. And, given the momentum of habit, making the advocated changes may require considerable and effort.

3. Significant Change Requires Participants to Adopt New Ways of Doing Things, When the Old, Habitual Ways Worked to Their Satisfaction

In many situations people have been using a different set of techniques to accomplish what the methods taught in the workshop are designed to do. Often those techniques had become habitual and participants could use them with relative ease.

So we're wise to expect that some people might be leery about giving up an ability that they are competent at and satisfied with for one that they're unfamiliar with, and they may be dubious about its practicality.

4. Participants Are Reluctant to Make the Effort Required to Master a New Skill

Acquiring a new skill entails a learning curve. Becoming proficient at a new way of doing things often requires considerable time and effort from participants, many of whom are already experiencing a pressured work life.

Figure 21-1. Training endeavors to instigate change and, as a result, is apt to trigger resistance.

No question about it: encouraging people to do things differently is a big challenge. But, through the years, we've all gained new knowledge, developed new and useful attitudes, and employed new behaviors, methods, and processes. And when you master the skills taught in this book, especially those in the next three chapters, you'll be able to significantly reduce the amount of resistance you encounter when training and better manage any vestiges that remain. That translates into improved learning for participants and more fulfilling and enjoyable training days for everyone involved.

The Reaction-to-Change Continuum

It's helpful to view resistance on a reaction-to-change continuum of open-minded responses, resistant responses, and obstructive responses, as portrayed in Figure 21-2.

Figure 21-2. The Reaction-to-Change Continuum

Open-Minded Responses	Resistant Responses	Obstructive Responses

Open-Minded Responses

The left end of the continuum represents participants in our workshops who come to learn. They give the information a fair hearing and put their best effort into practice sessions. They are a pleasure to work with and, thankfully, they usually constitute the majority of trainees in a workshop.

Resistant Responses

The center of the continuum represents participants who are skeptical of the value of what's being taught and thus far at least do not buy into learning or using it, but they're not trying to ruin the course for others or to undermine the trainer. When people are resistant, they're often being self-protective rather than aggressive. Their goal is to defend their own personal status quo.

Obstructive Responses

The right end of the continuum represents participants whose behavior tends to be uncooperative, discourteous, disruptive, bad mannered, rude, or hostile. Their misbehavior goes far beyond normal resistance. Some participants using obstructive behavior may feel vulnerable in the workshop situation, and their acting out may be their way of trying to protect themselves. But the way they're doing that interferes with the learning of other participants.

> There's a very practical reason for distinguishing between resistant responses and obstructive responses. As you'll see in Chapter 23, the best way to respond to an individual's distractive behavior is quite different from the most useful way of managing group resistance, which is covered in Chapter 24.

Factors Other Than Change that May Generate Resistance

There are a number of other factors that, separately or in combination, increase the likelihood that participants will become resistant to learning. When you are aware of and skillfully attend to these factors you can significantly decrease the amount of resistance you have to manage.

Factors in the Trainer

Often a trainer's behavior contributes to participant resistance. The number of ways a trainer can be disappointing could fill a book. Even the best trainers cannot execute all of the standards of our craft with skill and grace. There are so many standards for trainers to meet, that each trainer will excel at some and be weaker on others. For example, the trainer might present ideas too rapidly, or too slowly, with too few or too many examples. He may be too serious or too much of a comedian. Some trainer's lack of business experience may undermine their believability. They may seem too inexperienced and naive. Or the trainer may come across as too dogmatic and heavy-handed. At times the trainer's timing may be off, his energy low, his enthusiasm waning. If a number of participants in the group perceive the trainer to be lacking in credibility, too directive, unresponsive to participants, and so forth, resistance will begin to escalate. In these types of situations, to quote Walt Kelly's comic-strip character Pogo, "We have met the enemy and he is us."

Referring to a participant's behavior as "resistant" can be a way of refusing to acknowledge that our behavior may have triggered the resistance. To paraphrase therapist Sheldon Kopp, "Why do we label the participant 'resistant' when we should be labeling the trainer as 'inept'?"

Factors in the Participants

Many adults have mixed feelings about their elementary school, high school, and college education—some good, some bad. And, as adults, some of their experiences in training sessions may have been less than stellar. So, the experiences of some participants may bias them to have low expectations about the value of attending another workshop. Then, too, some participants may have a negative reaction to persons in an authority position.

Furthermore, a participant may be struggling with personal issues at work. He may have recently received a poor progress review or missed out on an expected promotion. Possibly the relationship with his manager is strained. In fact, he may be thinking that his manager who sent him to the training is the one who should be taking the course.

Personal stress—marital problems, troubled relations with children, illness of an elderly parent, and many other personal difficulties—may also distract some learners.

Factors in the Course Content

A participant may disagree with the content being taught. Others may be skeptical that what's being taught will work in their situation, and the more dubious participants may doubt that it will work anywhere. At times the content may repeat what the participants already have learned in a previous course.

Factors in the Administration of the Workshop

So much can go wrong with the administration of a workshop—inconvenient timing for the class, poor room selection or room setup, and so forth. Appendix III discusses potential administrative problems and how to avoid them.

Factors in the Participants' Workplace

No matter how professionally you are leading the workshop, events in the participants' workplace can have a strong negative effect on the participants' openness to learning. A merger, downsizing, and closing some work sites can seriously impact a person's learning. One of our most challenging training experiences was when, with no notification from our corporate contact, we found ourselves training people from a department in which everyone knew that their unit would be radically downsized in the coming week.

Learn from the Resistance You Encounter

Political analyst Walter Lippmann said, "Opposition is indispensable. A good statesman, like any other sensible human being always learns more from his opponents than from his fervent supporters."[8] And therapist Jeffrey Kottler advises, "Relabel resistance as helpful. Rather than see uncooperative behavior as oppositional, view it instead as feedback."[9]

You may be so occupied trying to manage the resistance during the workshop, that you may not be able to learn a whole lot from it at the time. But certainly after the workshop has concluded, you need to take some time to analyze when the resistance started, how it grew, and what was happening as it reached its peak. Were there earlier signs that you overlooked? What more could you have done preventatively? What are the changes you want to make in the material and design so you won't have a similar experience when you teach the course again? Even if few or no other participants agree with the resistant participant, try to find out what you can learn from her resistance. And keep in mind that the resistance that's raised about the content may really be about group process issues. Could you have managed the group process in a better way?

Coming Attractions: Methods for Managing Resistance

The next three chapters provide specific methods for avoiding the buildup of resistance and defusing it when it does arise. Chapter 22 discusses the basics of developing a training environment that eases participants' anxieties and makes them more open to giving the training content a fair hearing. Chapter 23 gives examples of disruptive individual behavior in training workshops and details a method for handling these types of situations in a respectful, constructive, and effective way. Chapter 24 shows how resistance can become a group phenomenon and provides a very specific way of handling the many forms of group resistance that you may encounter.

22

Maintaining a Positive Learning Climate

As educators . . . we must recognize that students are not only intellectual but also social and emotional beings, and that these dimensions interact within the classroom climate to influence learning and performance.

———Susan Ambrose, Michael Bridges, Michele DiPietro, and M. Lovett[1]

The trainer's ability to create a positive learning climate is one of the crucial factors for success in leading a workshop. An encouraging environment lowers participant anxiety and fosters a readiness to learn, which sets the stage for a smoothly running workshop. When you've succeeded in generating a positive learning environment, you're likely to overhear participants make comments such as the following:

"I was nervous about taking this training, but I actually feel quite comfortable here."

"Usually I don't say much in groups. This one is different. I feel like I can say whatever I want, even if I disagree with the instructor."

"This is a great group. We're all pulling for each other."

Virtually everything a trainer does either helps or hinders the creation and maintenance of a beneficial learning environment. Using the skills and methods covered in previous chapters goes a long way toward creating a milieu that is optimal for learning. However, these guidelines warrant special emphasis:

- Manage the physical environment.
- Be prepared.
- Make personal contact.
- Be yourself; don't take on the role of a stereotypical teacher.

- Be supportive.
- Be nonjudgmental.
- Deal constructively with viewpoints different from yours.
- Be enthusiastic but not dogmatic.

Manage the Physical Environment

Give thought to and make decisions about the best room setup for the particular course you're teaching. Set up the training area so that it's easy for participants to move around and to contribute to and listen to group discussions.

Comfort factors are an important part of a workable learning environment. When the workshop room is too hot, too cold, poorly lit, has uncomfortable seating, or other problems, the focus of the learners will be more on their discomfort than on the content to be learned. Some of these elements may be outside your immediate control. However, for the ones you can impact, do so as soon as possible. Contact the support staff to give a hand in improving the situation. Be open with the participants about any problems and ask for ideas to improve conditions. Even if the problems can't be ameliorated, you will have created a sense of "We're in this together; let's make the best of it." That will go a long way toward getting the participants' attention back to where you want it—on the course material.

Be Prepared

UCLA's John Wooden, perhaps the greatest college basketball coach in history, used to say, "Failure to prepare is preparing to fail."

When preparation is incomplete, you'll be preoccupied with details that prevent you from being available to participants as they arrive at the workshop. And when you're not accessible to arriving participants, you won't be able to do the essential work of building a positive learning climate at the crucial time when first, and often lasting, impressions are formed.

Thorough content preparation is the foundation for successful training. When you've prepared well, you are free to focus on participants rather than on your own anxiety about presenting the material. However, if you don't have a good grasp of the concepts you'll be teaching, are vague about their relevance to these participants, or lack a depth of knowledge that enables you to handle challenging questions, what are you doing in the training room?

Make sure that anything that can be done ahead of time is taken care of prior to the training day. And on each day of the workshop plan to be in the classroom at least a half an hour before the training begins. If you are new to training or if you're not confident that the setup you requested will have been done properly, arrive forty-five minutes early. That will give you time to track down missing materials or set up the room the way you want it if your instructions haven't been carried out. That extra time will also enable you attend to any last minute details and get yourself settled so you'll be centered and ready to welcome participants to the course.

Make Personal Contact

When your preparation is complete you are ready to greet participants as they arrive, introduce yourself, and learn the first names of some of them. Discovering something about each person and telling a bit about yourself helps put the participants at ease. You can join Ned, who is standing by himself, and after a bit of conversation hook him up with a small group. Then look for someone else who could use a little help in integrating herself into the group.

When you sense that everyone is doing reasonably well, do a casual visual survey of the group. You see that Norma has a good tan even though it is January and she lives in New England, you note that Aaron is talking about the big college basketball game last night, and that Jill is on crutches due to a skiing accident a few weeks ago. Noticing and mentioning specific things about the participants helps you establish personal contact with them. As you make one-to-one contact with the members of the workshop, you are building a positive learning climate one participant at a time.

Using participants' first names is another way of building rapport. Find out what name the person prefers to be called and use that name when you're having an informal conversation with him. And when you're in front of the group, you can say things such as:

"That's helpful, Bob; thanks."

"Lou's take on that is different from yours, Kate."

"Don, your experience seems to have been similar to Susan's."

"Seems like that piqued your interest, Andy."

Using people's names contributes to the workshop in several ways:

- It personalizes the instruction.
- It roots the names in your memory.
- It helps workshop members learn one another's names.
- It enables everyone to feel better acquainted and more relaxed.

Be Yourself: Don't Take on the Role of a Stereotypical Teacher

The *Dictionary of Behavioral Science*, second edition, defines *role* as "a pattern of behavior that is characteristic or expected of an individual occupying a particular position in a social system."[2] We all fill various roles in life—trainer, husband/wife, parent, coach, volunteer, and so on. When we fill those roles well, we do the expected behaviors competently while genuinely being ourselves. And while filling those roles we also adapt our behavior to stay in sync with the changing circumstances in which we find ourselves.

However, some people in the helping professions—medicine, psychology, religion, and education—take on the stereotypical role of how they think a person in that discipline should behave. It's not uncommon for trainers to succumb to that tendency. They behave like they believe a person in their role is supposed to behave. In the process of taking on a role, though, they suppress much of their individuality. When a person takes on a stereotypical role, her genuine self is stifled and she behaves in artificial and inflexible ways; without intending to, she has turned herself into a phony. Synonyms for the word "phony" suggest how damaging it can be to the learning climate when the trainer takes on the stereotypical role of "teacher":

Counterfeit   Bogus   Fraudulent   Fake   False   Spurious

How can you tell if you're taking on a role instead of being yourself? Your voice will change. It's that simple. Changes in the voice may vary from becoming singsong to becoming overly formal. Along with the change in the voice, language may become stilted. Body movements may change some too, but your voice is the key.

Trainers are most effective when they act no differently when teaching than they would in any other setting. They remain recognizably themselves. They act the same while teaching as they do on breaks or over lunch. No magical change occurs when they stand up to present or lead an activity or do a demonstration. Obviously, when you lead a group you need to engage in some different behaviors than when you are conversing informally with one or two people. You'll have to project your voice more and put a bit more energy into your body language. But make sure you avoid taking on an artificial "teacher voice" or other kind of hackneyed teacher behavior.

If you think this may be something you do that blocks your effectiveness, make a video of yourself in a normal conversation with somebody. Compare that video with one made when you were training. Listen for differences and similarities. You might also consider asking for feedback from an experienced colleague.

When a trainer avoids taking on a role, it makes a contribution to her being seen as genuine and trustworthy, which helps create the kind of learning climate that participants thrive in.

Be Supportive

Effective trainers behave in a warm and friendly manner, but beyond that there are specific behaviors they can do to be supportive. They can encourage participants as they practice new behaviors, show their enjoyment when successes come, and appreciate participants' efforts to learn especially when they are struggling. A supportive attitude conveys that the participant is important to the trainer and that the trainer is on her side, which helps build a climate in which it's safe to experiment with new behaviors.

Additionally, the trainer works to build a supportive group culture. At the beginning of a workshop, support comes mainly from the trainer. But competent trainers also use activities and methods that foster the development of supportive relationships among group members. When an encouraging classroom culture develops, participants increasingly feel, "It's safe to be myself here." They feel challenged, but that it's okay to try out some new behaviors.

Be Nonjudgmental

Even people who are generally supportive can become judgmental at times. That's a deadly tendency for a trainer. Few things can be as damaging to a learning environment as a trainer with a critical outlook. Psychologist Laurence Steinberg emphasizes that being judgmental seldom stimulates improvement:

> Criticism doesn't make people want to change; it makes them defensive.[3]

When people are learning new skills, they often make mistakes and need to receive developmental feedback. So, as described in Chapter 18, trainers need to cultivate the knack of being supportive and nonjudgmental even when providing developmental (i.e., corrective) feedback.

Deal Constructively with Viewpoints Different from Yours

As a trainer, one thing you can be sure of is that there will be times when people will disagree with what you are teaching, will be convinced that some or perhaps all of the methods you are advocating are impractical, or that your workshop—which they may have been forced to attend—is a total waste of time. These are likely to be a make-or-break moments in the development and maintenance of a positive workshop climate. These are the times that you really earn your salary.

During these moments all eyes in the room are watching intently: Is the trainer unsettled, irritated, insecure, or otherwise ill at ease? Does he show dislike or annoyance toward the disagreeing participant or participants?

A top priority of successful trainers is creating and maintaining a safe environment for all participants including any who may seem intent on discrediting the trainer or disrupting the workshop. It's part of your job to keep your poise during workshop crises. Maintaining your composure will enable you to reflect disagreements objectively, which typically will prevent differences of opinion from turning into arguments. Competent trainers demonstrate that they honor the right of each individual to hold her own opinion.

Nevertheless, once you have listened open-mindedly to opinions that differ from those you advanced, you've earned the right to concisely state or restate your point of view. Just keep it brief. Leave a moment for others to respond if they wish. Then you may succinctly recap the various points of view that have been expressed before pressing on with the remaining workshop material. Sometimes you just have to leave it at, "Okay, I guess here's where we agree to disagree," and move on.

Be Enthusiastic but Not Dogmatic

Accomplished trainers show enthusiasm for what they're teaching. Enthusiasm is partly conveyed by the amount of energy the trainer is putting out to the group. It's shown in the tone of voice, the volume and rate of speech, the gestures used, the eye contact made, and the body posture. If you're not enthusiastic about what you're teaching, why should anyone else care?

A trainer's enthusiasm, however, is not to be confused with an overly ardent approach to try to persuade participants to embrace what he's teaching. His phrasing and manner of presenting should communicate to participants that they have a free choice in what they will and will not believe or do. If they sense they are losing their freedom of choice, you can say goodbye to the positive learning climate you're trying to build.

By their words and their body language skilled trainers communicate this type of attitude:

> Here are some skills and concepts that I believe will help you become even more successful at work. That's why I'm enthusiastic about sharing them with you. I'm teaching these skills and methods so you can increase your options. Select those you think will be useful to you.

This attitude will help prevent power struggles between you and the participants that set up win/lose situations, can split the group, and are apt to end up having the trainer win the battle but lose the group. So be aware of the thin line between being enthusiastic in your teaching and attempting to convert participants to the methods, beliefs, and values you are teaching.

23

Intervening to Eliminate an Individual's Disruptive Behavior

It is important to remember that this is a discussion: two people are participating in a conversation. You are not lecturing someone.

——Ferdinand Fournies[1]

You've been teaching the class for half a day and your sense is that, by and large, things seem to be going well. The group has good energy, discussions have been lively, and questions and comments have been insightful. So far, so good.

Well, not quite. Although the group is going well, there is one participant, Jamie Baker, who makes no eye contact with you. He has not spoken in the group or mixed with other participants on breaks. He's also the last person to return from breaks. During your presentations his head is down as he reads some unrelated material. At other times during presentations he engages the people on either side of him in conversation. As you continue leading the group, you're aware that this is a problem that you'll have to do something about. But what?

This chapter answers that question by describing the following:

- Common sources of disengaged or disruptive behavior
- How to prevent much disengaged or disruptive behavior
- A series of increasingly potent interventions to manage problems

Common Sources of Disengaged or Disruptive Behavior

In everyday life people react to what's going on around them and these reactions often influence how they behave. That doesn't change when they enter a workshop.

In training, participants can be impacted by their reactions to one or more of the following:

- The company that employs the participant
- The training methods
- The trainer
- Other participants
- Factors in participant's life outside of the workshop

Positive or negative feelings emerge in reaction to these factors, and those feelings drive much of the behavior in the training room. Let's look at some participants who are having negative reactions to one or more of these factors despite the fact that the group is functioning well. (In these examples you are given the reason for the unwanted behaviors, but in training the only information you'll be able to consider is the behavior you are able to observe.)

Negative Reactions to the Organization that Employs the Participant

There's very stressful stuff going on in Jamie's life that the trainer is unaware of. Jamie feels unmotivated and angry because his company has been downsizing and he's afraid he may be one of the next to go. He hates what he sees as the secretive methods the company uses. It feels to him like they're playing with his life. In these circumstances, he's unmotivated to learn anything new. Additionally, he pictures the heavy workload piling up while he is wasting precious time in two days of training.

Negative Reactions to the Teaching Methods

Laurie Johnson is an exception in a group that is engaged in the various activities the trainer uses to enhance understanding of what they're learning. When the trainer introduces an activity, Laurie very reluctantly gets up from her chair and moves slowly and with obvious displeasure to join a group. When she finally sits in a group, she doesn't participate.

Laurie dislikes taking part in activities. Her preference is to learn through lectures and she is annoyed at having to get up and move around the room to work in small groups. She sees small-group activities as a waste of class time when she could be learning something that could actually help her at work. Additionally, the extra weight she is carrying makes it difficult for her to move about and she feels self-conscious.

Negative Reactions to the Trainer

Jeremy Jones interrupts the trainer with questions unrelated to the presentation. He also breaks in argumentatively to contradict or challenge a point she is making.

He leans forward in his chair when he interrupts, and uses strong gestures to punctuate his remarks.

Jeremy just plain doesn't like female trainers. He once had an incompetent female trainer who embarrassed him in front of the group. He now expects the same low level of expertise from this female trainer. His goal is to get her before she gets him.

Negative Reactions to Other Participants

Lucille Gambetta has not spoken in the large group for the first full day of training. She is avoiding interaction with other people in the group. Her facial expression is vacant and her energy level and involvement are low.

She feels wary and withdrawn because there are three coworkers in the group that she doesn't trust due to a recent bad experience with them. In a team meeting, the three women joined forces in shooting down two of her ideas that she felt were money savers and doable. She believes they didn't examine the worth of the ideas and discarded them because they came from her.

Negative Reactions to Factors in the Participant's Life

Eli Wagner spends much of his time in class looking out the window, looking down at the floor, rubbing his forehead, and sighing. He follows all directions and sits in on small-group activities but hasn't spoken in class discussions.

Eli is still coping with the recent diagnosis that his wife has cancer. He took a week off from work to take her to appointments and to support her during this rough time. Upon his return to the job he was scheduled to attend this training. It's hard for him to generate much interest in the class.

These examples demonstrate not only the kinds of disengaged or disruptive behavior that can be observed in the training room, but also how difficult it would be for a trainer to draw an accurate inference about what's causing the observed behavior. In these examples, as in life outside of training, it's unlikely that anyone can make an accurate guess about what is causing unwanted behavior. So remain an objective observer and be very cautious about making inferences about the behavior you observe.

When the trainer or the training methods seem to be triggering the disruptive behavior, the trainer may be able to make some changes in his behavior or methodology that may motivate the participant to reduce some of his dysfunctional behavior.

How to Prevent Much Disengaged or Disruptive Behavior

When you follow the recommendations in Chapter 22, you will have prepared well for the workshop, made sure the physical environment was comfortable, and made personal contact with everyone. On breaks you socialized and checked in with people by saying things like, "How's it going?" "Is this meeting your needs?" "Can you see yourself using this?" You were supportive of people's efforts, dealt constructively with viewpoints different from yours, and delivered the workshop energetically. When you do these things you'll prevent most but not all disengaged and disruptive behavior.

In many workshops there'll be participants who don't want to be there and who will demonstrate that with disengaged or disruptive behavior. The next section describes a four-level process of increasing potency of intervention that will enable you to appropriately manage virtually any difficult behavior you'll encounter in your workshops.

A Series of Increasingly Potent Interventions to Manage Problems

Dynamic trainers use four levels of increasing potency of intervention to deal with disruptive behavior:

Level 1: Check in

Level 2: Private feedback meeting

Level 3: Private confrontation meeting

Level 4: Termination of training meeting

Level 1: Check In

Research has shown that when someone is hostile toward another person, she has usually dehumanized that person. The person is not real to her. Psychologist George Bach labeled this type of dehumanization as "thinging" someone. When the person becomes more real—more human to the hostile person—it's difficult for her to continue the attack. Our goal at level 1 is for the trainer and the person who is doing the negative behavior to have a chance to humanize each other. That happens by checking in—spending a bit of time with the person and getting to know each other.

A natural response to negative behavior in the group is for the trainer to avoid the troublesome person. Go against those instincts and casually seek the person out. It's wise to check in as soon as possible after the unwanted behavior is noted. Make a decision to be with the person on break or to sit next to him at lunch if the lunch is a communal one. This interaction is a social one; there is no discussion of the participant's behavior. The purpose is to get to know each other better. Subjects such as where the person is from, what he likes to do outside of work, and an interest in current sporting events are safe. They don't call for much self-disclosure but they do help you know the participant better than you did before the conversation.

During this interaction you also make minimal self–disclosures in order for the participant to get to know you better. Think of the conversation as a balance of getting to know the participant and allowing him to know more about you.

Just getting better acquainted will help the humanization process and you may find that the two of you share some common interest or background that draws you closer together. Or you might pick up a clue as to why the behavior is occurring, although that is not the purpose of this intervention. The above example of the participant whose wife was diagnosed with cancer entailed a real-life conversation, and the disclosure about his wife was made at this level of intervention. Just sharing his problem and seeing that the trainer cared about what was happening in his life changed his behavior for the better in class. He became more engaged and focused.

If Needed, Provide Support or Problem Solving

Checking-in conversations sometimes uncover a problem that needs to be solved. For example, a participant in a sales course just learned that one of his clients is considering other purchasing options and he needs to be on the phone rather than in the seminar that afternoon. When problem solving, you might help the person figure out how he can catch up on the missed content if he needs to be out of class to talk with his client.

Sometimes you'll find that nothing can be resolved but you can still show your support. If a person tells you about a major upheaval in his department, when you've finished listening, you might reflect, "Sounds like you've got a lot on your mind right now. Let me know if there's anything I can do to make it easier for you to be here with so much going on back at work."

While checking in is a good first step when there seems to be trouble brewing, don't limit it to those occasions. Keep checking in with as many people as you can as often as you can. You will like the workshop more and your participants will too. And research shows that when participants find a workshop pleasurable, they learn more.

Level 2: Private Feedback Meeting

Resistance, if ignored, usually intensifies. If the checking-in conversation doesn't reduce or eliminate the negative behavior, you can't just let it go and pretend that everything is okay when it's definitely not okay. It's time to move to the next level of intervention. At this stage you find a way of having a private conversation with the participant in question. Meeting after class is best because you don't have the time constraint that you would have if you met during a break. Meeting over lunchtime is a second choice. Privacy is essential, so meet in a space that provides it. The steps of the private feedback meeting are as follows:

1. Say what you see.
2. Invite a response.
3. Listen reflectively until the participant has said everything she wants to say.
4. Summarize the problem.
5. Invite problem solving.
6. Evaluate the solutions and gain agreement on the adjustments.
7. Close.

Using the Jamie Baker example, here's an abbreviated script of how a private feedback meeting might go in his situation. Assume that the time and place for the meeting have been set and the trainer and Jamie are sitting down together after class.

Trainer: Thanks, Jamie, for taking the time to meet with me.

Jamie: No problem.

1. Say what you see.

Trainer: We've just finished our first day of training and this is what I've noticed. During my presentations you look through unrelated materials on your lap. At other times you engage the person on either side of you in conversation. And just before we ended this morning's session, you began reading the newspaper.

2. Invite a response and 3. Listen reflectively.

Trainer: Help me understand what's going on.

Jamie: Nothing is going on. I just don't like to sit still for so long.

Trainer: It's hard for you to be sitting so much.

Jamie: Yeah. I usually have a lot of action in my work.

Trainer: This is very different for you.

Jamie: Yes, it's especially hard now when so much work is piling up and I'm away for two days.

Trainer: You can imagine what's happening back at work.

Jamie: It doesn't take much imagination. My workload has doubled since the downsizing. And I'm stuck here supposedly learning stuff I'll never use when someone, somewhere, is putting my name on the list to lay off next.

Trainer: You're worried about keeping your job.

Jamie: Who isn't these days? I've seen times when the company has sent some of my coworkers to training and the next month, they're gone.

Trainer: So training could be an indicator of what's coming next for you.

Jamie: I don't know, but it could be. It really pisses me off. Everything is so secretive around here and my livelihood is on the line.

4. Summarize the problem.

Trainer: You have a lot on your mind to distract you from learning new skills.

Jamie: You've got that right.

Trainer: Thanks for telling me. It helps me understand where you're coming from.

5. Invite problem solving.

Trainer: We have another day of training tomorrow. Any thoughts on what you and I can do about the situation?

Jamie: Are you kidding? There's nothing to do. You can't change what's going to happen to me.

Trainer: I wish I could, but you're right—I can't. Maybe we can figure out a way to get through tomorrow so you get something useful from being here and I can go on teaching the group.

Jamie: I don't know.

(Silence)

Jamie: What do you want from me?

Trainer: You're kind of puzzled about what to suggest.

(Silence)

Jamie: Not really. I may have been a little rude to you. I don't need to do that. In fact, I'm sorry.

Trainer: Thanks, Jamie. That would help me out, but how about you? What could make the next day more useful to you?

Jamie: I don't know. Maybe you could show how I could use the new skills in my work and have me practice in my situations.

Trainer: Like customize the material to be more applicable.

6. Evaluate the solution(s) and gain agreement on implementation.

Jamie: Yeah. Can you do that?

Trainer: Maybe not in every situation, but I think I can adjust the material in several places so you can see the fit with you and your work. I might need your help on some of that. How does that sound?

Jamie: Not too bad.

Trainer: Okay. So as far as our working together tomorrow goes, we've agreed that I'll do some customizing of the material so you can see practical applications to your work and you'll help me out on that when I need your help.

And you won't thumb through or read materials or have side conversations during class time. Right?

Jamie: Right.

7. Close.

Trainer: Thanks for partnering with me on this, Jamie.

Jamie: No problem.

Trainer: See you tomorrow.

Three Major Characteristics of a Private Feedback Discussion

1. The trainer is not accusatory, blameful, or attacking. She sticks to a clear description of Jamie's behavior. How different the conversation would have been if the trainer said, "I think that you're being rude in the class. You're inconsiderate of others who are there to learn and certainly you're interfering with my efforts to teach." It would be all downhill from there.

2. The trainer uses reflective listening. Whenever Jamie made a response, the trainer refrained from correcting him or judging what he said. When replying to Jamie, she didn't try to persuade him to change. Instead, each time Jamie spoke, she reflected his thoughts and feelings. She showed that she understood what he was saying.

3. The trainer encourages participant to come up with the solution to the problem, gets an agreement about what each will do and then sets up a working relationship that makes the trainer and the participant a team.

Level 3: Private Confrontation Meeting

In twenty-eight years of training we've never had to progress to a private confrontation meeting after having had a private feedback meeting. However, in training as in life, anything can happen for the first time so we'll briefly discuss how to deal with this type of situation.

Keep in mind that prior to this meeting you've created a positive learning climate. When the participant displayed disruptive or disengaged behavior, you did the check-in intervention. When that didn't change the behavior, you set up a private feedback meeting with him. Despite his agreements in that meeting, Jamie's disruptive behavior soon reappeared. So now you are having a level 3, private confrontation meeting, with him, in which you will follow a procedure similar to what you used in the level 2, private feedback meeting.

There are two differences between the way a trainer would communicate in a level-2 meeting and how to communicate most effectively in a level-3 meeting:

1. The trainer will now use stronger body language and a firmer tone of voice than was used in the level-2 meeting.

2. The trainer now focuses on the broken agreement rather than the disruptive behaviors. There are two reasons for focusing this conversation on the broken agreement rather than on the disruptive behavior:

    a. You want to be sure that in the future Jamie realizes that when the two of you have an agreement, it's a serious commitment that you expect to be honored.

    b. When he follows through on this agreement, he will, in the process, stop the distracting behaviors in the workshop.

At the meeting, the trainer states the agreement:

"When you and I have an agreement about what I will do to make the class more useful to you and what you will do to participate in a more positive way . . ."

then states the problem:

". . . and you don't do your part,. . ."

then states how she feels about the negative effect on herself:

". . .it's frustrating because I have a tougher job teaching and the class is held back from learning all that it could."

The trainer then listens with the same respect and effort to understand Jamie as in the previous meeting. She waits for him to either renew their original agreement or to modify it with a change that's acceptable to her.

The trainer explains that if Jamie doesn't abide by this agreement, there is no benefit to his being in the class so he's free to leave. Tell him that you will have to notify his supervisor (or whoever signed Jamie up for the workshop) about Jamie's incompletion of the class.

Level 4: Termination of Training Meeting

As we never had an occasion to engage in a level-3 intervention, we've never needed to implement level 4 either. But it's comforting to know that you have this option in your hip pocket if the need should arise.

Ending participation might occur at level 3, depending on how disruptive the participant is.

Here's Level 4 in a nutshell. When a trainer has acted appropriately at the first three levels of intervention and there has been no improvement in the participant's behavior, the trainer has a final meeting with the participant to let him know that as a consequence of his continued disruption in the class he will have to leave the training immediately, and his supervisor or other contact person will be notified of his departure and the reasons for it.

This final meeting has two of the same characteristics of previous interventions—discussing behavior in a non-blameful, non-accusatory way, and treating the participant with respect through listening open-mindedly to understand his perspective. However, the third characteristic—inviting the participant to come up with his solution—is no longer an option. The decision that he has to leave the training and that his supervisor will be notified has been made and was communicated clearly.

When a trainer has these four levels of potent interventions to work with, she doesn't have to become a victim in her own classroom. She can maintain a good relationship with the class while respectfully and effectively intervening when an individual engages in disruptive behavior.

24

Observing Group Process and Intervening to Improve Its Functioning

Where observation is concerned, chance favors only the prepared mind.

——Louis Pasteur[1]

You've already read about group process in Chapter 2 as well as in many of the other chapters describing methods and attitudes that promote positive group process. In fact, you can prevent many potential workshop difficulties by employing competencies described throughout this book

The ability to generate effective group process and to repair a faltering one is a key ability that separates a first-rate trainer from a mediocre trainer. Since this is such a crucial aspect of training, we'll do a mini-review of the difference between content and process. Then you'll see that rather than focus your attention primarily on delivering the course content, it's important to also be proactive in generating positive group process. Next, we'll discuss what to look for when observing group process and how to intervene when group process is deteriorating and interfering with learning.

The Difference Between Content and Group Process

Content is what is taught: it's the subject matter of the workshop—the concepts, attitudes, methods, and/or skills that are to be learned.

Process focuses on how the training group is functioning. It's composed of two related aspects of group experience:

- The emotions the individuals in the group are experiencing
- The ever-fluctuating interaction of participants as they encounter each other, the workshop content, and the trainer

Process is always present in training and inevitably contributes to or detracts from learning.

Be Proactive in Generating Positive Group Process

Trainers generally have considerable content to deliver and, unless there's a crisis in the group, the typical workshop leader focuses the bulk of his attention and energy on delivering the content well. In the meantime, he's apt to pay scant attention to group process. However, the research is clear: good group process facilitates learning; poor group process undermines learning. So a high priority of savvy trainers is to be proactive in developing positive process in their workshops.

A trainer who is focusing on generating positive group process asks himself questions such as the following:

"What can I do to increase participants' comfort with what we're doing?"

"What can I do to get participants more involved?"

"Would a change of pace increase the group's energy?"

"Does the group need a break?"

And well before any problems appear, he asks the group some checking questions:

"How are things going so far?"

"Have I been clear about this?"

"How useful does this seem to you?"

"Is there something you would like to add?"

How to "Read" Group Process

When taking the pulse of a group, look for the following:

- Indicators of positive process
- Indicators of mediocre process
- Indicators of negative process

Indicators of Positive Process

When a group's process is effective, it is characterized by attentiveness, high energy, humor, and questions to clarify anything that is not understood—in short by good "vibes." There's also a general camaraderie among participants. This is the kind of group in which learning is enjoyable, positive relationships are formed, and people complete the workshop with a sense of accomplishment and motivation to do better on the job. Although when leading webinars, group process is harder to read and is less front and center than in a workshop, it is still important to remain aware of process, as you'll see later in the chapter.

Indicators of Mediocre Process

In a group with mediocre process, people take a "wait and see" attitude. There's a minimum of either positive or negative contributions. People may be simply marking time until they decide whether or not this training is worthwhile. Although a few participants may be attentive and interacting, the group is emotionally flat; blah.

Indicators of Negative Process

When several of the characteristics and behaviors listed below are present, the group you are working with is exhibiting negative process and it's likely that learning has deteriorated significantly. When signs of negative process begin to appear, they're often nonverbal. If they're not addressed quickly and successfully, you're likely to soon find yourself coping with vocal criticism of the course and/or yourself.

Nonverbal Indicators of Negative Process

When group process has deteriorated significantly some or all of the following symptoms will appear:

1. Low level of energy. Participants slump in their chair, yawn, sigh, and show little positive emotion. A listless quietness settles over the group.
2. Slow to move into activity, practice, or discussion groups. Participants take unnecessary time to gather their materials, get up from their chairs, find a partner, and settle into their activity, practice, or discussion.
3. Late in returning on time from breaks and lunch. Although timing guidelines have been presented clearly, a pattern emerges in which a number of participants repeatedly straggle in several minutes late.
4. Subgroups may form. Discontented students often cluster together in ways that retard workshop cohesion and performance.
5. Overt lack of interest in the workshop. Several people look out the window or leaf aimlessly through the materials to show their lack of interest and boredom. Someone might be reading the newspaper during your presentations.
6. Lack of eye contact. There is little eye contact with the trainer or with other participants.
7. Avoidance of the trainer during breaks or lunchtime. A number of participants make it clear through their blatant avoidance that they are not going to interact with the trainer.

Verbal indicators of Negative Process

1. Little verbal participation or group interaction. Few trainees make comments or ask or answer questions. During practice sessions, many chat rather than practice.
2. Making excuses. Participants are far more likely than usual to make excuses for arriving late, leaving early, or not completing classwork or homework.
3. Being argumentative. Participants debate excessively, contradict, and assume a challenging point of view regarding much of the workshop content.
4. Attacks on the course. Some participants may derogatively refer to the training as "charm school" and proclaim that what's being taught will never work in the "real world."
5. Inappropriate humor. Sarcasm directed at the trainer and or the course content.
6. Verbal attacks on the trainer. Occasionally, the situation may turn so ugly that a few of the more hostile participants attempt to discredit the trainer as a person who is unqualified to lead the workshop. Or they may put him down in other ways either publically or in private conversations.

Dealing with Negative Group Process

One of the biggest mistakes a trainer can make is to pretend that nothing is wrong in a workshop when everyone knows that things are going badly: the trainer knows, the participants know, and anyone just dropping in would know. So why would a trainer ignore the obvious problems and not address the situation?

Fear and ignorance often combine to be a formidable influence to do nothing. The ignorance is about not knowing how to handle the difficult situation. And the fear is of the bad things that could happen if the trainer addressed the problem in the group. If fear and ignorance win out when dealing with negative group process, the workshop will soon plummet out of control.

Learning to identify negative process and mastering the skill of successfully intervening when the group is floundering will banish whatever ignorance and fear a trainer may have about dealing with negative group process.

The Seven-Step Method for Restoring Positive Group Process

Although you have worked diligently to create a positive group process, as we've discussed, there'll be times when you find yourself leading a group in which many members are using nonverbal as well as verbal behaviors that negatively affect group process. You realize that you'll have to intervene to restore positive process. Here's a time-tested way to proceed:

1. Observe the behavior of the participants.
2. Stop teaching, pull a chair to the front of the group and the center of the room, and sit down.
3. Say what you see and invite a response.
4. Listen attentively until everyone who wants to have a say has said it.
5. Summarize the problem and invite problem solving.
6. Evaluate the solutions and gain agreement on any emerging redesign adjustments.
7. Close, and take a brief break.

1. Observe the Behavior of the Participants

The ability to distinguish between a behavior and an inference is essential for this step of the intervention. As noted in our book, *People Styles at Work . . . and Beyond,* second edition:

> Behavior is what a person does that can be seen and heard and therefore is observable. Behavior includes posture, gestures, facial expressions, the actions we take, and so forth. . . . There are many inner qualities that lie beneath the surface—thoughts, feelings, attitudes, motives, beliefs, and values. These inner qualities cannot be observed. No one can know for sure what's taking place in someone's inner world. We can only infer—guess—what someone else is thinking or feeling.
>
> . . . When asked to observe and then describe behavior, people often report inferences. In our workshops, for example, before defining and giving examples of the distinction between observation and inference, a trainer often explains that he will do some behaviors and afterward will ask participants to describe the behaviors they observe. The trainer will then take some action like stomping across the room while shouting and shaking a fist. When asked what behaviors they observed most people tell the trainer, "You were angry." Without realizing it, they stated their inference (that the trainer was angry) instead of reporting the trainer's behaviors (stomping across the room and shaking a fist).

When observing a group, focus your observation strictly on behavior. Avoid the tendency to jump from observation of behavior to assuming what thoughts or feelings may be driving the behavior. You may automatically make inferences about what triggered the behavior; but don't include those inferences in your description of the behavior.

2. Stop Teaching, Pull a Chair to the Front of the Group and the Center of the Room, and Sit Down

When you decide to intervene, stop teaching. Become silent. Typically you will have been standing in the front of the room. When you shift to sitting down, it signals that something different is about to happen and participant's attention is heightened.

3. Say What You See and Invite a Response

Here's how to say what you see and invite a response in a training program. Describe the behavior that's interfering with the learning. For example, "I noticed that some of you are coming back late from breaks, others move very slowly into work groups, and there's no discussion of the questions I raise. This leads me to think that I'm missing the mark with you." When saying what you see, make it clear, nonjudgmental, and brief.

Then ask for the group's help in understanding what's happening. Asking for it might sound like this: "Help me understand what's going on." Then discipline yourself to remain silent until someone responds to your request.

Typically, everyone will be silent for a while. You may be tempted to fill the void by saying more about what you are asking and why. If you give in to that urge, you'll undercut your intervention. If you remain silent, someone will speak up.

4. Listen Attentively Until Everyone Who Wants to Have a Say Has Said It

As you hear the various responses you may feel your defensiveness rising. However, this is not the time to justify yourself or the workshop. Nor is it the time to agree or disagree with what's being said. Instead, use the skills of listening that you learned in Chapter 12. No matter what comes up, continue listening until you sense that the group is finished. To be sure that everyone who wants to speak has spoken, at what seems to be the end of the sharing, you can ask, "Anyone else?"

5. Summarize the Problem and Invite Problem Solving

If five or six people are talking about the same problem but saying it differently, make an integrated statement of the issue. Add to that statement any other problems that were raised. For example, "It seems that several of you feel overloaded in your work and that attending this training is causing you some stress. Others feel frustrated because you've already taken training with some of this content. A third piece of the problem seems to be . . . "

Thank the group for their openness. Then say, "I think if we put our heads together we can come up with some ideas to get us back on track. How can we work this out?" Say it optimistically; show that you have confidence that the group members have the ability to solve the problems they just described.

If you have ideas about how to solve the problems that were raised, hold back and let the group solve the problem. The group's ownership of the problems and the solutions will motivate participants to make them work. If a suggestion is made that would be unacceptable to the client or to you, say so. However, wait until the end of the discussion when you and the group are evaluating the solutions. If you interrupt the flow of ideas with comments about what will and won't work, you'll reduce the group's problem-solving momentum. As the discussion is winding down, if you have something to contribute, this is a good time to say it.

6. Evaluate the Solutions and Gain Agreement on Any Emerging Redesign Adjustments

Invite the group to put together ideas that will meet the needs of the group, the trainer, and the client (whose needs will usually be voiced by the trainer since the client is unlikely to be in the room). Write the final product on an easel chart for future reference.

7. Close, and Take a Brief Break

This is a time to signal that the interaction is over. Thank the participants for their help. A break (typically ten minutes) gives both the trainer and the group a bit of time to shift gears. The trainer can use some of this time to figure out how to start making some of the changes that the group called for and how to get back on schedule. As far as possible incorporate what the group decided to change as soon as you can. That will demonstrate that you are taking the group's input seriously.

Chapter 25 discusses dealing with this kind of situation, which if you are a career trainer you'll undoubtedly experience from time to time.

Trusting the Method

Course leaders in our training firm were taught the seven-step method described above. The crux of the training followed our regular teaching method that's described in Chapter 3: tell how, show how with debriefing, practice, and feedback.

Tell how: The leader described a situation in which the participants were disruptive and disengaged and described how to handle such a situation successfully.

Show how: The leader demonstrated the method with the other trainers acting as participants in the class and then debriefed the demonstration.

Practice: Each trainer practiced the method using the other trainers as their participants.

Feedback: The trainers who were acting as participants gave feedback to the practicing trainer.

Each trainer had one practice as well as the opportunity to observe each of the nine other trainers practice and receive feedback.

The following week, a team of two from this group was scheduled to co-lead a workshop: Louise, with years of experience in the lead role, and the second trainer, Bob, prepared and capable but inexperienced.

Within the first hour of the training it was clear that this group was not willing to participate in a constructive way. On the first break the trainers huddled. Louise summarized the challenge they faced and began searching for solutions. Bob listened, then suggested that they use the seven-step method they learned last week.

"Are you serious? I'm not facing this contentious group with a method I've never used before," Louise responded.

Silence followed. Then Bob said, "I think I learned the method pretty well and I'm willing to use it if you think it's worth a shot."

After weighing the options, Louise gave her okay.

When the participants reluctantly returned to class, Bob pulled his chair to the front of the room and sat down. He observed the group until everyone was settled in their seats and giving their full attention. Then Bob said what he had been seeing: "I noticed that many of you were not making eye contact with either Louise or me when we were presenting the course material. Some of you were thumbing through books, while a couple of people were reading newspapers. Others were looking out the window or had their eyes closed. Can you help me understand what's happening?"

Bob waited silently for a response. He did not rephrase the question nor did he use any techniques to encourage an answer. After a little over thirty seconds a participant named Jack said, "It's not that anything is exactly happening. We're just not a gung-ho group."

"Just a generally quiet group" Bob reflected.

"You've got that right," said Jack.

Bob waited through another long pause.

"This is getting pretty silly." said Alice.

"A little ridiculous," reflected Bob.

"Well yes," continued Alice, "I mean we're all adults here. Why can't we just tell him the truth? He happened to hit us with this training at a particularly sensitive time."

"Timing for this training is way off," Bob reflected.

"I would have told Bob that," said Jack, "but I wasn't sure how everyone would feel about discussing this salary dispute in class. Maybe we should just move on and forget about it."

"Some things might be better left unsaid," Bob reflected.

"Or maybe not," Kevin interjected. "It looks like we're going to waste a whole day of training if it continues like this."

"Seems like the group has a choice about how to proceed," Bob reflected. He paused briefly and added, "How are we going to solve this problem?"

The participants vented some of their anger about the company trying to rene-gotiate a new wage scale when the employees thought that was a done deal. After discussing a bit they decided that the training room might not be the best place to deal with that problem and agreed to set the wage dispute aside for now and get down to the business of learning the content of the workshop.

Bob summarized the agreement, thanked the group for their forthrightness, and announced a break before resuming the training. The group returned from the break filled with lively conversation and ready to participate in the remainder of the train-ing program.

Bob's ability to describe the group's behavior, his nonjudgmental tone of voice, and his neutral facial expression lowered the group's tension and kept their defen-siveness from rising. When he waited for someone to respond he was able to be patient because of his confidence that someone would eventually speak. Without this foundation undergirding the seven-step method, the likelihood of success is limited.

A participant wrote in the final evaluation, "The highlight of the workshop for me was when Bob sat down with the group and had a frank discussion about the fact that things weren't going well. I see that this is a great ability for me as a super-visor to have."

The news of that incident spread through our trainer network. In describing the episode to her colleagues in our training network, Louise said that an unforgettable learning from that episode was to "trust the method." Before long the phrase "trust the method" had become a catch phrase for using the seven-step method whenever positive group process was seriously eroding.

PART IV

MATURING AS A TRAINER

25

Redesigning a Troubled Workshop While Teaching It

If you want to give God a good laugh, tell Him your plans.

——Yiddish Proverb

Wouldn't it be great if every workshop you led was a roaring success, if every participant wanted to be there, and if every course you taught was well-designed and a perfect fit for the group? You'll enjoy that type of experience when leading many workshops.

But some courses you lead will undoubtedly be poorly designed. On other occasions, you may have a well-designed course but one that's not a good fit for the group you're leading. Later in this chapter we'll describe a number of other troublesome factors that can undermine the effectiveness of your workshop. Due to factors like these, an important training skill is being adept at revising the workshop design at the same time you are teaching the course. This process is often termed *emergent redesign*. In this chapter we discuss these issues:

- What is emergent redesign?
- Situations that require emergent redesign
- The foundations of emergent redesign
- A three-step method for rescuing a troubled workshop
- Redesigning prior to the workshop

The chapter concludes with a brief discussion of adapting the course to the participants prior to the opening of the workshop, when time is available.

What Is Emergent Redesign?

Sometimes when a redesign is needed, you don't have the luxury of redesigning the course prior to delivering it. You may be asked to lead the course on the spur of the moment because the trainer who was scheduled to teach it called in sick. Or you may not know about serious morale problems in the unit the participants are drawn from, which are negatively affecting their involvement in the workshop you are leading. When problems like these surface during a workshop, emergent redesign is imperative.

The American Heritage Dictionary of the English Language defines emergent as "occurring as a consequence of." In training, emergent redesign is called for when a group feels that its needs are not being met and, as a consequence of its dissatisfaction, balks at participating constructively in the training. The group's discontent is palpable. The trainer recognizes that the needs of the group are not being met and that it's time to take a detour from the original workshop design. It's a bit like when you are driving and come upon an unexpected detour sign on the highway. At first you are surprised. Then you take in the information, make the necessary adjustments, and go on.

Situations That Require Emergent Redesign

Here are a handful of examples of situations that we or our colleagues faced that required emergent redesign:

- A group of customer representatives (reps), who chose their field because they did not want to sell, were put in a sales course. Their management wanted the reps to be able to respond effectively to sales opportunities that arose during customer service calls. The reps were irate and were completely closed to learning what the trainers were expected to teach. (This situation is described more fully in Chapter 1.)
- A group of supervisors, in conflict with their managers who were initiating many unwelcome changes, were livid about being sent to a two-day Change Management workshop.
- A group of graduate students at Notre Dame were scheduled for a Communication Skills workshop that conflicted with an on-campus UCLA vs. Notre Dame basketball game during March Madness.
- During a major corporate downsizing, a group of managers who were struggling with the firing of many of their employees were scheduled for a Management Communication Skills course. The managers wanted to get more help on these difficult conversations along with what was already in the course.

We're embarrassed to mention these examples because none of those snafus would have occurred if we had done a good job of installing the training. After a few of these mishaps, we learned our lesson and became diligent about effectively installing every training program so that these preventable mishaps would not happen. Appendix III discusses what we learned about installation.

The Foundations of Effective Emergent Redesign

There are two prerequisites for being competent at emergent redesign:

- You must know your material thoroughly.
- You must be keenly attuned to the group process you are working with.

Both of these fundamentals require preparation.

Know Your Material Thoroughly

The trainer needs to be so soundly prepared that he can improvise his way through unpredictable and challenging situations and still maintain the constancy of purpose to achieve the goals of the course. Thorough preparation provides a base from which you can improvise while retaining a sense of where you've been in relation to where you are and where you need to be.

Awareness of Group Process

While solid planning is essential to doing emergent redesign, the ability to face facts and the flexibility to adjust to the current reality are just as vital. Chapter 24 discussed how to ascertain what the problem is and how to deal with it. Many times the issue will be that the group's needs are not being met in some ways. When the problem is aired, the stage is set for emergent redesign.

A Three-Step Method for Rescuing a Troubled Workshop

One of the essential abilities of a good trainer is the ability to salvage a dying workshop. When a workshop is in trouble, do the following:

1. Listen diagnostically. The crucial first step in redesign is listening attentively to participant's dissatisfaction with the course. You learned (or revisited) the essential training skill of reflective listening in Chapter 12. You'll now see how to apply that skill to rescue a troubled workshop.
2. Know the changes that can make a positive impact. When doing emergent redesign, the trainer typically alters one or more of the following:
   a. The pacing of the workshop
   b. The activities employed

    c. The length of the training or other scheduling changes

    d. The content

    e. The methods

    One of the big challenges of emergent redesign is that these adjustments are made in real time—during workshop hours and with the participants present.

3. Invite participants to partner in the workshop redesign. You have the best resources to help you do an effective redesign sitting right in the workshop. Invite participants into the redesign process by asking for their ideas of how to make their time in this workshop more productive. For example:

    "Within a broad definition of this course, what would be most useful for you to learn?"

    "Let's share some thoughts about what it is you really need to benefit from this course."

    "What do we have to do to make this workshop worthwhile for you?"

Redesigning Prior to the Workshop

The workshop has been selected, scheduled, and assigned to an experienced in-house trainer. The trainer begins preparation and becomes uneasy because he sees that the course material is neither well designed nor a good fit for the group. Any trainer charged with delivering a workshop that's poorly designed and/or ill-suited for the group is facing a major challenge. These types of problems are best addressed during the selection and initial adaptation of the course—well before the trainer begins preparing to deliver the course. In some cases, however, this just doesn't happen and the ill-fitting workshop becomes the trainer's problem.

When a trainer begins preparing to lead a workshop and discovers that presentations are not applicable enough to participant's needs, or that not enough time is devoted to practice, or that two of the activities are in another course that some participants in the target population have already taken, she knows that there's plenty of redesign work ahead. Appendix II describes how to do that proficiently.

The good news is that if the trainer started her course preparation early enough, there is still time to make changes that will improve a lackluster course dramatically. As President John F. Kennedy said, "The time to repair the roof is when the sun is shining."

26

Avoiding Trainer Defensiveness

The play was a great success, but the audience was a disaster.

——Oscar Wilde, playwright

Like resistance in participants, defensiveness in trainers is a protective strategy to ward off anticipated, perceived, or real attacks. It's an effort to guard yourself against actual or imagined criticism, injury to your ego, or exposure of your shortcomings. People don't plan to be defensive—it just seems to pop out of them. Even so, as you'll see in this chapter, there's much you can do to manage your defensiveness effectively.

Being human, we all have our defensive moments; to some degree we resemble the New Testament lawyer who, "desiring to justify himself, said . . . "[1]

Each of us has been somewhat defensive all our lives, beginning in the preschool years. When a parent tells a young child, "Stop hitting your brother," the probable response— regardless of the facts of the situation—will be, "I didn't do anything" or "He started it." When you stop to think about it, most of us have had decades of practice at being self-protective. So defensiveness is in each of us waiting to be aroused.

At times, defensiveness does us a real service. That's why it remains part of our evolutionary heritage. When people are mercilessly critical or uncaringly judgmental, defensiveness typically comes to our aid and blunts the withering attacks. It's a great ally when needed. As therapist Howard Clinebell points out, "All of us have and need defenses to cope with the pressures and crises of our lives. . . . It is important to remember that people *have* defenses because they still *need* them, or believe they do."[2]

However, we're all inappropriately defensive at times. And some people have developed more than average self-protectiveness. Until you've learned to handle excessive defensiveness, it's like a time bomb waiting to explode. Sooner or later, the trainer who hasn't mastered his defensiveness will surely fail in the training room.

Consequences of Excessive Trainer Defensiveness

When a trainer experiences disproportionate self-protectiveness, and instead devotes her energy to shielding herself or defending the content she is presenting, she's in trouble. It is important to realize that when we're triggered, as the saying has it, "We don't have our defenses, they have us."

Typically, when the trainer is defensive everybody loses—participants suffer through an unsatisfactory workshop and the trainer has a failed leadership experience.

Managing your defensiveness can be one of the biggest challenges you'll face in your work as a trainer. Sooner or later, the trainer who hasn't learned to handle her defensiveness will surely fail in the training room. The good news is that trainer defensiveness can be diminished and much of the remaining defensiveness can be managed by using the methods described in this chapter.

As your awareness of the dynamics of defensiveness increases, your ability to function in less defensive ways should increase, with the result that your workshop leadership becomes more productive and your participants' learning is greatly enhanced.

Two Types of Defensiveness—Chronic and Triggered

It's useful to distinguish between

- chronic defensiveness and
- triggered defensiveness.

Chronic Defensiveness

A person with chronic defensiveness is considerably more susceptible than the average person to being wary about the intentions and behaviors of others and behaves accordingly. Chronic defensiveness tends to generate self-protective behavior before the trainer even meets the participants; he's armored as he waits for them arrive. When participants begin filtering into the room, he reacts to a number of them based on past experiences with people they remind him of. He behaves more warmly to some, more distantly toward others—often irrespective of their attitude toward the workshop or the trainer. In other words, chronic defensiveness can be preemptive as well as reactive.

Subtly the defensive vicious cycle described by Jack Gibb is initiated. Participants aren't drawn to the trainer. The trainer becomes a bit more defensive, doesn't connect with the trainees, gets busy arranging materials, and finally begins to go through the motions of training. It's hard to relate well to others when you're focused on yourself. The defensive trainer's self-protectiveness inches toward scuttling the effectiveness of the workshop. Consequently, a chronically defensive trainer will tend to have one mediocre to poor training experience after another.

Triggered Defensiveness

A trainer with triggered defensiveness tends to be reasonably non-defensive most of the time. Sometimes, however, situational factors—certain persons or certain situations—are apt to trigger his defensiveness. However, as you'll soon see, our defensive incidents aren't caused by something outside of us. What's "out there" is merely a stimulus—a trigger—rather than what caused the defensive reaction. For instance, an incident that hooks us at one time might not bother us at all at another time. And although certain people and situations may have a greater likelihood of inciting defensiveness in you or us, other people may not be ruffled by them at all.

When a trainer experiences disproportionate self-protectiveness, he tends to shift from trying to understand what participants are experiencing and instead devotes his energy to shielding himself or defending the content he is presenting. It's important to realize that when we're triggered, "we don't have our defenses, *they have us.*"[3]

When Defensiveness Encounters Resistance—The Push-Pushback Phenomenon

Self-protective behavior in one person tends to increase self-protectiveness in other people. And, sure enough, in our field, trainer defensiveness is often triggered by participant resistance. Here's an example: A participant has had a negative reaction to a new process that the trainer was presenting to use in his work. The participant looked uninterested and vigorously shook his head from side to side, indicating his strong disagreement. A few minutes later he butted into the presentation saying in a sarcastic tone, "Have you ever been down to see how our department works?"

That pushed the trainer's button and he said, "What's that got to do with what I'm presenting?"

The trainer's response stiffened the participant's resistance, which in turn boosted the trainer's defensiveness. The pattern continued as the participant's intensified resistance generated more defensiveness in the trainer. A vicious cycle had been set in motion; real communication stopped, and the interaction became a kind of "king of the hill" scuffle.

To demonstrate this type of dynamic, course leaders in the Craft of Training workshops sometimes do a demonstration of what's been referred to as the push-pushback phenomenon. The demo goes like this:

Introduction: "I need a volunteer to do a brief nonverbal demonstration with me. It will take only forty seconds, you won't have to say a word, and you are guaranteed success."

[Wait for the volunteer.]

Directions: "Put palms of both hands out in front of you at shoulder height, making a stop signal. I am going to do something and I want you to respond by doing whatever comes naturally."

Activity: Place your hands against the volunteer's hands and push. If the volunteer backs up, move with him and keep pushing. The volunteer will eventually push back—if only because he is up against the wall.

As soon as the volunteer visibly pushes back against you, stop the activity and give the volunteer a round of applause.

Debriefing: Ask the volunteer, "What just happened? Did you stop to think, 'Hey this person is pushing me. I'll stop this. I'll push back'?"

The answer is always, "No." So, without thinking, the volunteer pushed back.

The trainer then says to the group, "When resistance occurs, it's generally an automatic reaction rather than a conscious decision. So don't take it personally. And don't hold it against the person."

The push-pushback phenomenon can also occur between a group and the trainer. Group members may be unresponsive to the trainer's questions, may drag their feet when asked to do an activity, or demonstrate by other actions or words that they don't want to take part in the workshop. When the trainer notes that, but pretends nothing unusual is happening, he has begun his defensive response. He pretends to ignore what's going on but begins to justify or overexplain the main points of his presentation. Or, he may withdraw into himself and rush through material just to get it over with. In a defensive mode the trainer will do everything but deal with what is actually happening, gain cooperation in identifying the real problem, and work effectively to address it.

One of the biggest mistakes a trainer can make is to pretend that nothing is wrong in the workshop when everybody knows things are going badly. The trainer knows, the participants know, and anybody just dropping by would know. So, why would a trainer ignore the obvious and persevere even under these terrible conditions? Because his defensiveness kicked in due to fear and ignorance:

Fear of the unknown—what bad things would happen if he really faced the problem?

Ignorance—not knowing how to handle the tough situation even if he acknowledged it.

Fear and ignorance create a powerful force that leads many trainers to become anxious and deny the problem. Reactive trainer defensiveness is the beginning of the death of a workshop.

Forewarned Is Forearmed

Here's another type of preparation that leaders of the Craft of Training workshops sometimes use to help trainer-participants avoid being hooked by their defensiveness. They ask the trainer-participants to think of a person who triggered them in a workshop or in daily life. Then each person briefly describes what it was about that person that "got" to them. That activity generates lots of insights—and much hilarity. Among other lessons, it quickly becomes apparent that what triggers one trainer might not faze another trainer at all.

Once a trainer is aware of the kind of person or persons he's apt to be hooked by, he can act preventively. For example, he can be proactive in establishing a relationship with that sort of person as early in the workshop as possible.

Methods of Managing Triggered Defensiveness

There are two general approaches to managing one's defensiveness:

1. Prevention: take steps to avoid being triggered.
2. Learn the six ways of managing your defensiveness once your self-protectiveness begins to interfere with your training—or other aspects of your life.

Prevention: Take Steps to Avoid Being Triggered

The saying *an ounce of prevention is worth a pound of cure* applies in spades to keeping your defensiveness from interfering with your training. Although these common-sense guidelines have been mentioned earlier, it's worth briefly repeating the following three ways of enhancing your management of defensiveness before entering the training room:

1. Be well rested.
2. Be in good physical condition.
3. Have your tension level under control.

If you open a workshop feeling fatigued, with low stamina, and a fair amount of tension in your body, you're more vulnerable to becoming defensive. You just don't have what it takes to stand on your feet for eight hours a day, presenting and relating to twenty to twenty-five people. Instead, enter the workshop well-rested, with high energy, and good spirits. That will take you a long way in keeping your defensiveness low and managing it if you feel it beginning to creep up on you.

Know Your Material

The first few times of teaching a new workshop, you're more vulnerable to defensiveness than if you're an old hand at it. You might skip a key point, your presentations don't hang together the way you want them to, or you get a question that you don't know how to answer. Your confidence may go out the window and your defensiveness is likely to surge.

To prevent this from happening when you teach a new course, you want to be at ease in all aspects of leading the course: presentations, demonstrations, activities, and skill practices. You want to know the big picture of the course and have command of the details. This investment up front in your course preparation will pay big dividends—especially if difficult people challenge you or other negative events materialize.

Excel at Creating and Maintaining a Positive Learning Climate

Trainers who are able to develop a supportive, friendly, and open classroom seldom have to manage their defensiveness. That's because the learning climate they've created decreases the participants' resistance and helps things run smoothly. Chapter 22 contains most of what you need to know about this subject.

Be Okay with Not Being Perfect

As Rosalynn Carter said, "Once you accept the fact that you're not perfect, then you develop some confidence."

What to Do When You Sense You're Getting Hooked

When it comes to defensiveness, prevention is the strategy of choice. But since we're human, there'll undoubtedly be times when you get hooked by a participant. Here are six ways of managing these situations. Four are internal—ways of thinking and managing your self-talk. When using the other two methods the trainer deals with the whole group. It's sometimes useful to combine two or more methods.

Work on Yourself

The first four methods are done internally: nothing is mentioned to the participants about the triggering incident or your reaction to it.

1. Maintain Your Professionalism

As a trainer, when you stand up in front of a class, you have left behind the luxury of allowing yourself to be triggered by a cantankerous individual, a vocally hostile subgroup, or even a whole class of uncooperative people. When the going is difficult, remind yourself that you are a professional—and that a professional is a person who "rules his spirit."[4]

Japan's Sadaharu Oh was one of the greatest baseball players of his time. In his autobiography he described his thoughts and feelings as he stood alone in the locker room in the moments immediately before his last game. He was crying and gripping his cap so tightly in both hands that he was in danger of tearing it. He was clearly in no condition to go out on the field.

He tells us what happened next:

> I am a professional baseball player, I told myself. A professional. The word has meaning for me as few others in my vocabulary do. There is a standard performance you must maintain. It is the best you are able to give and then more—and to maintain that level of consistency. No excuses for the demands of your ego or the extremes of your emotions. It's an inner thing. I held myself to that standard for twenty-two years. It is my proudest achievement.

Impressive, right? Yet no less is expected of a professional trainer. As a professional, when leading a workshop you have given up the option of reacting in a defensive mode against a person who triggers you. Your role is to strive to protect every participant's well-being, including the well-being of the person or persons who may be disrupting the workshop. A key to doing that is to try to treat everyone in the workshop in an approximately equal but not identical way.

It's important to note that if you defensively push-back against a triggering participant the group may turn against you. They'll see that you are using your power as group leader against a person in a weaker position. Hold yourself to the high professional standard of not getting triggered into using behavior that you'll be sorry for.

2. Manage Your Self-Talk

Understanding how self-talk works can be very helpful in managing the kinds of feelings that often activate trainer defensiveness. Basic to the self-talk concept is the assumption that the feelings you experience in consequence of what another person says or does may be less about the incident itself than it is about how you interpret the meaning of the incident. This interpretation of the event is called self-talk since it is what you say to yourself about the incident.

A stands for Activating event that occurred.

B stands for trainer's Belief about the the meaning of the event.

C stands for the Consequence which is the trainer's feelings of defensiveness triggered by the Belief.

D stands for the trainer's resulting Defensive reaction.

The radical aspect of this concept for trainers is that our feelings of defensiveness that we often think are triggered by a participant's disruptive behavior are really triggered by what we say to ourselves about the disruptive behavior. Contrary to common opinion, psychologists have found that our feelings and the behaviors they tend to generate are not caused by the other person's behaviors but by our inner thoughts about the situation.

Making your self-talk more accurate and constructive generally leads to more productive feelings which lowers your defensiveness and enables you to cope better with difficult people and challenging situations. For example, in a Train the Trainer workshop, a class member described a time when her defensiveness was hooked:

A, the event:

"One participant in a People Skills for Managers workshop spoke more often, longer, and with stronger opinions than other participants. He dominated group discussions and interrupted my presentations with long comments—like how to redesign the agreement practice which I had just led!"

B, the self-talk:

"Oh my God; here we go again. This guy is out to get me. Talk about rude. . . ."

C, the resulting feelings:

"In a defensive, self-protective mode I felt impatient and non-accepting of him."

D, the trainer's consequent defensive reaction:

"When he spoke I tensed up. I tended to avoid eye contact with him and was more abrupt in dealing with him than I was with others in the class."

Here's how the trainer could have used self-talk to alter her frame of mind about the situation and come up with a more effective way to manage the interaction regarding the same event:

B, the self-talk:

This participant has not yet learned how to be an effective member of a group—that it's not okay to dominate, interrupt, and sidetrack what we're focusing on. It would be good if I could help him eliminate or decrease that kind of behavior. For now, I'll just deal with his sidetracking (redesigning workshop exercises). I'll have to think more about how to show him an option to use instead of dominating and interrupting.

C, the resulting feelings:

Relieved to have a plan of action—just deal with his sidetracking for now.

D, the trainer's non-defensive response:

"Sounds like you have some interesting ideas. Could we talk about them on break so we can finish our work on getting agreements?"

3. Reframe the Situation

Reframing involves looking at a situation from a different point of view. Barlow and Moller's book, *A Complaint Is a Gift*, provides a useful way of reframing participant's criticisms. As they put it, "The criticism we receive probably has some truth in it, even if it feels unfair or like an attack."[5]

It's often been said that you can learn more from your enemies than from your friends. So when a disgruntled trainee criticizes you, listen up.

4. Suppress Your Defensiveness

Suppression involves consciously but temporarily pushing certain thoughts and feelings to the back of your mind until you have the time and energy to deal with them.

A therapist described how he uses suppression when he's counseling people. When he finds himself beginning to get distracted, he says:

> I temporarily put those thoughts and feelings on hold. . . . I conjure up an image of an empty chair and seat whatever I want to put on hold in that chair. In my mind I say to my anger, frustration, anxiety. . . , "I hear you. Now sit here and be quiet. I'll get back to you later."

Suppression involves consciously ignoring an incident, thought, or feeling for the time being—until you are free to think about or deal with it. Suppression is a great tool for trainers for dealing with trainer defensiveness.

Although the trainer is cognizant of the problem, he makes a decision to set the problem aside and not deal with it. Your defensiveness is lowered when you decide that you are not going to enter into an argument, or give a person a dirty look, or in some other way show your displeasure with what was said. Suppression too helps you maintain your professionalism.

When You Choose to Reply

The remaining two methods are ways of handling situations that come up in the whole group and generally are best dealt with in and to the whole group.

5. Neutrally Acknowledge a Participant's Hostile Comments

When someone makes a remark that you perceive as attacking and you feel your defensiveness rising, the simplest thing to do is to acknowledge the comment and move on. Here are a few examples of neutrally acknowledging a participant's antagonistic remarks:

"I hear you."

"I see."

"Thanks."

"Thanks for telling me. I know that's not easy."

This type of courteous response enables the participant to feel that he was heard without your having agreed or disagreed with him. And, although you take the information in as feedback, you don't consume valuable class time with your comments and the possibility of an unnecessary dialogue that likely will only be of interest to one of your twenty or more participants.

It's not wise to reflect his comments at this point because the participant might take that as an opportunity to continue her attack.

6. Reply Non-Defensively to Criticism

A participant's body language had made it clear that he was dissatisfied with the workshop. After a while he spoke up:

Participant:

I don't know how much homework you've done on our company, but it doesn't seem like you know what we're all about. If you are going to teach people, it would help for you to get smart about the history of the company, what made us successful, and what's happening today.

Defensive Response:

As it happens, I *have* done my homework. I'm very aware that XYZ Company is sixteen years old and was started by an engineer who never envisioned this kind of rapid success. Etc. Etc.

Non-Defensive Response:

I guess I haven't demonstrated the type of background you are looking for. It sounds like that is important to you. Let's see if I can do better on that from now on. And if you think I'm missing some important context feel free to jump right in and add it.

A final word: Defensiveness in a trainer severely undercuts group process and triggers and intensifies resistance in participants. And, who wants that.

27

Three Trainer Qualities that Facilitate Learning

The facilitation of significant learning rests upon certain attitudinal qualities which exist in the personal relationship between the facilitator and the learner.

——Carl Rogers[1]

Carl Rogers, a leading psychological clinician of the twentieth century, emphasized that *respect, empathy,* and *genuineness* are three "core conditions" in teachers that spur growth in learners. Educational researcher David Aspy and his colleagues conducted a major investigation into whether these qualities actually improve teaching effectiveness. Aspy's team recorded and assessed more than 3,500 hours of instruction from 550 teachers in various grades of elementary and secondary school. This large and well-designed investigation found that students make greater gains in learning when their teachers exhibit high levels of respect, empathy, and genuineness. Significant measurable improvements were produced in such diverse areas as reading achievement, cognitive growth, creative interest, self-confidence, productivity, and grade point average.

Today, sixty years after Rogers first published his findings, it is firmly established that this triumvirate of growth-enhancing characteristics in teachers and other helping professionals is crucial to the success of their efforts to help people develop. *Respect* is the foundation; *empathy* demonstrates caring and informs connections with participants; *genuineness* is the what-you-see-is-what-you-get unpretentiousness of effective teachers.

We've personally witnessed the growth-facilitating power of these core characteristics. When we managed a cadre of fifty trainers, we studied the research of Rogers, Aspy, Carkhuff, Truax, and other psychological investigators who focused on the profound impact these three qualities have in facilitating human development. Impressed by the research findings, we applied them to the selection and development of our firm's trainers. As the research predicted, those of our trainers who embodied high levels of respect, empathy, and genuineness achieved by far the best results in their training. Thereafter, we rigorously employed these criteria to our trainer selection and development processes, and the quality and consistency of our trainer's performance improved markedly.

This chapter describes each of these core conditions of effective teaching and their application to training adults.

Respect

Respect for participants is the foundation on which all effective training efforts rest. This is not to suggest that you have to like or agree with every participant. But respect does involve interacting courteously with each person regardless of your personal feelings about the individual.

What Respect Entails

Respect has typically been thought of as a positive feeling of admiration for a person due to his good conduct, exemplary achievements, and/or high status in his field or in society. In other words, respect should be accorded to those deserving of our respect. But for some decades now many people have realized that respect should be democratized—that every person should be treated respectfully, that every learner—the reluctant as well as the eager, the slow as well as the quick, the disruptive as well as the facilitative—should be accorded our respect.

What Respect Does

Respect is an amazingly powerful quality. International mediator William Ury says, "Respect . . . is the key that opens the door to the other's mind and heart." He goes on to say:

> An obvious reason to give respect to the other is *because it works*. In my own work as a mediator in ethnic wars, I have had to deal with leaders who have blood on their hands. I do not approve of their behavior, I may not like them personally, but if I want them to accept a No to violence—bring about a ceasefire, save the lives of children—the only way I have found that works is to approach them through basic human respect.[2]

Abraham Lincoln was noted for treating others respectfully even when they acted rudely disrespectful to him. For example, Edwin Stanton, the U.S. attorney general of Lincoln's predecessor, President James Buchanan, put Lincoln down in the most abusive terms. He described Lincoln to others in such terms as a "low cunning clown . . . the original gorilla." Despite Stanton's many put-downs of the president,

Lincoln treated Stanton respectfully and picked him to be his second secretary of war. Even as a cabinet member, Stanton referred to Lincoln as a fool. Lincoln, however, continued treating his vehement detractor with respect. When told of Stanton's insults, Lincoln brushed the matter off saying, "Did he call me that? Well, I reckon it must be true then, for Stanton is generally right." The Great Emancipator's respect finally won out: their relationship became increasingly mutual. And when Lincoln died, the grief-stricken Stanton spoke of the president as "the greatest ruler of men the world has ever seen."

Trainer Respect

Fortunately, we trainers are not faced with the need to express such heroic respect as William Ury, President Lincoln, and many others have had to summon up. But a trainer's respect for participants must permeate his approach to training. It's a low-key way of making a powerful impact. Jane Dutton, professor of business administration and professor of psychology at the University of Michigan, suggests:

> Small acts of respectful engagement infuse a relationship with greater energy while at the same time sending signals and modelling behavior that gets picked up by others.[3]

Demonstrating Respect in the Normal Course of Training

Here are some examples of ways trainers can embody respect in their training:

- Complete the preparation for the workshop on the day prior to delivering the course in order to be free for informal discussion with participants:
  - In the classroom prior to beginning the workshop
  - During breaks
  - During meals
  - After the workshop (when requested)
- Develop a relationship with each individual.
- Throughout the workshop, listen for participants' needs, and work to problem-solve back-at-work situations with individual trainees as needed.
- Tap individual and group wisdom by actively inviting input in ways that demonstrate your desire to hear the wisdom and knowledge of the participants.
- Reflect participants' views, opinions, and suggestions—whether or not their positions contradict the material being presented.
- React non-defensively to criticism of the course and yourself.
- You can respond by simply saying, "Thanks for your input. Any other reactions?"
  - Or make a brief reply when appropriate.
  - And, when fitting, apply the suggested improvement as soon as possible.

When you find yourself internally disagreeing with a participant's statement, consider saying:

"Help me understand what you see."

"Tell me more about your point of view."

Respond Respectfully to Disruptive Participants

Chapter 23 described a proven method for handling disruptive participant behavior constructively and effectively. Here we'll describe how to implement that method by relating respectfully with the disruptive participant.

Make no change from the way you were responding to a participant when everything was going well. Continue to do the following:

- *Stance:* Face the participant with your shoulders "squared off" to parallel the speaker's shoulders. Keep the same distance from the participant as you normally do when responding to a participant.
- *Eye contact:* Maintain eye contact by looking the participant in the eyes with a calm and rather steady gaze.
- *Facial expression:* Show interest. Avoid grimacing or appearing worried or disgusted.
- *Tone of voice:* Use the same tone of voice you usually use when responding to questions or comments.
- *Word choice:* Use no judgmental or derogatory words.
- *Use constructive self-talk:* Tell yourself things like, "This person is using behavior that he's learned to use over the years. I can help him learn another option by the way I treat him right now."

The remaining hours of the workshop will go much better when you demonstrate respect for each person in the workshop including participants who have been behaving disruptively.

Empathy

Empathy is another powerful facilitative quality. It serves as a lubricant that smooths interactions and enhances relationships.

What Empathy Entails

The word *empathy* surfaced in the 1890s. It stems from the Greek word, *empatheia,* which means "feeling into." Since the word *empathy* is sometimes mistakenly equated with *sympathy,* it's important to stress the fact that the words have significantly different meanings.

Sympathy is feeling sorry for another person. Unfortunately, that may weaken the recipient—often at a time when the person most needs to rely on his strength.

In contrast, *empathy* involves trying to perceive the world from the other person's perspective, accurately taking in the *facts* and the *feelings* that he or she is experiencing. Empathy is the primary tool we have for understanding and communicating effectively with others. As Atticus Finch tells his daughter Scout in Harper Lee's *To Kill a Mockingbird,* "'You never really understand a person until you consider things from his point of view . . . until you climb into his skin and walk around in it.'"

The evidence is clear: when people feel empathically understood, their mental and emotional capabilities are invigorated. Empathy, one of the key qualities for relating well to others is clearly a must-have trainer characteristic.

What Empathy Does

Carl Rogers writes, "The research evidence has kept piling up, and it points strongly to the conclusion that a high degree of empathy in a relationship is possibly the most potent factor in bringing about change and learning."[4]

It's not only in fields like therapy and education that empathy contributes enormously to one's effectiveness. It also makes a powerful positive impact in every field in which individuals must work together to achieve common goals. Take professional basketball—a rather distant example. In his book, *Sacred Hoops: Spiritual Lessons of a Hardwood Warrior,* coach Phil Jackson writes that empathy was a powerful performance enhancer in his successful effort to integrate outstanding individual basketball players into a cohesive, world championship team:

> In my work as a coach, I've discovered that approaching problems of this kind from a compassionate perspective, trying to empathize with a player and look at the situation from his point of view, can have a transformative effect on the team. Not only does it reduce the player's anxiety and make him feel as if someone understands what he is going through, it also inspires the other players to respond in kind and be more conscious of each other's needs.[5]

Expressing Empathy in the Normal Course of Training

Here's what empathy looks like when it's an integral part of the trainer's interactions in a workshop:

- The trainer helps each individual sense the relevance of the course content.
- The trainer speaks to business concerns with pertinent applications.
- The trainer employs high-quality listening, receives what's said open-mindedly and thoughtfully, and, when appropriate, concisely reflects his understanding.

- The trainer responds sensitively to particular stresses that may impact a given group—such as staff reorganization, staff downsizing, corporate financial problems, etc.

How to Respond Empathically to an Objection

Typically, the best way to deal with an objection is to make sure that you, the objector, and the rest of the class all have the same understanding about the precise nature of the disagreement. To achieve that common understanding:

1. Temporarily suppress your own perspective.
2. Accurately tune in to the *content* and the *feelings* the person is expressing.
3. Succinctly communicate to the group your understanding of the participant's point of view—making sure that the person who raised the concern is satisfied with your phrasing.
4. When appropriate, explain to the group your perspective on the issue.

1. Temporarily Suppress Your Own Perspective

Empathy involves temporarily suppressing your own point of view to tune in to someone else's. It means identifying with the other person's situation, feelings, and motives to gain a level of insightful awareness greater than ordinary understanding.

That takes some doing. As a trainer you come to this workshop after days of concentrated preparation. Your mind is bursting with the information you've committed to present. And suddenly, during one of your presentations, someone in the group interrupts, saying in a loud voice, "That will never work." A number of others in the class murmur their agreement.

You're in the midst of teaching a module on active listening, a skill that has proven useful in innumerable types of work situations. You've already trained several people from the skeptic's department who, after using these skills on the job, have told you how useful this way of listening has been. You strongly want to let the person who voiced the objection and others in the class know how useful these same abilities have proven to be on their very own turf.

But don't do it—at least not yet.

At this moment, your job is to swivel your mind and heart from presenting to listening.

2. Tune in to What the Other Person Is Expressing

Once you've stepped out of your own perspective, try to understand where the other person is coming from. Try to see the matter as the speaker sees it—from within his frame of reference. As you follow along with him, focus on the following:

- *The content of the message*—the point he is making, the issue he is raising. Think along with the speaker and follow his train of thought.
- *The emotional flavor* of the participant's comment—the feeling(s) he is experiencing.

3. Communicate Your Understanding of the Participant's Point of View

Although understanding is the crux of empathy, by itself understanding is insufficient. To complete the empathic process, your understanding must be communicated to the person who spoke. (In group situations your understanding of the message is usually communicated to the group in which the person who spoke is a participant.)

For instance, this interaction took place in a communication skills workshop:

Participant: If you think that sounding like a psychologist is going to make me a better supervisor, you're living in a different world than I am.

Trainer: "You don't want to learn skills that could make you sound like a shrink. You might lose your credibility if you talked that way.

4. When Appropriate, Give Your Input

After an interaction such as this, participants in our workshops often raise the issue that it sounds like the trainer is agreeing with the participant. The trainer doesn't want the individual or the class to be left with the false impression that he thinks the objecting participant is correct—yet he doesn't want to make the participant look bad in front of the group. To accomplish both goals, his response could be something like this:

It makes sense to question the validity of new ways of doing things until you've proven to yourself that they work for you. These listening methods have been found to be useful in many work situations as well as in people's personal lives. We've just started learning it. How about you give it more of a chance and then, if you find it's not for you, that's your choice.

You've perhaps noticed that the above four steps are essentially a brief recap of Chapter 12.

Empathize with Your Most Difficult Participants

Empathizing with your most difficult participants may at first seem to be a human impossibility. It has, however, proven not only to be possible but also to be a highly effective skill in many conflict-ridden situations. In fact, it is the tactic of choice of innumerable police departments across the country, thanks in part to the work of psychologist and former police officer George Thompson, who teaches cops how to relate empathically to murderers and other dangerous criminals. In his book, *Ver-*

bal Judo, Thompson says "the single most powerful concept in the English language [is] *empathy.*"

> Here is the bottom line of all communication, Empathy absorbs tension. . . . This is the communication warrior's real service: staying calm in the midst of conflict, deflecting verbal abuse, and offering empathy in the face of antagonism. If you cannot empathize with people, you don't stand a chance of getting them to listen to you. . . .
>
>   If you take a moment to think as another might be thinking, then speak with his perspective in mind, you can gain immediate rapport. Ill-fitting as his shoes may be, walk a few steps in them. Only then can you provide real understanding. . . . Only then can you help that person see the consequences of what he is doing. . . . Only then can you help him make enlightened decisions.[6]

Verbal Judo describes one incredibly dangerous situation after another that Thompson or other police officers successfully resolved by empathizing with their adversaries.

The international disputes between nation states is another conflict-ridden arena where empathy is desperately needed but where it is seldom employed. Robert McNamara, drawing on his experience as the longest serving U.S. secretary of defense, said:

> What is becoming clear . . . based on the detailed study of the Cuban missile crisis and the Viet Nam War, is that empathy is an absolute fundamental element in determining success or failure in foreign policymaking. If it is present, as it was *at the end* of the Cuban missile crisis . . . war can be avoided, peace established, understanding achieved. If it is absent . . . outcomes are possible that are far worse than even so-called "worse-case" analyses predict.

McNamara concludes, "'Rule No. 1' in international conflict management is, 'Empathize with your enemy.'"[7]

If empathy is seen as the tool of choice for police dealing with armed criminals and leaders of democracies in their relationships with military dictators with hostile expansionistic tendencies, trainers can surely empathize with resistant participants.

One last point: we stand behind everything we've written about empathy, but we would be remiss if we didn't mention that there are some people who are so naturally empathic that, at times, no words are needed. A mere facial expression can communicate deep empathy. For example, when describing an event, a participant said, "It was like being hit with a ton of bricks. I just couldn't believe it." The trainer spontaneously jammed her eyes shut and tightened her mouth as if she was being hit. That said it all.

Genuineness

Genuineness is another trainer quality that's especially facilitative of participant learning and development.

What Genuineness Entails

Genuineness entails being honest with ourselves and being natural and open with others. It is being "dependably real" in that what you say and do closely matches what you think and feel. This quality of genuineness is sometimes encapsulated in the phrase, "What you see is what you get."

When leading a workshop, the genuine trainer doesn't put on a special "teacher persona"—she's the same person on coffee break as when making a presentation. "At the very minimum," says Robert Carkhuff, "we present no façade that would misrepresent ourselves. We present no mask from a professional or other role."[8]

What Genuineness Does

As a trainer, the more you can avoid taking on a role and instead be genuinely yourself, the more impactful the training will be.

Through the ages, leading thinkers underscored the importance of being genuine. Buddha said, "A man should direct himself in the way he should go. Only then should he instruct others." Shakespeare wrote, "To thine own self be true, and . . . thou canst not then be false to any man." And Ben Franklin said, "A good example is the best sermon."

Five Ways to Integrate What You Teach into Your Lifestyle

Here are five things we can do to ensure that that we not only verbalize effectively how to do the ability that's being taught, but that we also incorporate what we teach into our lifestyle as an example of how the content we are teaching can be capably applied:

1. Avoid using a "teacher voice" or body language.
2. Internalize the content.
3. Walk the talk: to the degree possible, integrate the skills you are teaching into the leadership of the workshop as well as in your daily life.
4. Demonstrate strong conviction and enthusiasm about the skills without being absolutist or evangelical.
5. Incorporate your own experiences without drawing attention to yourself or seeming to put yourself up or down (and without overemphasizing personal applications of the course content).

1. Avoid Using a "Teacher Voice" or Body Language

In elementary schools, secondary schools, and college classrooms, some teachers take on certain vocal, postural, and gestural mannerisms when they teach. It's obvious to students that they're taking on a role rather than being themselves when they're presenting. Some trainers also rely on this tactic, and it greatly diminishes their effectiveness.

2. Internalize the Content

In all likelihood, most of the workshops you deliver will have been designed by someone else. Your job, then, is to internalize the content—make it your own. Put your own stamp on it.

Goethe, the famed German poet, dramatist, novelist, and scientist, put it this way, "All truly wise thoughts have been thought already several thousand times; but to make them truly ours, we must think them over again honestly, till they take root in our personal experience." Then, when we teach, we must cast them in our own words, use our own analogies, and rely mainly on our own examples.

3. Walk the Talk

When a trainer's actions don't match his message, it's the trainer's actions that are heeded; the useful methods of the workshop are disregarded. But when a trainer's actions are congruent with his words, they're likely to be taken seriously. In fact, walking the talk can prove to be one of the clearest and best messages you'll ever send.

Albert Schweitzer, the German, later French physician and musicologist, spent decades working as a medical missionary in Africa. One of his biographers summed up Schweitzer's lifestyle by stating that the great missionary gave the natives the message of Jesus, "one day [of the week] with his lips as he was already giving it seven days a week with his life."[9] Week in and week out, Schweitzer walked the talk. Then, on Sundays he talked the talk. And though it happened in a remote part of the earth, the sincere talk and the skilled and dedicated walk captured the world's imagination and Schweitzer received the Nobel Peace Prize in 1952.

4. Demonstrate Strong Conviction and Enthusiasm About the Skills

As we've emphasized before, enthusiasm is a crucial trainer capability. If you aren't enthusiastic about what you are teaching, it's unlikely that participants will muster up much motivation to learn. At the same time, there's a fine line between being wholesomely enthusiastic about the good things you are teaching and going overboard and taking an evangelical or absolutist stand.

5. Incorporate a Few of Your Own Experiences

A small amount of self-disclosure by the trainer can make her seem more accessible to the group. Although overdoing self-disclosure can be off-putting, well-selected, pertinent personal experiences shared sensitively can make the trainer seem more approachable. For example, a trainer might say:

Years ago when I was in a counseling course, the instructor kept telling us how important it was to listen, but he never taught us how to do the kind of listening that would be helpful in a counselling situation. It was very frustrating for me because I knew I should be doing something different, but couldn't figure out exactly what.

Respect, empathy, and genuineness, the three trainer qualities that enhance participants' learning, are the same qualities that strengthen all human relationships. So, as you mature as a trainer by developing these qualities, you will also strengthen all your relationships. That's very good news indeed.

APPENDICES

Appendix I
Course Preparation Worksheets

E ven though you may have either a moderate-size or extensive study guide for any given course you teach, to make the course your own, we recommend that you create course preparation worksheets for every activity, presentation, demonstration, and practice that you do. It may take four or five rewrites to get the worksheets into the concise form that will be maximally useful to you. An additional benefit of rewriting them is that trainers who write and rewrite the material in their own words become more integrated with it. These course preparation worksheets are also excellent for a quick review of the major points you want to remember.

In this appendix we provide the four course preparation worksheets that are referred to in the corresponding chapters of this book:

- Activity Worksheet
- Presentation Worksheet
- Interpersonal Skills Demonstration Worksheet
- Practice Worksheet

Activity Worksheet

Module: _____

Title: _____

Time: _____ to _____ Length: _____

INTRODUCTION

Transition In:

Purpose: (unless it gives away the lessons)

Preview: "You'll be doing _____, in groups of _____, for _____ minutes."

DIRECTIONS

Logistics:

- Materials (and page numbers):
- With whom:
- Where:
- (pause)

Instructions (by role in chronological order, including timing of each part):

OBSERVE/GUIDE

DEBRIEF

CONCLUSION

Summary:

Transition Out:

Presentation Worksheet

Module: _____

Title: _____

Time: _____ to _____ Length: _____

INTRODUCTION

Transition In:

Attention getter:

Preview:

BODY

2–5 Points with supporting examples, stories, quotes:

CONCLUSION

Wrap-up signal:

Review:

Concluding Statement:

Transition Out:

Interpersonal Skills Demonstration Worksheet

Module: _____

Title: _____

Time: _____ to _____ Length: _____

INTRODUCTION

Transition In:
Purpose:
Preview:

DIRECTIONS

The situation:
The volunteer's role:
The other person's role:
Equipment, materials, etc.:
Specific things to watch and listen for:

ASK for a VOLUNTEER

DISCLAIMER

DEMONSTRATE

DEBRIEF

The People in the Demo (optional):

The Workshop Participants:

TRANSITION

Summary:

Transition Out:

Typical Questions and Comments of Participants:

Potential Trouble Spots:

Practice Worksheet

Module: _____

Title: _____

Time: _____ to _____ Length: _____

INTRODUCTION

Transition In:

Purpose:

Preview: "You'll be practicing _____

_____, in groups of _____, for _____ minutes."

DIRECTIONS

What:

Where:

Who:

How:

Timing:

Materials:

Trainer's Role:

OBSERVE/GUIDE

DEBRIEF

CONCLUDE

Summary:

Transition Out:

Appendix II

Adapting the Workshop to Fit the Participants

W hen you read the title of this appendix, you may wonder why, in a book for trainers, there would be an appendix about rewriting trainer outlines and other workshop materials to make the training a better fit for the intended audience. Isn't that a function of the workshop development staff? It often is. But in smaller organizations the trainer may need to be a Jack—or Jill—of all trades. And larger organizations often expect their trainers to have some design skills. Also, it's a natural progression for a trainer to be involved in upgrading training manuals and revising participant materials to make them a better fit for the target population. With first-hand knowledge of what it takes to lead successful workshops, a trainer has much to contribute to improving a workshop's outcome by adapting the course a bit so it better meets the needs of the participants.

After briefly discussing off-the-shelf courses, this appendix focuses on three increasing degrees of adaptation of course content to better suit the sponsoring organization and the user population:

- Tailored workshops
- Customized workshops
- Redesigned workshops

Next, we discuss six guidelines that can help trainers and training administrators determine the appropriate level of workshop adaption for a given situation. Finally, we briefly discuss monogramming a course—making the look of the training materials a good fit with the corporate colors and logo.

Off-the-Shelf Courses

Off-the-shelf courses are designed for a broad spectrum of industries, companies, and employees. With the possible exception of a trainer's ad-lib reference to the current participants' situations, off-the-shelf courses are not adapted in any way to the organization or its training population. However, an off-the-shelf course often provides a good starting point for a workshop that you'll adapt to a greater or lesser degree to make it more relevant to the group you'll be teaching.

We're not fans of using unmodified off-the-shelf training for groups. When you consider the fixed costs of most training programs, which often include participant transportation to and from the workshop, participant food and lodging, the trainer's salary and expenses, participant materials, and the lost productivity due to the participants' time away from the job, the organization has already made a significant investment in the workshop. It's usually wise to make the most of that investment by adapting the program to fit the goals of the corporation and meet the needs of the trainees.

However, off-the-shelf resources like books, DVDs, and CDs can supplement workshops and may also be useful for individual participants.

Three Tiers of Course Adaptation

There is no universal agreement in the training community regarding the number of tiers of workshop adaptation to the client population or on the terminology used to discuss such things. For example, terms like *tailored* and *customized*, which have distinctly different meanings for us, are sometimes used interchangeably by other seasoned trainers.

We've found it useful to work with three levels of adaptation of a workshop to the needs of the sponsoring organization and the training population. The levels of adaptation, from least to most modification, are *tailored*, *customized*, and *redesigned*. Most off-the-shelf training can be improved significantly by using one of the three levels of course adaptation portrayed in Figure II-1 and discussed in the remainder of this appendix.

Tailored Workshops

When seasoned trainers are knowledgeable about the course content, the user organization, and the training population, they're equipped to tailor the training program by altering presentations and demonstrations so that they are more applicable to the corporation's culture and terminology as well as to the participant's situations.

Figure II-1. The course adaptation continuum indicates the specificity of the design to the user population which incurs different amounts of design time, administrative effort, and cost.

Course Adaptation Continuum

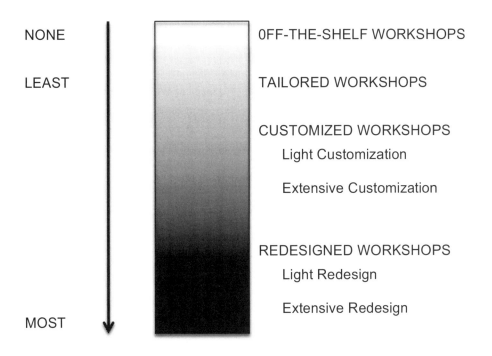

NONE — OFF-THE-SHELF WORKSHOPS

LEAST — TAILORED WORKSHOPS

CUSTOMIZED WORKSHOPS
Light Customization
Extensive Customization

REDESIGNED WORKSHOPS
Light Redesign
Extensive Redesign

MOST

Corporate trainers usually have the information required to do this. When a training company sells a workshop that's to be tailored, the sales rep often gathers the information that's required to tailor the workshop.

Occasionally, it may be desirable for the person who will be doing the training to conduct a tailoring interview. While its best to do the tailoring interview face-to-face, today's technology provides other viable options such as audio conferencing, web conferencing, and video conferencing. Although it's fitting to be businesslike in the tailoring interview, building rapport is an important part of these conversations.

In a tailored workshop, all visual aids and other hardcopy materials remain unchanged. Any visual aid or hardcopy that's not relevant to this particular group of participants is simply not used.

Customized Workshops

Customized workshops include the types of alterations to demonstrations and presentations that were discussed in the description of tailored workshops. Additionally, in customized courses, some or all of the following training resources are revised to be better suited to the purchasing organization and its participants:

- Workbooks
- Handouts for activities and practices
- Charts or power point slides

As in tailored workshops, the course outline remains unchanged; no part of the course is expanded, contracted, or altered in significant ways.

We distinguish between two levels of customization: light and extensive. *Light customization* involves developing new role plays and demonstrations and sometimes making a few other minor changes. *Extensive customization* involves significant revision of the hardcopy training resources, but does not alter the structure or timing of the course.

Redesigned Workshops

A redesigned workshop is characterized by one or more of the following:

- Altering the content and often the length of the course by adding or changing demonstrations, practices, and perhaps adding new modules.
- Combining parts of two or more courses.
- Adapting course material to a different occupational group or level of management.

Redesigns can be light or extensive, depending on the extent of changes. *Light redesign* modifies the trainer's materials but leaves the participant materials unaltered. *Extensive redesign* revamps both the trainer's materials and the participant's materials. When extensive redesign requires the development of one or more new modules, it often necessitates additional time to train the trainers to lead the revamped course. Also, in an extensively redesigned program, a pilot workshop with a revision loop may be needed to detect and remedy aspects of the redesign that need to be strengthened. Extensive redesign is often called for when the client has a unique set of training needs.

It's often cost-effective to customize an extensively revised course for the first outing. Customization should boost the course evaluations a bit and enhance word-of-mouth recommendations, which are especially important when recruiting participants for future outings of an extensively redesigned course.

Highly redesigned programs require more of the training staff's time and a greater financial outlay than any of the other options we've discussed. It's often worth the additional cost and effort, however, when the pool of trainees is large or when there's sufficient value added for a training population that's rather small.

Guidelines for Determining the Appropriate Level of Workshop Adaptation

When determining the appropriate level of course adaptation for a given course to be delivered to a specific population, you'll want to do the following:

- Assess the potential effect of the training on the organization's effectiveness.
- Choose an outstanding workshop design.
- Consider the size and the composition of the population to be trained.
- Address administrative issues.
- Manage possible financial trade-offs.
- Develop a realistic rollout schedule.

Assess the Potential Effect of the Training on the Organization's Effectiveness

The more crucial the training is to an organization's effectiveness, the more likely that extensive course adaptation will be appropriate. For instance, a new CEO was brought in to rescue a floundering midsized company. One of his first acts was to hire a consulting firm to extensively redesign the consulting firm's Management by Objectives (MBO) program so that it fit the corporation's needs. Because the training was so vital to the organization's survival, a course textbook and workbook were written detailing the specific way that MBO would be done in that organization. The textbook and workbook were obligatory reading for everyone in the organization from the CEO to the group leaders.

Following the book's formats for writing Key Results Areas, Objectives, and Actions Plans, the CEO developed his Job Plan, and shared it with the vice presidents on his top team. Each of the VPs then made a first pass at his own Job Plan, discussed that with the CEO and discussed and made agreed upon changes. In a step-by-step manner, the integrated planning cascaded through the organization. The effort was successful and today—over a decade later—the organization is thriving and the extensively redesigned MBO workshop is recognized as having been an important contributor to the corporation's revitalization. When the stakes are high, anything less than an extensive adaptation of the training program is likely to be an inadequate intervention.

Most training interventions, however, don't require a full-court press like the one just described. For instance, among the courses taught by the training organization that we are associated with are workshops on interpersonal skills. Extensive redesign of this type of course is seldom warranted. However, there are programs such as performance review workshops that combine training in the pertinent communication skills with the corporation's performance review system and therefore require redesign.

Choose an Outstanding Workshop Design

For every outstanding workshop design there are a host of mediocre ones. It's often difficult to tell an exceptionally good workshop from a mediocre one by comparing sales literature and listening to competing salespeople. As you've undoubtedly experienced, flashy literature and convincing salespeople seldom are reliable resources for evaluating a training program that's a possible addition to your curriculum. A better practice is to attend the workshop yourself with two or three representatives from the population to be trained and see for yourselves whether this training is likely to achieve what you want it to.

Choosing good representatives is important. Don't send problem performers to see if the training can help them. Rather, select people who are highly respected by others in their departments. They will be your best barometer. And, if you decide to use the program, the endorsements of these well-regarded employees will undoubtedly encourage attendance when the program is offered.

Consider the Size and the Composition of the Population to Be Trained

The size and the composition of the population to be trained generally have significant impact on the degree of course adaptation that's feasible. The more people to be trained, the lower the per participant cost of course adaptation. And the nature of the target population may affect the amount of course adaptation that is practical. Organizations typically are willing to spend more per person on training people in higher salaried positions than on those who receive less compensation.

Address Administrative Issues

Schedules need to be set up and monitored, interviews arranged, rooms reserved, pilot programs set up and evaluated, and so forth. The administrative effort needed to make a workshop successful can sometimes be a burden for training departments whose administrative personnel may be overtaxed already. So it's important to note that each succeeding level of workshop adaptation from light customization to extensive redesign generally requires more administrative time and effort than the previous level. And experience has proven that shoddy administration can undermine the effectiveness of a workshop.

Manage Possible Financial Trade-Offs

For the most part, the more extensive a course is adapted, the more directly it addresses a specific population's issues, talks its language, and is relevant to its world; and the lower the resistance to learning, the higher the level of interest, the better the practice sessions, and the greater the transfer of learnings.

Highly specific adaptation, however, is likely to severely narrow the scope of the population that can be served unless additional adaptations are developed for other segments of the organization—which from a financial and staffing perspective may or may not be acceptable.

Fortunately, some types of course adaptation are quite inexpensive. Some training firms don't charge for tailoring a workshop. One firm that we know tailors its workshops at no cost to the client and increases its income by doing so! Here's how they accomplish that: Good tailoring normally improves a workshop significantly enough that training managers and line managers alike hear lots of good reviews. The stronger than usual positive scuttlebutt drives repeat business without incurring the usual sales and marketing costs. With this approach, everybody wins.

Factors such as the type of client population, the geographical location, the training organization's client list, and numerous other factors affect pricing significantly, so it's inappropriate to comment on this important issue here. Suffice to say, the more changes required, the more expensive the course adaptation will be.

Develop a Realistic Rollout Schedule

Once the decision is made to train a group of people, there's often a desire to begin the training as soon as possible. So, when customization or redesign is employed, a hurried revision is often made. Training frequently suffers from the hasty compromises that generally result.

Customizing a course typically involves the following:

1. Interviewing
2. Writing
3. Editing
4. Initial client review
5. Rewriting
6. Re-editing
7. Proofing
8. The final client review
9. Producing the final product

And that's if everything goes according to plan! So there's more to doing even minor customizations than one would think. Redesign, of course, takes much more time. Furthermore, redesign often requires a pilot workshop and a revision loop. And for heavy redesign, time needs to be factored in to train or retrain the trainers. So if a course is to be customized or redesigned, be sure to schedule enough time to do it well. And remember Murphy's law: Anything that can go wrong, will go wrong. So build a bit more time into the schedule than you think the course adaptation will take.

Monogramming Training Programs

Monogramming training programs entails making cosmetic changes in the courses' publicity, audio visuals, workbooks, handouts, etc., to create a match or to coordinate well with the "look" of the client's printed materials. Monogramming is usually done at the customization or redesign level. As one company executive said in regard to monogramming, "I like monogramming because our people must see the immediate connection of the training to the company. They have to get that this is who we are."

Appendix III

Installing the Training Properly

The effects of training cannot be considered separate from the environs of the worker. You cannot create a behavior change which violates the culture in which the behavior is embedded.
————James McCroskey, Carl Larson, and Mark Knapp

In a comprehensive survey of research on transfer of learning to the job, Timothy Baldwin and Kevin Ford note the pittance of transfer that results from most training.

> There is growing recognition of a "transfer problem" in organizational training today. It is estimated that while American industries annually spend up to $100 billion on raining and development, not more than 10% of these expenditures actually result in transfer to the job.[1]

How discouraging to realize that even when you lead a highly evaluated workshop, it's unlikely that much good will stem from your efforts.

Many of the barriers to transfer of learning stem from ineffective installation of the training. This appendix describes how to install training in ways that support the application of what was learned in the workshop.

The Installation of Training

Here's what we mean when we speak of the installation of training:

> The installation of training refers to a three phase set of crucial activities that are performed
>   • before,
>   • during, and
>   • after training

to promote the successful transfer of learning from the workshop to the workplace. It involves a set of collaborative activities that involve trainers, managers/team leaders, and participants.

(Henceforth we'll use the terms *team leader* or *leader* to designate persons who are often termed managers or leaders in their organization.)

The crucial importance of solid installation was highlighted in a 2006 study of training failure by the American Society for Training and Development (ASTD), which attributed

- 20 percent of training failures to circumstances prior to the training,
- 10 percent to poor delivery of the training program, and
- 70 percent to an "application environment" that either prevented participants from using what they had learned or failed to reinforce participants' use of new knowledge, methods and skills.

Despite these research findings, most training departments focus the bulk of the trainer's time and attention on delivering training, which leaves little time available for other things important to the workshop's success, such as arranging for

- participants before the workshop preparation, and
- participants after the workshop transfer of learning to the workplace.

Unless other options are provided for accomplishing these needs, the lopsided allocation of trainer time is a formula for failure of the learning to make a difference in the workplace.

Obviously, for transfer of learning to occur, it's important for the training event itself to be successful. But if the transfer opportunities in the other two installation periods are shortchanged, the effectiveness of the training will be seriously compromised.

Every major problem that we've encountered in a workshop was traced, at least in part, to one or more installation problems. Why? Because installation problems can rear their ugly heads at any moment, especially when you least expect it. They're always lurking in the background, ready to pounce if installation is ineptly done.

Be wise. Install properly. Or live to regret it.

Whose responsibility is it to ensure the effective installation of training? If the training was purchased from a salesperson on the staff of an outside training firm, the salesperson and the trainer who will deliver the course can team with the company contact person. Responsibilities can be agreed to and a pre-workshop conference call can be held to ensure that these details have been completed.

If a company trainer is leading the course, he can team with personnel in the training-and-development group to make sure that all the steps of installation are accomplished.

This three-phase (before, during, and after) approach to installation obviously requires collaboration among

- the trainer,
- the participants' leader(s), and
- the participants.

Thus, training is best installed as a three-phase/three-role endeavor. It's often up to an in-house trainer to manage the three-phase/three-role process. The remainder of this appendix describes what needs to be done in each phase of this collaborative installation process in order to promote successful transfer of learning. When using an external training firm, it's important for vendor's trainers to be aware of your installation policies and procedures and how they contribute to the workshop's overall effectiveness.

Before the Workshop

More than half of the steps of installing a workshop occur before the workshop opens:

1. Develop an accurate understanding of the group.
2. Inquire about current or pending departmental or company problems.
3. Ensure that a critical mass of participants receive the training within a short period of time.
4. Discuss with team leaders their role in preparing participants for the workshop.
5. Stress the importance of team leaders using the course information.
6. Keep the training separate from corporate evaluation of participants.
7. Link the course content to the participants' work world.
8. Check on administrative details relating to the workshop.

1. Develop an Accurate Understanding of the Group

Some of the most awkward training experiences stem from a failure to fit the training to the participants. Here are a few examples:

- An international sales group asked for product training but was given a sales communication course instead.
- A group of staff people who had no subordinates were given a course on people skills for managers.
- Service personnel who had not been told that they would have sales responsibilities suddenly found themselves in a sales course in which they learned that as of the conclusion of the course they would be responsible for achieving sales targets as well as meeting their current customer relations objectives.

Trainers skilled in handling group resistance and in doing emergent redesign (both discussed later in the book) were able to turn each of these potential disasters into positive learning experiences. But in each case, proper installation would have made the training not only more powerful and successful but also less problematic for everyone involved.

Subtle aspects of a group understanding can also have a positive effect on the training. Knowing the group culture, the buzz words, and the sensitive issues can help trainers tailor their presentations and responses so that they are clearly addressing the people in the room.

2. Inquire About Current or Pending Departmental or Company Problems

Trainers need to know what's going on in the company that may have an impact on the participants. Are products being dropped, benefits being changed, older employees being encouraged to take early retirement? Is a general downsizing being discussed? Are departments being eliminated? Is the company being sold? These are important issues that can interfere with participants' receptivity to the workshop. The trainer who is blind-sided by these emotionally laden challenges will wonder what's wrong with the training, the participants, or the trainer himself. When the trainer is aware of the current situation, he can use appropriate disclaimers and show empathy for what the participants are facing. When the trainer is out of the loop, he appears clueless, which greatly complicates creating a positive learning climate.

3. Ensure that a Critical Mass of Participants Receive the Training Within a Short Period of Time

When only one person in a work unit is trained, he often returns to a work environment that's inhospitable to the use of what was taught. Long-established group norms are apt to undermine her individual efforts to apply the new learning.

When introducing change, therefore, it's highly desirable to train a "critical mass" of the target population within a fairly short time period. A *critical mass* is a sufficient number of trainees who work together to receive the instruction in the same general time period. When a critical mass is trained, individuals can support one another in their effort to employ their new knowledge. By training a critical mass of employees, the ability that's taught generally becomes "the way we do things around here." So it behooves those from the training function who are involved in a training to work with line managers to cobble together a critical mass of participants that will be sufficient to promote transfer of the course knowledge.

When it's not possible to train a critical mass of people, trainers can help team leaders connect people in different departments as groups or pairs so that they can support one another in using new methods and skills.

4. Discuss with Team Leaders Their Role in Preparing Participants for the Workshop

Preparation for training increases participants' readiness to learn; it gives them mental hooks on which they can hang their new knowledge and skills. Promise of support and follow-up after training further motivates participants by showing strong management commitment to their growth and development.

Trainers can provide those in a supervisory capacity with information about the course and discuss the connection between the training the participants will experience and the work they do. Appropriate handouts tend to increase the impact of these brief discussions. Ask the team leaders to schedule both a pre-training meeting and a post-training meeting with their participants to discuss how this training can be most usefully applied to their job responsibilities. Offering managers the following ideas for such conversations makes it more likely that the before-the-course interactions will take place:

> "Let's talk about how this training can help you in your work."

> "Here's a list of the content of the training. Let's highlight the parts that you see as applicable to your work."

> "What do we need to do to support your use of what you learn when you return to work?"

5. Stress the Importance of Team Leaders Using the Course Information

Probably the most effective way to change a person's behavior in the workplace is to change her leader's behavior. If the leader is not using the knowledge, methods, and skills of the workshop herself, it's unlikely that her team members will see much value in the new ways or have much commitment to applying them at work. Ideally, the leaders will have been trained and will be applying that new ways of doing things before their team members receive the training. When the late William Weisz was chairman of Motorola, an outsider asked, "How does top management show its support for training?" He replied, "First by our example. We participate. We go through training ourselves to set an example."

6. Keep the Training Separate from Corporate Evaluation of Participants

Some organizations request feedback on how individual participants performed during a workshop. And sometimes team leaders request that type of information.

We believe that it's crucial to have a policy explicitly separating training and corporate evaluation of individual's performance in a workshop. Evaluation of an individual's workshop participation for other than his own growth inevitably degrades the learning climate of a workshop. To the extent that participants believe they are being evaluated, their focus often shifts from learning to self-protection.

This is such an important training issue that some of our colleagues risked losing major contracts because of their insistence on maintaining a strict confidentiality policy. However, most training managers realize that what's important for their organization is not how a person performs in training but how he performs on the job.

7. Link the Course Content to the Participants' Work World

The course needs to be a good fit with the participants' world of work. If the number of participants to be trained is moderately large, light customization of course materials may be done. If the number of people to be trained is very large, extensive customization of the workshop may be provided. These extra steps will ensure that participants have less of a struggle to transfer the new methods and skills back to the job. Because of the time and expense involved, however, customization usually is limited to high-level personnel or special situations. Appendix II provides guidelines for when and how to customize a course.

It's often left to the trainer to gain an understanding of how the training fits with the participants' work responsibilities and to weave that into the fabric of the workshop. Much of that knowledge can come from communication with the team leader.

8. Check on Administrative Details Relating to the Workshop

Having a successful workshop relies heavily on top-notch administration. Many details need to be handled on time, accurately, and thoroughly. Such details include the following:

- Generation of a class list
- Distribution of pre-course work
- Selection of an appropriate training site
- Selection of the size and number of rooms
- Room setup
- Distribution of course materials including the timely delivery of pre-work
- Provision of supplies and equipment
- Arrangement for any needed accommodations, lunches, breaks, dinners

The trainer is seldom directly responsible for arranging these administrative details. However, she needs to be sure that these tasks have been accomplished.

Installation During Training

During a training session the following training policies improve learning:

1. Establish the norm of confidentiality.
2. Don't allow observers in the workshop.

3. Set limits on permissible absence from training.
4. Include action planning in the workshop.

1. Establish the Norm of Confidentiality

In a context where the trainer and participants agree to keep personal information confidential, participants feel free to let their guard down. Everyone may speak more candidly than normal about problems they are facing—and about how what they are learning may or may not help resolve or reduce those problems. This kind of open communication encourages the application of learning to real-life situations. Confidentially helps learning become more practical and specific, which aids the transfer of learning.

2. Don't Allow Observers in the Workshop

A number of people interested in the success of training may want to drop in on the class to see how it's going. Some may even want to sit in the back of the room to observe the entire course. While larger interest in and commitment to the training is an important part of installation, having nonparticipant observers in the training room disrupts the learning process for participants. It also violates the confidentiality and separation of training from corporate evaluation of individual employees in training that was alluded to earlier.

3. Set Limits on Permissible Absence from Training

Ideally, all participants will be present for the entire training session, but reality often intervenes. Ever hear of one of the following occurring?

- A manager calls a participant out of training to be at a meeting.
- A participant has a medical appointment taking half a day out of the training.
- A participant leaves a half-day early due to travel arrangements.

These occurrences can be avoided by establishing a policy that defines maximum permissible absence, perhaps a quarter of a day or less for a four-day course, a couple of hours or less for a shorter training. Participants who miss more time than the policy stipulates need to be rescheduled to participate in a different training session.

4. Include Action Planning in the Workshop.

One way trainers can support participants' efforts to transfer what they've learned is to include action planning in the workshop agenda. There are a number of ways to do action planning in a workshop. After the workshop, the action plan can be discussed and possibly revised in a face-to-face discussion between the participant and her leader. If no action plan was developed at the end of the workshop, the plan can be developed after the workshop as part of the post-workshop discussion with the leader.

Establishing the norm of confidentiality, not allowing observers in the workshop, setting limits on absence from training, and including action planning in the workshop agenda are aspects of installation during a workshop that foster the transfer of learning.

Installation After Training

The period immediately after the workshop is pivotal for the transfer of learning. The ASTD study, cited earlier, found that a whopping 70 percent of training failure was due to an "application environment" that either prevented participants from using what they had learned or failed to reinforce participants' use of new knowledge, methods, and skills. Although we only have two types of action to take here, they are of major importance.

Changing work habits requires concerted effort. But when participants return to their jobs, they typically tackle a backlog of work that accumulated while they were in training. Under these circumstances, it takes real commitment to make the time and put forth the effort to implement the new learnings.

If we want to improve training results, we need to increase the amount of time, energy, and creativity that we spend on improving the application environment.

Two kinds of installation interventions are available to trainers after the conclusion of a workshop to foster greater application of workshop lessons:

1. Encourage team leaders to reinforce the training.
2. Refresh the training through coaching, memos, or brief reinforcement courses.

1. Encourage Team Leaders to Reinforce the Training

This may be the most important of all the recommended installation steps. One study found that unless there was immediate application and feedback, only 5 percent of workshop training persisted. But with immediate utilization, timely feedback, and support, 90 percent of the training endures.

Recommend that team leaders meet with trainees immediately after training, debrief the experience, and mutually identify barriers to transfer as well as opportunities for utilization. This discussion highlights the importance of the training and pinpoints on-the-job use of the abilities. And it's a time to offer help, "Let me know what I can do to help you implement what you learned."

Consider reminding the team leaders that the learning process does not entail consistent progress. Instead people tend to take two steps forward and one step back. And sometimes it's one step forward and two steps back. And even when the transfer of learning is fairly successful, participants ultimately tend to reach a plateau where the learning is sustained but there's little if any improvement. Realistic expectations ward off discouragement and help maintain the training.

2. Refresh the Training Through Coaching, Memos, or Brief Reinforcement Courses

Like other types of education, training tends to suffer from a "fade-out" effect, in which the knowledge, methods, and skills that participants are able to use immediately after a workshop tend to wither away over time. Coaching enables people to continue to be trained on the job and is a powerful way to counteract the fade-out effect. See Chapter 18 for information on using the key skill that's required for this type of coaching.

A series of memos can provide timely reminders about how and when to employ a newly learned method. A brief refresher course can help participants polish their skills and motivate them to continue their efforts to improve their performance.

Notes

Preface

1. Henry Adams, *The Education of Henry Adams* (privately printed, 1907).

Chapter 1: The Challenge of Training

1. J. Holt, *How Children Learn* (New York: Pitman Publishing, 1968), p. 3.

2. See for instance, J. Bruner, *The Process of Education* (Cambridge, MA: Harvard University Press, 1960).

3. R. Kegan and L. Lahey, *Immunity to Change: How to Overcome It and Unlock the Potential in Yourself and Your Organization* (Cambridge, MA: Harvard Business School Press, 2009), p. 316.

Chapter 2: Content and Process

1. The terms *confluent teaching* and *confluent education* were in fairly common use by educators several decades ago but fell into disuse as other terms took their place. We've reinstated them for use in discussing dynamic training because they so closely depict blending of content and process, the two fundamental aspects of this approach to training.

Chapter 3: A Universal Structure for Skill-Building Workshops

1. J. Barzun, ed. Morris Philipson, *Begin Here: The Forgotten Conditions of Teaching and Learning* (Chicago: University of Chicago Press, 1991), p. 112. Emphasis in the original.

2. C. Hannaford, *Smart Moves: Why Learning Isn't All in Your Head,* 2nd ed. (Salt Lake City: Great River Books, 2005).

Chapter 4: How to Open a Workshop

1. D. Brooks, *The Social Animal: The Hidden Sources of Love, Character, and Achievement* (New York: Random House, 2011), pp. 8–9. In a similar vein, researchers found that they could predict the outcome of gubernatorial races with considerable accuracy by merely looking at ten-second silent video clips of the candidates talking.

2. *Ibid.*, p. 9.

3. K. Campbell, "Does Fashion Matter?" *New York Times Magazine*, October 24, 1993.

4. R. Pike, *Creative Training Techniques Handbook: Tips, Tactics, and How-to's for Delivering Effective Training,* 3rd ed. (Amherst, MA: HRD Press, 2003), p. 224.

Chapter 5: Using Activities to Engage Participants

1. L. Shulman, *The Skill of Helping: Individuals, Families, Groups, and Communities* (Pacific Grove, CA: Brooks-Cole, 2008), p. 37.

2. "Workshop time" is the time on the wall clock in the training room. If there is no wall clock in the room, the trainer usually makes sure her watch is accurate and announces that will be workshop time and asks participants to synchronize their watches with hers during the workshop.

Chapter 6: Debriefing to Gather the Learnings

1. A. Huxley, *Texts and Pretexts: An Anthology with Commentaries,* repr. ed. (Westport, CT: Greenwood, 1976).

2. B. Pascal, *Pensees,* 2nd ed. (Paris, 1620; English ed. 1688).

Chapter 7: Organize Your Presentations

1. Montaigne, *Essays, 1588.*

2. T.S. Eliot, *Selected Essays 1917-1932* (New York: Harcourt, Brace and Company, 1932).

3. Some definitions of the terms *impromptu* and *extemporaneous* match our usage in this chapter. However, we acknowledge that some dictionaries, books on public speaking, and people who are knowledgeable about this topic might not agree with all aspects of our manner of distinguishing between *impromptu presentations* and *extemporaneous presentations*.

4. L. Wittgenstein, *Philosophical Investigations* (1953). The Baruch poll rated this, "the most important book of the 20th century."

5. Z. Ziglar, *Better Than Good: Creating a Life You Can't Wait to Live* (New York: Thomas Nelson, 2007), p. 134.

6. The capital letters are ours.

7. D. Brooks, *The Social Animal: The Hidden Sources of Love, Character, and Achievement* (New York: Random House, 2011), p. 338.

8. *The Soul of F. W. Robertson* (New York: Harpers, 1947), p. 113. This is a paraphrase of a sentence from a sermon by Frederick W. Robertson of Brighton, one of the most notable preachers in English history. We used the term *outline* where Robertson used the word *arrangement* because we think it best translates Robertson's meaning into today's terminology.

Chapter 8: Creating and Using Flip Charts

1. Using Flip Charts, www.usingflipcharts.co.uk/, a website developed by Graham Jones.

2. Here's an earlier example of the use of visuals to enhance productivity. In the late 1700s and early 1800s, Welsh-born industrialist Robert Owen used visuals to provide productivity enhancing feedback. Above each machinist's workstation he had a cube installed with different-colored faces that indicated the quality of the work and the amount produced. The worker—and his coworkers and supervisor—could see at a glance how his productivity compared with that of others. It was a hugely successful innovation, and Owen became a very wealthy man as well as a generous philanthropist.

3. M. Twain, "The Art of Composition," *Life as I Find It: A Treasury of Mark Twain Rarities*, ed. C. Neider (New York: Cooper Square Press, 2000).

Chapter 9: Creating and Using PowerPoint Slides

1. *Bloomberg BusinessWeek*, September 3–9, 2012.

2. W. Earnest, *Save Our Slides: PowerPoint Design that Works* (Dubuque: Kendall/Hunt Publishing Company, 2007), p. 1.

3. For more information see Edward R. Tufte, *Envisioning Information*, Graphic Press, 1990.

4. R. Altman, *Why Most PowerPoint Presentations Suck: And What You Can Do to Make Them Better*, 3rd ed. (Create Space Independent Publishing Platform, 2012), p. 33.

5. This builds on Cliff Atkinson's approach to creating slide presentations that is described in his book, *Beyond Bullet Points: Using Microsoft PowerPoint to Create Presentations That Inform, Motivate, and Inspire,* 3rd ed. (Redmond, WA: Microsoft Press, 2011).

6. Altman, *Why Most PowerPoint Presentations Suck,* p. 41.

7. B. Gabrielle, *Speaking PowerPoint: The New Language of Business* (Sevierville, TN: Insights Publishing, 2010), p. 130.

8. N. Duarte, *slide:ology: The Art and Science of Creating Great Presentations* (Sebastopol, CA: O'Reilly Media, 2008), p. 145.

Chapter 10: Fine-Tuning Your Delivery

1. Plutarch, Demosthenes, VII. The translator used the word *declaim* where we used *public speaking*.

2. V. Woolf, *Orlando* (1928) (New York: Oxford University Press, 2008).

3. K. Bain, *What the Best College Teachers Do* (Cambridge, MA: Harvard University Press, 2004), pp. 118–119.

4. M. Twain, Autobiography of Mark Twain, vol. 3, eds., H.E. Smith and B. Griffin (Oakland: Univ. of California Press, 2015), p. 170.

Chapter 11: Using Disclaimers to Sidestep Resistance

1. D. Peoples, *Presentations Plus* (New York: John Wiley, 1988), p. 147.

2. J. Heinrichs, *Thank You for Arguing: What Aristotle, Lincoln, and Homer Simpson Can Teach Us About the Art of Persuasion* (New York: Three Rivers Press, 2007), p. 32.

3. Quintilian, *Institutio Oratoria*, IX, ii, 14–17.

4. B. Kafka, *Microwave Gourmet: The Only Microwave Cookbook You Will Ever Need* (New York: Morrow, 1987), p. 11.

5. *Ibid.*

6. G. Kemp & E. Claflin, *Dale Carnegie* (New York: St. Martin's Press, 1989), p. 153.

7. R. Heilbroner, *The Worldly Philosophers: The Lives, Times, and Ideas of the Great Economic Thinkers* (New York: Touchstone, 1999), pp. 58–59.

Chapter 12: Listening Actively to Stay in Tune with Participants

1. B. Klatt, *The Ultimate Training Handbook: A Comprehensive Guide to Leading Successful Workshops & Training Programs* (New York: McGraw-Hill, 1999), p. 308. Unfortunately, despite this strong endorsement of the importance of listening in training, the author's treatment of listening is very brief.

2. R. Nichols and L. Stevens, *Are You Listening?* (New York: McGraw-Hill, 1957), pp. 5–6.

3. C. Osgood, *Osgood on Speaking: How to Think on Your Feet Without Falling on Your Face* (New York: William Morrow, 1988), pp. 45–46.

4. L. Steil, J. Summerfield, and G. de Mare, *Listening: It Can Change Your Life—A Handbook for Scientists and Engineers* (New York: John Wiley, 1983), p. 3.

5. J. Brownell, *Listening: Attitudes, Principles, and Skills,* 3rd ed. (New York: Pearson, 2006), p. 89.

6. L. O'Heren & W.E. Arnold, "Nonverbal Attentive Behavior and Listening Comprehension," *Journal of the International Listening Association*, 5, 86–92.

7. E. Atwood, *I Hear You: Listening Skills to Make You a Better Manager* (New York: Walker and Company, 1992), p. 21. This summarizes A. Ivey and J. Hinkle, "The Transactional Classroom," unpublished manuscript, University of Massachusetts, 1970.

8. K. Singh in M. Brody, ed., *The Wisdom of Listening* (Boston: Wisdom Publications, 2003), p. 195.

9. G. Goodman and G. Esterly, *The Talk Book* (Emmaus, PA: Rodale Press, 1988), p. 38. R. Lefton, V. Buzzotta, M. Sherberg, found that prior to training, 98% of managers they observed "never use reflective or summary statements . . ." *Improving Productivity Through People Skills* (Cambridge, MA: Ballinger, 1980), pp. 200–201. Although their observation was made several decades ago, we and our colleagues find that it's still a rarity for people to reflect what they're told when that's an appropriate response.

10. The several dictionaries that we've consulted for the definition of the word *paraphrase* do not limit the role of a paraphrase to feeding back the *factual content* of the speaker's message. However, when teaching listening, we've found that it's very useful to have a one-word label for reflecting factual content. Since there's no commonly accepted designation for this important listening skill, we've commandeered the word *paraphrasing* for the job.

11. Not all teachers of listening agree with this guideline. Some think that paraphrasing with questions is largely a gender issue since some women, in an effort to avoid being dogmatic, often phrase statements as questions. Other communication trainers teach that, regardless of gender, it's okay or even preferable to couch paraphrases as questions.

We and our colleagues have tried both approaches and have taped and played back paraphrasing practices for over thirty years. From these observations, as well as from our everyday experience, we've found that paraphrases that are phrased and voiced as statements are more productive than those that are framed as questions.

Experience shows that the speaker will let you know if you got the message right without your asking. Since the speaker is likely to let you know whether or not your paraphrase is on target, wording it as a question is unnecessary.

Obviously, if an occasional paraphrase is worded as a question, it's not apt to do much harm. But if your paraphrases are usually phrased as questions, your effectiveness as a listener will be significantly diminished.

Chapter 13: Responding to Questions, Comments, and Objections

1. J. Kotter, *Leading Change* (Boston: Harvard Business School Press, 1996), p. 102.

2. E. Biech, *Training for Dummies* (Foster City, CA: IDG Books, 2005).

3. A. Gilman and K. Berg, *Get to the Point: How to Say What You Mean and Get What You Want* (Dubuque, IA: Kendal Hunt Publishing Co., 1995), p. 114.

4. P. Johnson, *Choice Words* (Portland, ME: Stenhouse Publishers, 2004), p. 56.

5. W. Steele, *Presentation Skills 201: How to Take it to the Next Level as a Confident, Engaging Instructor*, (Denver: Outskirts Press, 2009).

6. M. Twain, Life on the Mississippi. (Boston: Osgood, 1883).

7. J. Boswell, *The Life of Samuel Johnson*, 1791 (entry for 1755).

Chapter 14: Making Presentations Interactive

1. K. Bain, *What the Best College Teachers Do* (Boston: Harvard University Press, 2004), p. 126.

2. M. Nystrand, *Opening Dialogue: Understand the Dynamics of Language and Learning in the English Classroom* (New York: Teachers College Press, 1997), p. 57. We substituted the word *learning* for his word *achievement*.

3. F. Fournies, *Coaching for Improved Work Performance,* 3rd ed. (New York: McGraw-Hill, 1999), p. 89.

Chapter 16: Demonstrating What You Teach

1. R. Carkhuff, *Helping and Human Relations: A Primer for Lay and Professional Helpers, Vol. II: Practice and Research* (New York: Holt, Rinehart, and Winston, 1996), pp. 3 ff., esp. p. 25.

Chapter 17: Leading Practices: Dress Rehearsals for the Real Thing

1. Oh, Sadaharu and Falkner, D., *Sadaharu Oh: A Zen Way to Play Baseball* (New York: Times Books, 1984), p. 165.

2. Publilius Syrus, *Maxims*, 439. First Century BC.

3. M. Silberman and Carol Auerbach, *"Active Training": A Handbook of Techniques, Designs, Case Examples and Tips,* 3rd ed. (Hoboken, NJ: Wiley, 2006).

4. C. Hannaford, *Smart Moves: Why Learning Is Not All In Your Head* (Salt Lake City: Great River Books, 2005), p. 22.

5. M.H. Alderson, *Reader's Digest*, February, 1955.

Chapter 18: Providing in-the-Moment Feedback

1. R. Thaler and C. Sunstein, *Nudge: Improving Decisions about Health, Wealth, & Happiness* (New Haven: Yale University Press, 2008), p. 90.

2. No. 1 leadership thinker. The ranking was by the Biannual Thinkers 50 Ceremony sponsored by the Harvard Business Review.

3. M. Goldsmith and M. Reiter, *What Got You Here Won't Get You There: How Successful People Become Even More Successful* (New York: Hyperion, 2007), p. 112.

Chapter 20: Ending the Workshop

1. R. Pike, *Creative Training Techniques Handbook*, 3rd ed. (Amherst, MA: Human Resource Development Press, 2003).

Chapter 21: Understanding Resistance

1. R. Maurer, "Resistance and Change in Organizations," *The NTL Handbook of Organization Development and Change* (Pfeiffer, 2006), p. 121.

2. J. Jellison, *Managing the Dynamics of Change: The Fastest Path to Creating an Engaged and Productive Workforce* (New York: McGraw-Hill, 2006), p. 28.

3. N. Machiavelli, *The Prince*, 1532, Ch. 6.

4. W. Bagehot, *Physics and Politics*, 1869, Ch. 5.

5. M. Planck, *Scientific Autobiography and Other Papers*, 1948. Translated by Frank Gaynor.

6. W. Schiemann, "Why Change Fails," *Across the Board*, April, 1992.

7. Herbert Spencer, *Social Statistics* (London: John Chapman of London, 1851).

8. W. Lippmann, *Atlantic Monthly*, August 1939.

9. J. Kottler, *Compassionate Therapy: Working With Difficult Clients* (San Francisco: Jossey Bass, 1992), p. 190. Philosopher John Stuart Mill wrote, "He who knows only his own side of the case, knows little of that." *On Liberty*, 1859, Ch. 2.

Chapter 22: Maintaining a Positive Learning Climate

1. S. Ambrose, M. Bridges, M. DiPietro, and M. Lovett, *How Learning Works: Research-Based Principles* (New York: Jossey-Bass, 2010), p. 156.

2. *The Penguin Dictionary of Psychology* tells us that, from the perspective of social psychology, the word *role* "refers generally to any pattern of behavior involving certain rights, obligations, and duties which an individual is expected, trained, and indeed encouraged to perform in a given social situation. In fact, one may go so far as to say that a person's role is precisely what is expected of him or her by others and ultimately, after the particular role has been thoroughly learned and internalized, by the person him or herself."

3. L. Steinberg, quoted in M. Goulston, *Get Out of Your Own Way at Work* (New York: Perigee, 2006), p. 21. Psychologist Abraham Maslow pointed out that the Bruderhof, a Christian sect, considered criticism to be an application of Christian love. They taught that it was unloving to let someone go on making the same mistake again and again because others aren't willing to be lovingly honest with him. [F. Goble, *The Third Force: The Psychology of Abraham Maslow* (New York: Pocket Books, 1980), p. 33.] So don't ban developmental feedback from your repertoire; just make sure that you keep your positive feedback and your developmental feedback in balance. And, when you do offer developmental feedback, be sure to say it sensitively and then listen open-mindedly to the other person's response.

Chapter 23: Intervening to Eliminate an Individual's Disruptive Behavior

1. F. Fournies, *Coaching for Improved Performance*, 3rd ed. (New York: McGraw Hill, 1999), p. 168.

Chapter 24: Observing Group Process

1. L. Pasteur, Address given on the inauguration of the Faculty of Science, University of Lille, December 7, 1845.

Chapter 26: Avoiding Trainer Defensiveness

1. Luke 10:29.

2. H. Clinebell, *Contemporary Growth Therapies* (Nashville: Abingdon, 1981), p. 39.

3. *Radical Collaborations: Five Essential Skills to Overcome Defensiveness and Build Successful Relationships,* James Tamm and R. Luyett, (NY: Harper Business Reprint, 2005).

4. Proverbs 16:32.

5. J. Barlow and C. Moller, *A Complaint Is a Gift: Using Customer Feedback as a Strategic Tool* (San Francisco: Berrett-Koehler, 1996), p. 124.

Chapter 27: Three Trainer Qualities that Facilitate Learning

1. C. R. Rogers, "The Interpersonal Relationship in the Facilitation of Learning," in T. Leeper, ed., *Humanizing Education: The Person in the Process,* ed. T. Leeper (National Education Association, Association for Supervision and Curriculum Development, 1967), p. 3.

2. W. Ury, *The Power of a Positive No: Save the Deal, Save the Relationship, and Still Say No* (New York: Bantam, 2007), pp. 81 and 83.

3. J. Dutton, *Energize Your Workplace: How to Create and Sustain High-Quality Connections at Work* (San Francisco: Jossey-Bass, 2003), p. 22.

4. C. R. Rogers, *A Way of Being* (New York: Mariner Books, 1980), p. 139.

5. P. Jackson and H. Delehanty, *Sacred Hoops: Spiritual Lessons of a Hardwood Warrior* (New York: Hachette, 1995), p. 53.

6. G. Thompson with J. Jenkins, *Verbal Judo: The Gentle Art of Persuasion* (New York: William Morrow, 2013).

7. J. Blight and J. Lang, *The Fog of War: Lessons from the Life of Robert S. McNamara* (New York: Rowman & Littlefield, 2005)

8. R. Carkhuff, *The Art of Problem Solving: A Guide for Teachers, Counselors, and Administrators* (Amherst, MA: Human Development Press, Inc., 1973).

9. H. Hagedorn, *Prophet in the Wilderness: The Story of Albert Schweitzer* (New York: Macmillan, 1949), p. 109.

Appendix III: Installing the Training Properly

1. T. T. Baldwin and J. K. Ford, "Transfer of Training: A Review and Directions for Future Research," *Personnel Psychology* 41 (1988).

Index